I0159930

The One and the Many

OTHER WORKS
BY ROBERT BOLTON

The Order of the Ages:
(World History in the Light of a Universal Cosmogony)

Keys of Gnosis

Self and Spirit

Foundations of Free Will

Person, Soul, and Identity

Robert Bolton

The One
and the Many

A Defense of
Theistic Religion

*And be ready always to give an answer to every
man that asketh you a reason of the hope
that is in you, with meekness and fear.*

1 Peter 3 : 15

ANGELICO PRESS
SOPHIA PERENNIS

First published in the USA,
Sophia Perennis, 2008
Second, revised edition, 2011
Angelico Press/Sophia Perennis edition, 2024
© Robert Bolton

All rights reserved

Series editor: James R. Wetmore

No part of this book may be reproduced or transmitted,
in any form or by any means, without permission

For information, address:
Angelico Press,
169 Monitor St.
Brooklyn, NY 11222
angelicopress.com

ISBN 978-1-59731-081-9 (pbk)
ISBN 979-8-89280-062-4 (cloth)

Cover design: Michael Schrauzer

For, instead of worshipping the true God who gives and establishes
my personal identity, it is easy enough for me to worship an idol
which robs me of identity and puts its own ugly self in my place
Then, in the name of religion, I want to reduce everybody else
to my own non-entity so that my idol's empire may
be further extended."

H. A. Williams,
Poverty, Chastity and Obedience

CONTENTS

Introduction

Metaphysical Religion

The nature of the relation between the One and the Many is a specially contentious issue for most religions. Does unity possess a degree of reality which makes the Many an irrelevance? Or is multiplicity real, while the One is just an abstraction, or is there an equal necessity for both of them? The ways in which these questions are answered are vital for any understanding of the way in which God and the world are related. Those who may still think that this is just a matter of delving into abstractions for their own sake should remember that there is nothing abstract about the results of ignoring such issues. Every social agenda is set in accordance with some kind of theory, no matter how wrong or how badly understood. The manner in which the relation of the One and the Many is understood, however confusedly, has an influence which extends even to politics. It is also at the heart of the issue between Theistic religion and Pantheistic religion.

What I have called metaphysical religion has this range of influence, however indirectly, so that it has wider effects than religious practices which engage only the will and the feelings. In spite of this, the metaphysical basis of religion is of interest to very few people, and those who have some understanding of it are mostly under the influence of impersonal mysticisms from Eastern traditions, where metaphysical thought is believed to survive more than in the West. Consequently, for many Westerners, spiritual wisdom is taken to mean a supremacy of the One to an extent which makes everything else unreal. This is true of the monistic and non-dualistic ways of understanding which are taken to be the inner meaning and substance of all religions for those who are driven by a passion for simplification in the belief that simpler must mean more true. For those who believe in divine revelation, this can only mean that revelation does not really reveal anything, since this approach equates the contents of revelation with externals and inessentials. The resulting divergence from orthodoxy is thus too deep to be explained away.

The aim of what follows is to question the idea that the Absolute Reality must mean the unreality of everything else, and to spell out some of the peculiar consequences that must follow if non-dualistic religion were true. To those who are content with such consequences, there is no more to be said, because all religious beliefs are influenced by one kind of subjective choice or another. A critique of monistic religion is by no means an advocacy of pluralism, because the conceptions of duality and multiplicity necessarily include an underlying unity, which in some way embraces their diversities, and enables us to form distinct ideas of them. Monism is an extreme position, and therefore not difficult to define, whereas certain varieties of it, like non-dualism, can be confusing to those who are unfamiliar with it. For the present, it is enough to say that non-dualism allows some quasi-reality to exist besides the One, so the Many are not an illusion purely and simply, but the overall tendency is still 'monistic', in the customary sense of the word, and so I shall frequently speak of monism and non-dualism under the joint concept of 'monistic religion' for convenience' sake.

The Psychological Background

The adoption of any belief system, however metaphysical, is relative to pre-existent subjective conditions, and monistic religion is no exception in this respect. The human conditions which make people receptive to it are very widespread today, and have often been remarked upon. One of them is an attitude of deliberate subjectivism with its preference for private feeling over objective truth. This state of mind has arisen in reaction against the belief in objectivity at any price which dominated a previous era, although that does nothing to justify it. Feeling is on the borderlands of the private and the public, because it is more easily shared than, say, understanding or imagination, and it gives a sense of freedom which one does not easily find in reason.

Logically, this preference would result from a disbelief in the reality of the outside world, and from a confusion between objective and subjective. Indeed, the very distinction of objective and subjective would be rejected as part of the dualistic scheme of things which is to be overcome in the unity of feeling. The same could be said for the distinction between public and private, since the activity of the intelligence is private to an extent which is not matched by the other mental functions.

These subjective conditions are also manifest in a hostility and suspicion towards individualism, despite the fact that individualism is equally powerful for good or evil, like any other positive attribute. In its best forms, it is the source of everything of lasting value, whether spiritually or naturally, but it is necessarily rooted in the objectivity and duality which modern minds want to deny. Such conditions are the seedbed for mystical religious cults which deny the value of personality and deny the distinction between the sins of the self and the self as such. It is as though the moral tension which belongs with personality was no longer experienced as an adventure and a challenge, but only as a burden. In such cases, there are many who are willing to see the sublation or cessation of individual selves as the fulfilment of the desire for a life without moral tension, rather as though there were something artificial about personhood as such.

The religious orientation resulting from this will be one that feels only impatience with the idea that there should be any absolute distinctions on the spiritual level, be they between one person and another or between man and God. This point of view gives one an apparent right to reject rational argument and verification, and external authority. The spiritual convergence of all things on God is thus understood by subjectivists as though it were an ontological convergence, like the confluence of tributaries into the same river, because physical and spiritual reality are not distinguished. Inevitably, this point of view does not distinguish between God as such and God as experienced by human beings, or between God and the world, or between primal man and fallen man, or between the created and the uncreated.

The Two Faces of Simplicity

As a rule, monistic religion has little or no attraction for those who definitely believe in God and for those who definitely do not believe in God, but those who have not resolved the question as to whether they believe in God or not are often attracted to it, because it offers a simple solution to their dilemma, and which seems to leave them at no disadvantage in relation to those with orthodox convictions. In a similar way, the hard alternatives of either personal immortality in the next life or personal extinction can also be similarly avoided by a conception of divinization which is in effect a compromise between the two, and which, from a personal point of view is a quasi-survival.

All alternatives are by definition forms, and if ultimate reality is without attributes and thus form-less, one may suppose oneself to be operating on a level where choices like belief and unbelief cease to be relevant. If this were justified, one would be not just equal to orthodoxy, but superior to it. This is why monistic forms of religion can be engaged in without what orthodox religion means by faith, even though they are in other respects based on something spiritually positive. This positive aspect is another result of the simplifying function of monism. It is owing to the way in which its theoretical scheme of things reflects the moral teachings of nearly all religions.

For this reason, it can easily appear to be the logical conclusion at which all religions are aiming, whether people see that clearly or not. Thus the ideal of there being ultimately only one real substance is in line with a common factor of all spiritual life, namely, the process of simplification and concentration of the life as it is lived more fully in relation to God. The natural life by itself always tends to greater multiplicity, and therefore to self-dissipation, in a way similar to the ever-divergent property of animal life, which has no center upon which it could revert. In human life, this tendency leads to the fragmentation of one's identity until it is like a collection of different selves. This condition makes an effective or motivating belief in God impossible, since that requires a whole self.

Consequently, it can seem reasonable to believe that a form of religion which teaches the ultimate simplification, the identification of God and man, Creator and creature, must coincide with the most complete truth. The problem with this conclusion is that it is one of those final logical steps which undo those that went before it. Such an extreme degree of simplification becomes self-contradictory because it destroys the 'uniands' (i.e., the things to be united), and therewith the union itself. Instead of discarding the inessential and making the essential stronger, both are sublated equally in a reality which excludes that of other things.

Simplification, if the word means anything, must be a simplification of *something*. In the abstract, it is a negative or reductive process, so that if it is made an end in itself or an absolute, as non-dualists usually appear to do, it is reduced to nothing. Here is the issue upon which the neo-traditionalism of the non-dualistic kind coincides with the entropic reductionism of modern culture. Because of this area of coincidence, one can be ideologically anti-modern while still having an essentially modern mindset. Of course, the passion for simplification which is peculiar to modernity has nothing spiritual about it, only a world-weariness with no sense of any other world. It is as though Ockham's Razor were a divine law, and as though the existence of real differences and distinctions were an affront to the desire for truth. Monistic and non-dualistic thinkers are more at home in this ethos than they care to admit, and they play their part in the prevailing cult of reduction, no matter how unintentionally, while they want to express the wisdom of tradition.

I draw attention to this negative simplification because it is characteristic of the modern world, which forms the end of a very long world-cycle. Since it is the final prolongation of a universal era, it brings with it the realization of all the most spiritually negative possibilities of the cycle, as I have explained elsewhere (see R. Bolton, *The Order of the Ages*). This is why, the present age being 'the age of the realization of the impossible', as Schuon calls it, there is no point in expecting to see any profound new flowering of the spirit in our time. Nevertheless, some such thing is irrationally believed in by many non-dualists, in defiance of their own doctrine of the dark cycle. One may by grace escape the prevailing forms of corruption, but that hardly carries one to the highest levels of sanctity or super-angelic perfection. If such things as that were possible today, the end of the present world-age would be delayed for ever, and there would be no conceivable order or structure in the cosmic process.

Who Are The Vedantists?

Some readers may mistake what follows for an attack on Hinduism as well as on the traditional conception of religion, particularly those who think that the doctrine of the great Vedantist Shankara ought to be beyond the scope of rational critique. If they should think so, it could only be owing to an ignorance of the real Hindu religion. The three greatest of the masters of the Vedanta are Shankara (700–750 AD), Ramanuja (1017–1137 AD), and Madhva (1197–1276 AD)

These three authorities do not form a succession like that of Justin, Clement, and Origen in early Christian Patristics, because Ramanuja and Madhva both reacted strongly against Shankara's monistic interpretation of the doctrine. Madhva made much use of the fact that the central faculty of the individual self is its self-reflective principle, because this is not subject to sublation, since it is equivalent in potentiality to a world. This is the reality on which Descartes was to base his *Cogito* argument four hundred years later, and it also informs the kind of thinking which is applied to the question of the One and the Many in this book. Thus the doctrinal development of Hinduism clearly contradicts the belief that Hinduism is to be equated with the *Advaita* or non-dualist school of Vedanta founded by Shankara.

Nevertheless, this belief has been taught directly and indirectly in the works of a number of respected authors in the field of metaphysical religion, as though it had no rival. It appears that they have done so simply because they felt that it would be good for people if they could be made to believe in the truth of the *Advaita* doctrine, and to take it for a universal orthodoxy. In reality, Shankara's doctrine held the dominant place in Hinduism for not much more than two centuries, mostly in the ninth and tenth centuries AD, after which the Hindu tradition as a whole has been moving steadily away from it during the last thousand years. There are nevertheless those who want to equate Shankara's doctrine with tradition as such, but their conflict with the historical record appears to be insoluble.

Far from being an attempt to treat spiritual doctrines from an individualistic point of view, therefore, this book follows a traditional path in its method and its objective. While it is not overtly theological for the most part, the theoretical basis of religious belief as understood by Christians, Jews, and Muslims is defended, and analyzed only for the purpose of revealing its strength. Where the thinking appears Cartesian in inspiration, it is in any case rooted in a traditional conception, employed by both Augustine in Western tradition, and by Madhva in Vedantic tradition.

The sceptical treatment that will be given to Shankara's doctrine is thus in line with the teachings of some of the most revered teachers of Vedanta who saw no reason to treat the *Advaita* school with reverence. It is too seldom understood that both Ramanuja and Madhva deny that the famous dictum, 'He is the Self; That Thou Art' is in any way a rigorous statement of identity. For Ramanuja it simply denotes the analogical relation between the Self and all finite selves, (E. Lott, *Vedantic Approaches to God*, p 33) just as an identity-statement like 'You are wise' means that you participate in the quality of wisdom, and not that you and wisdom are one and the same thing, or 'You are a teacher' means that teaching is one of your attributes, not that you are nothing but an instance of the act of teaching something.

Among Advaitists who are aware of these historical facts, there are those who attach no importance to such facts on the grounds that the later Vedantists were merely arguing for more limited points of view than that of Shankara. F. Schuon has judged the matter in this way, (see *Spiritual Perspectives and Human Facts*, chap. 4), but without explaining what he means by limitation in this context. In fact, this kind of argument amounts to pure question-begging, since it requires that one first equate limitation with differentiation while prescinding from its positive content. Such specious reasoning can easily be turned round against those who use it, if one starts by defining limitation as deprivation of attributes. Obviously, anything must be limited if it lacks what most matters to oneself. Greater or less limitation can only be a genuine issue where both sides of the issue want the same thing, and there is little sign of that here.

However traditionalists may judge this attempt to apply criticism to Shankara's doctrine, they should now be aware that their judgment will be similarly applicable to some of the principal figures in the Hindu tradition. This, I hope, will appear reasonable to all except those who wish to equate the idea of tradition with one school of thought.

Note to Reader

Readers who are unfamiliar with the religious context in which these observations are made would do best to begin by looking at what has been said in the debate in Chapter 8. That was the original exchange of ideas which led to my writing this book. Those who are theologically-minded should bear in mind the fact that the dualism I argue for here is solely what results from the nature of knowledge, not of ethics, and has nothing to do with Manichaean or Gnostic dualism, or with any attempt to make evil the equal counterpart of good.

1

The Question
of Idolatry

Monism and Non-Dualism

Any connection between idolatry and monistic forms of mysticism can easily appear to be fantastical or even self-contradictory. Nevertheless, this connection is a real issue, as I shall try to make clear, when the main ideas involved have been defined. Such terms as monism and non-dualism will often be used rather loosely, but this is only because the standpoint taken here is not identified with either, and not because they are taken to be just the same. The difference between these varieties of what might be called the 'pantheistic spectrum' is important for those whose ideal is involved with its religious overtones, but not for those who see them as members of a common genus.

Monism is the easier of the two to define, since it teaches that there is only one real substance, regardless of appearances, whether that substance be understood as spiritual or material, and whether or not it is identified with God. All other things which are taken to be separate substances, agents, or entities are ultimately unreal, and so are illusory appearances. The modification made to this conception by the term non-dualism is best understood if one can see it in the light of Plato's idea of the material principle. As the complementary principle to the Forms, which are immune from change and instability, this conception of matter (*hyle*) has no inherent identity, but is in a constant flux, admitting everything and retaining nothing. It has

neither being nor non-being, but consists in a to-and-fro movement between them, receiving and manifesting the Forms, but
in ways which are never stable, lasting or very true.

Thus matter is only a quasi-reality, and this is just the kind of
conception which non-dualists enlarge until it embraces everything other than the Absolute. The reality owing to the presence of the Forms is discounted in favour of the aspect of
endless flux which the world presents to the senses, as though
the senses were the key to the mysteries. Thus the whole range
of realities that common sense takes for reality is reduced to the
evanescent marginal position which materiality has for Platonism. It is an open question, therefore, as to whether any reality other than the Absolute is really being conceded; under one
aspect it is, under another it is not, but this suffices to conceal
the hard outline of strict monism for theological purposes.

Stated as bluntly as possible, therefore, the difference between
Monism and Non-Dualism amounts to this: monists say that, in
the end, the only reality is God or the Absolute, whereas non-
dualists say that, in the end, the only reality is God plus a mote of
dust which is not quite sure whether it is you, me, or somebody
else. Non-dualists believe that that doctrine keeps them within
religious orthodoxy, although its only 'active ingredient' is
monism.

The Role of Logic

In what follows, I shall attempt a number of critical examina-
tions of what could be called pantheistic religion if monism and
non-dualism are not referred to specifically. To some minds, any
such undertaking must be misconceived because this kind of
doctrine is of too high an order to be treated as though it were
one more variety of philosophy. It belongs to a level of being
which is above that of the formal objects to which logic is applicable, so that critiques like this one must be at best naive and
possibly presumptuous. From this point of view, to apply logical
criteria to monistic mysticism is to be like someone trying to
sound the ocean with a six-foot pole; such probings must be an

irrelevance to those who are acquainted at first hand with the interior reality itself.

Nevertheless, this supposed right to bypass logic on account of the supra-logical reality is really a misunderstanding. The reality above formal relations is of course not tied to any of the particular processes of logic, but on the other hand it contains eminently the truths at which logic aims. Therefore, although in many cases it cannot validate logical conclusions in the way in which they are valid in this world, in other cases it will not only validate them but determine them even more strongly. Failing this condition, supra-formal reality would be no different from the irrationalities of our subjective nature, and not the source of objective reality which it must be. In this case, to expect the transcendent to exemplify or vindicate monistic thought because it is not subservient to logic (although it is the cause of logic) is as mistaken as expecting it to vindicate every other variety of the irrational as well.

One significant fact about both monists and non-dualists is that they both conclude that the phenomenal world is illusory as a consequence of their premise that only the Infinite is real. This is obviously a logical deduction, one which shows that they too believe that reason rules even at the highest levels of reality. Otherwise, if supra-formal and supra-natural reality was beyond logic as such, they would be able to affirm both the reality of the world and the exclusive reality of the Infinite at the same time, and never mind the contradiction. Why not, if only formal relationships are involved? The fact that they will not do this is a good indication that they only object to logic when it does not serve their purposes. The doctrine of illusion is admitted to be contradictory, but in that case it is accepted by its proponents.

Where it is held that, despite any counter-arguments, there is a direct experience of monistic transcendence which must make it proof against criticism, it should be realized that the word 'experience' in this context must mean something completely different from what it means anywhere else. Experience is by definition a relation between a subject and an object, whence there cannot properly speaking be a monistic or non-dualistic experience. To adapt an argument of F.Schuon, the argument that a given doctrine is too high for reason is one which could have been used at any time in past ages, but in fact it was not used until belief in God began to wane in modern times. The adequacy of reason was not doubted in traditional cultures.

However, the fact remains that the monistic interpretation of mysticism which is being examined here is one of the most respected and influential forms of thought today, and is held by many of those with the deepest knowledge of religions and their doctrines. When, therefore, would-be critics are members of traditional religions, ought not the most appropriate attitude for them be one of reverent acceptance toward ideas which may after all only seem wrong because of one's own limitations? There is no shortage of writings by atheists who show that they dislike religion too much for them to bother to learn much about it. Thus critics of Oriental mysticisms could be in a similar position to that of most atheists, one which shows itself in a desire to criticize what one does not understand. In view of this possibility, they must have a reason for what they are doing which is undeniably more substantial than any personal con- cerns. Such a reason certainly exists, and it will not only suffice to dispel suspicions about subjectivity, but will be seen to be a major issue for both theists and for non-dualists equally, in the light of what I shall say about creation.

The Meaning of Hope

On a human level, there is obviously reason enough for criticism of monistic religion, not least because of the ever-present desire for a religion which allows ultimate meaning for hope. All such concerns for hope and therefore happiness are usually dismissed by the masters of the non-dual doctrine as being just so many more parts of the illusion which their doctrine serves to dispel. F. Schuon has said that there was nothing profoundly human in his writings because nothing human was profound, as though he knew that God could not act through or by means of limited human beings. (The question of how free from limitation one *ought* to be for God admits of no answer, unless one maintains that no agent less than God could serve His purposes.)

This view that the human is necessarily trivial can be refuted on its own ground, starting from the fact that there are all kinds of purely human reasons for reacting against things which are typically human, such as the desire to be happy and the consequent need to be able to hope. Despite all denials, the desire to be happy remains in those who deny it as much as in those who accept it because it is part of the will to live, and because a capacity for hope is a normal part of sanity. Denials of its validity as a spiritual value are at best a result of a confusion between happiness as such and immoral and deluded forms of it, and at worst hypocrisy. Hope is in any case one of the Theological Virtues, regardless of its human character, so that it is rightly a criterion of orthodoxy.

Since hope and happiness are inseparable, hope could not be a virtue unless happiness were the goal of life, granted only that it is by no means wholly identifiable with what is possible in the life of this world. On the basis that man is created, therefore, the purpose of his creation must lie in his happiness, since supposed alternatives to it are incoherent. In this case, there must logically be a right to be able to hope, whence these things are both human and profound, inasmuch as they result from the origin of our being, contrary to the ideas of non-dualists like F.Schuon.

Conversely, for those who do not believe in creation, or those who regard it as just a complication in the process of emanation, there is no reason to see any grounds for either hope or happiness except as parts of the purely natural and mortal life. This is one issue which divides those who believe in creation from those who do not, and other fateful consequences of this divide will be shown presently.

The Self and the Ego

A further reason that could be offered against a critique of this kind is that monists and non-dualists understand the subordi-

nate position of the ego in spiritual life as well as in the scheme
of things. They at least cannot be deceived into over-rating it
because of the importance it has for practical matters. In a spiritual dark age like the present time, it is assumed that people are
their egos and nothing else, as though this were a self-evident
truth, and this delusion of modern culture has invaded orthodox religion. Too often therefore, religion itself is assumed to
be solely a matter of the ego and its relations to the outside
world, and in this way tradition gets taken over by anti-tradition.

In opposition to this, non-dualists have led the way in exposing its falsehood, and in showing how true religion must involve
the whole person in ways that transcend the activities of the
ego, tied as it is to externals. The belief that persons are only
their egos is so much at the heart of modern corruption that it
has been attributed with some justification to the work of the
devil. (Joan O'Grady, *The Prince of Darkness*, chap. 14, p142, Element Books, 1989)

In view of this, those who work to restore the mind and soul
of religion and to expose the falsehoods attached to it should, in
principle, receive support rather than criticism. But unfortunately, the issue is not as clear-cut as that, because this crucial
insight into the lower status of the ego is largely neutralized by
an extremist conviction that the ego is nothing but a natural
phenomenon with no ultimate meaning, just because it is not
the highest of realities. One extremism begets another. This is
why non-dualist and pantheistic thinking opposes that of materialistic modernity in a way which just turns it upside down and
inside out, and is therefore unwittingly a derivative of it. The
truth cannot be reinstated by such simplistic means, and modernity cannot be corrected by a mindset which is still part of it.

The intellectual service given to spiritual religion is thus
compromised by a reductive idea of reality which would dissolve
the distinction between the natural and the supernatural, and
indeed all other distinctions as well, as though they revealed
nothing of their metaphysical origin. This is nevertheless not so
serious an issue as that of idolatry, and it is still not clear how any
such thing could arise in this context. Idolatry is any form of

religion in which a created thing is put in the place of its Creator, no matter whether it is material or a created soul or spirit, or idea. This is something mystical monists are never suspected of as a rule, since their system implies a radical negation not only of the ego, but of the natural world to which the ego relates. Their doctrine of illusion should be enough to exclude any scope for idolatry, and it would be if their denial of reality to the world were complete, but there is one thing that escapes it, and that is consciousness. Pantheistic systems depend completely on consciousness and its possibilities, and it is here that its challenge to theistic religion encounters its biggest problem.

The Denial of Creation

For sophisticated minds, the teaching that the world is created often sounds like an explanation for ignorant or immature minds. The explanation they frequently believe in is a kind of emanation, in which the world results from higher causes through an impersonal process. From this point of view, the idea that the world is designed, willed and created by a personal God appears to be a popular way of expressing something too difficult for popular consumption. Creation is thus supposed to be an anthropomorphic account of an impersonal and even unconscious cosmic process. This would mean that God or the Absolute was the highest part of the scale of being, and not its creator, and the main religious consequence to follow from this is a contemplative spirituality which leads to a state where the distinction between the human and the divine ceases.

Even though it is denied that an individual could reach such a state except under the guidance of a master who was believed to have accomplished this transition already, this does not alter the fact that the denial of creation is a necessary part of an idea that all mankind are on a continuum of being with God, with consciousness as the connecting principle. Such an idea is closely allied to a conviction that all religions teach the same thing, by which one means this doctrine.

Most of those who are influenced by Oriental religion are

liable to see things in this way, but for all the appeal of this idea to an intelligence seeking the most economical answer, its foundations are deeply insecure. To explain why, I shall refer to what has been said specifically in regard to Buddhism by Paul Williams in his article 'Aquinas Meets the Buddhists' in *Aquinas in Dialogue* (Jim Fodor and Frederick Christian Bauerschmidt ed., Blackwell Publishing, 2004). Williams begins with an account of Buddhist authorities such as Santideva and Candra-kirti where they argue against the existence of God. For them it is clear that the idea of a personal creator could mean only existing natural forces under a different name, or else the addi-tion of an extra cause to those of nature, and one which is easy to dispense with.

These refutations of God are circular inasmuch as their idea of causality is equated with natural efficient causality alone. On this basis, it is a tautology to say that the idea of God as the cause of the world is meaningless. But this is to ignore the fact that the conception of causality includes that of creation, as Williams points out. For this reason, Buddhist refutations of God are invalidated; in none of them do Buddhists conceive the idea of the world (the total context of all natural causal interactions) as being created, i.e., intentionally brought into being by omnipo-tence. Conversely, God and Creator are so much at one in Christian thought, that the statement that God is the Creator of the world tells us something essential about God, even suppos-ing reason alone could say no more than that. This is why deni-als of creation by both Buddhism and *Advaita* must mean a denial of God equally.

In an uncreated world, one can readily conceive an ideal of life as a process toward sublation and mergence with a universal reality from which the world differs only by the illusions of human minds. Such a scheme of things could be allowed to have absolute finality if there were no other reality external to it, like a Creator, but that is something Buddhists and Vedantists have no idea how to prove.

The Affirmation of Creation

Williams comments on Buddhist criticism of belief in God that it very effectively disproves idolatrous conceptions of God, where God is assimilated to some part of the natural world. But that is emphatically not the God of traditional theologians like Aquinas. The Creator God whom they understood was never supposed to provide reasons as to why specific things took place in nature, except where miracles were in question. On the contrary, God was exclusively the cause of the total system, physical, psychical and spiritual, the cause of spirits as much as of material things. God is in this case the answer to the question 'How come there is anything at all?' As a question assuming causality, this question is legitimate and coherent, since the question 'How did X come to be?' is not logically tied to the size of the object in question. It can as well be a mole on someone's chin, the rings of Saturn, or the whole of reality.

Those who deny creation may object that one cannot say God caused the world because, since causality belongs to nature, we cannot expect to find it if we look outside the whole natural order. But this still only amounts to the truism that the causality by which God creates the world cannot be of the same kind as the forms of causality which operate in nature, between one creature and another. Even in this world, there are forms of causality other than efficient causality, such as moral causality, as well as formal and final causality, as Aristotle defined them.

To ask 'What, in the nature of things, caused X to come into existence?' is of course not the same kind of question as: 'What caused this nature of things, within which X came into existence?' The second of these questions assumes that at least something of this 'nature of things' extends beyond the world as we know it, which is a normal conception in Platonism. Such a causal relation is what should be expected if God creates through archetypal realities. In that case, the causality which governs natural forces would be a material image of the eternal causality by which the world comes from God.

In view of the different kinds of causality which exist even in this world, human behavior can have physical causes as studied by science, or it can have subjective, irrational causes, or intellectual or Divine causes. Causality is thus a genus with a variety of species in it, and so there is no reason to suppose that this world contains all of them. Therefore, if God creates the world through a kind of causality that no created being could employ, this both would and would not be causality as we know it, but would still be causality. It could be replied that this only shows that the world's being caused or created by God is a possibility, so that non-creationists would have just as good a chance of being right. But the case for creation is stronger than that, because the world can be seen to be a contingency, that is, both as a whole and in its parts it can be conceived as not existing, without any problem in logic. Consequently, it cannot be self-caused, but can only be caused by an agent who really is self-existent. Those who fail to see this are confusing the world with God.

The causal relations which exist in the world are reflections of or pointers to a causal relation which embraces the world as a whole. Conversely, if causality were not necessary to explain the world itself, one could with as much reason deny the reality of causality within it as well as outside it. Philosophers such as Hume have done just that, and proposed to reduce causality to mere regular sequences. But for Buddhists and Advaitists, that would be anathema, since Karma is essential to both of these doctrines, so deeply rooted are they in the conception of causality linking all lives. Yet despite this commitment to causality within the world, they deny that there is any cause for the world as such. Their passion for causality suddenly evaporates just where causality approaches its most significant consequence.

In the article referred to earlier, Williams emphasizes the point that the final destiny of all beings cannot be separated from their origin, and that if we hold that all things are created by God, this final destiny must likewise be in God. Conversely, if there were no Creator, there would be no origin and therefore no ultimate destiny for existing beings. In this case, *Advaita* and Buddhism could not be said to offer salvation; they may claim to offer something beyond salvation, but the difference between that and nothing would seem to be beyond the possibilities of experience.

Where there is no creation, there is no relation between the world and Divinity (however understood), and therefore there is no reason why even the most holy or spiritual life should ever connect with the Divine. To assume that it must do so could only be the result of a kind of blind faith. Along with what was said about our origin and destiny, the consequence was drawn that our being created, if true, must be the deepest ontological truth about us (ibid., p106). In this case, religions which deny creation would thereby deny any hope of valid self-knowledge, which is ironic, because they typically are devoted to self-knowledge above all else. Even if creation is admitted only as a possibility, spiritual systems which are centered on the deepest self-knowledge possible must therefore fail by their own criteria if the world is in fact created. A supposed enlightenment which is blind to its own origin could only be a new kind of illusion.

Williams next quotes the teachings of Saint Catherine of Siena, according to which belief in creation determines our ability to acquire real virtue. Without this belief, no one can understand the goodness of God in relation to himself, and without that, no one can be capable of gratitude. The gratitude taught by non-theistic religions is confined to the gratitude which one owes to other persons in this world, and has no relation to the gift of existence itself. Without gratitude for existence, the spiritual dimension of gratitude is absent, but when it is there, it is the basis of both humility and charity, according to both Saint Catherine and Saint Thomas, these being necessary in turn for all the other virtues if they are to have any spiritual meaning. This is why belief in creation is necessary for salvation according to Christian doctrine, and this is sharply opposed to the belief that all religions teach the same thing.

A Mystical Idolatry?

To deny or ignore creation is to assume that the world depends on nothing else, and this is implicitly to put the world in the place of God, regardless of the evident fact of its contingency discussed above. For this reason, Christianity is bound to teach that monism and non-dualism have an orientation to paganism, one which is manifest in the way in which they merge the human and the divine and the natural and the supernatural. Their stock answer to this is to invoke the doctrine of illusion, and deny the reality of the created world, in which case one could not be accused of making a false God of the world. But when people, even non-dualists, speak of 'the world' they usually think of the aspects of it which engage the imagination, and not of its psychical and spiritual content.

In reality, the greater part of the world consists of the consciousness of spiritual beings, and there are serious problems with saying that consciousness is all part of the world-illusion, especially for non-dualistic religion, which consists in the development and refinement of consciousness to very high levels. Consciousness, they believe, can under the right direction, prove to be one with God. Here is where creation is the main issue, because Advaitist beliefs require that consciousness as such be outside both creation and illusion equally. It has to be real in order to convict the rest of the world with illusion, and be uncreated so as to be divine.

But if there is even a fifty percent chance that the soul and its consciousness are created, there must likewise be a fifty percent chance that treating an exalted state of consciousness as though it were God would really be an act of idolatry. There is a gulf between the idea of a created being in close relation to the Creator and a created being who is taken to be the Creator, and as far as the argument has been presented at this stage, non-dualists and monists would have no more than one chance in two of not being idolaters, given the possibility of creation. There is an element of Pascal's Wager in this dilemma, because the non-creationist option is fraught with spiritual danger, especially if it is adopted with the intention of denying God and creation, whereas the creationist option is centered on a wholly positive idea of God. The former option, if false, would be implicitly damnable, whereas the latter, if false, would be at least no worse than nothing.

While the chances of creation being true are just one in two, if we take it simply as a possibility apart from any supporting arguments, the same must apply to the non-creationist position, *Advaita* likewise having one chance in two of being the truth. This is more damaging for it than for creationism, because it claims to be above all a way of knowledge. What sort of knowledge could it be that has only a fifty percent chance of being knowledge? That is in fact the best chance it could have, and I shall give reasons later on as to why its chances of being really knowledge are even less than that. The stakes could not be higher with this issue: to be wrong about creation is to be wrong about everything.

Some non-dualists try to refute the implications of creation by saying that of course they believe in it, as indeed they hold all religious beliefs, only with the difference that creation be a subordinate reality within a system where the difference between creature and Creator is finally overcome. The Creator is thus said to be the 'first determination' after the Absolute, and creation would be a special complication in the pattern of an illusory world-order. This is an instance of the familiar assumption that the Creator and the Absolute are different beings. Nevertheless, this larger system in which creation is a component, as are the mental faculties which conceive it, could just as well be created as any of the realities more immediately known to us. Therefore, it too has only one chance in two of not being created. (Creation is the origin of things or it is nothing.)

The perspective of creation implies no limitation on the rigor or objectivity of the knowledge we are capable of. We inhabit a world of space and time, in which innumerable natural and logical and mathematical laws can be seen to operate, and many of those who reject creation are unable to see that these dimensions and laws are all equally parts of the created world. This is because their thinking is tied to sense and imagination, to things which can be pictured, and not to what can simply be conceived, the vast extent of non-material reality, along with souls and intellects. But once the latter is recognized in the context of creation, the denial of it is a mere assertion of meaninglessness, such as one might expect from materialists.

Many of those who deny creation in favour of monistic emanation are inclined in this direction by an unconscious materialism. This gives rise to the assumption that the non-material part of reality must be a kind of 'free zone,' to which even God could have no access or relevance. In such thinking, the non-material reality gets split off from the material and unwittingly put in the place of God, and so becomes a kind of idol.

The essence of this idol is consciousness, and consciousness betrays the fact that it is a created thing, or at least that its origin is outside itself, by the fact that it cannot explain what it is. I will enlarge on this in Chapter 3, but for now suffice it to say that consciousness does not comprise the self-subsistent nature which would be proper to a divine and therefore self-existent being, which exists by necessity. In other words, consciousness manifestly lacks a precondition for the role it is given in Advaitist and Buddhist religion, where everything depends on it.

In view of this central role of consciousness in monistic types of religion, a non-human observer might expect that its teachers would have a special respect for the source of consciousness, which is invariably the psycho-physical individual, but needless to say, they do not. They may prefer to say that its source is really the source of these individuals, namely God, but the fact that God cannot or will not bring consciousness into this world except in individual persons must imply something about its essential nature. If one respects the Creator, one must respect his creature. This issue could only be set aside if consciousness were *ipso facto* divine, and only needed to be rid of everything else for its true nature to be realized, but it has just been indicated that it is lacking in the self-explanatory independence that would be consistent with Divinity.

If it were a creature from the start, it could not be anything else when it had reached its highest destination. In just the same way, by no conceivable feat could a character in a novel turn into the author of the novel. Advaitists and Buddhists both believe that consciousness will continue to exist after the personalities in which it originated have ceased to exist. One should note that this is not at all like believing that the soul will still exist when it is separated from its body, because the soul is the source of both personal identity and consciousness, while the body is a constant material flux. In this case, it is simply a question of a substance continuing to exist after losing something of itself. Conversely, a supposed continuation of consciousness without either soul or body would be a continuation of an activity without its agent, which is a self-contradiction, not a doctrine.

There is a clear parallel between this religious conception and that of the scientific materialism which is supposed to be its opposite, because the latter is similarly unable to take account of the fact that all science and the scientific scheme of things is the product of human minds which have no place and no meaning in it; that it is a product of consciousness while consciousness is the activity of minds or souls. Thus the whole conceptual world of science is absurdly imagined as functioning just the same as though none of those minds which create sciences were part of it, and in the same way religious anti-personalism imagines a perfect consciousness without any conscious person. This parallel between them is so close that the two systems may well proceed from the same deep flaw in human consciousness, a selective mental blindness.

Scientific materialism and mystical impersonalism are also alike in the way they avoid belief in God and idolize something created to fill the gap. In the one case, this created divinity is an elevated consciousness, and in the other it is a world-order devised by consciousness, and though these two sects may despise one another and appear to outsiders as opposite extremes, what they have in common is more important than their differences. Their denial of both God and personality, and their worship of intelligence in one form or another are of the essence of the modern mentality, and keep it in being.

Appeals to Authority

Non-dualism, together with its allied conceptions is seldom argued, but rather assumed and employed as though it could not be confused with pantheism or monism. Explanations and definitions are avoided, but at the same time support for it is offered in the form of appeals to traditional authority. This has been done by both R. Guénon and F. Schuon (and many others also), whose writings contain countless citations of 'Hinduism' and 'the Vedanta' in support of their monistic doctrines, and many others have done the same. Although it is never said directly, such interpreters always make it appear that the whole Hindu tradition is dedicated to this kind of doctrine as its basic orthodoxy. This, if true, would be the most powerful argument in favour of Shankara's doctrine, and it is willingly believed by those whose knowledge of Hinduism is limited to texts prepared for Europeans who are presumed to want to believe in some kind of pantheism.

In reality, the citations of Hinduism and Vedanta in Guénon's and Schuon's works nearly always mean 'Shankara's doctrine,' which, if openly professed, would have convinced very few people of the truth of their doctrinal position. It is therefore hard to see how the misuse of the name 'Hinduism' could have been accidental, because one cannot imagine that Guénon and Schuon read only popularizations of Eastern religion. They knew the truth about Hinduism, but decided that this truth was not enough for the purposes of the non-dualistic mysticism which they wanted to present as the essence of all traditional religion. Their doctrine was in need of an unimpeachable authority, and this appeared to be provided by a nineteenth century idea of Hinduism which is still prevalent in the West.

But for those who are willing to see, there is no shortage of scholars who try to correct Western man's stereotyped beliefs about Eastern religion:

> It is clear that the Hindu tradition has become increasingly theistic and has for approximately the last thousand years

taken centrally the theistic-devotional form of bhakti. Indeed the Bhagavad Gita, which is dominated by the idea of the personal Lord, and which has long been India's most influential scripture, was written before the time of Christ. (John Hick, Foreword to *Vedantic Approaches to God*, by Eric Lott, The Macmillan Press Ltd., London 1980)

Similarly, according to the Cambridge Lecturer in Comparative Study of Religion,

Many Westerners also believe—alas this is true for too many of the modern Indian intelligentsia as well—that the great Advaitin Shankara is representative of Hindu religious thinkers. Now this belief strikes me as manifestly indefensible. He (Shankara) is hardly representative of Hindu theologians or even Vedantins.' (Julius Lipner, *The Face of Truth*, SUNY, 1986, Preface)

According to a follower of a Theistic branch of Vedanta,

Scholars of South Asia have largely ignored the Madhva School of Vedanta. The result has been a false identification of Vedanta with either *Advaita* or Visistadvaita Vedanta and misconceptions and generalizations about the ways that Hindus think. 'All Hindus are monists who want to merge with the divine,' is the incorrect refrain that I often hear from students and teachers alike. Why has this stereotype persisted? Why has Madhva Vedanta been eclipsed by its predecessors?... As will become clear, some Hindus, namely Madhvas, are theists and firmly believe that they are and will always remain different from God, that is, Vishnu. (Deepak Sarma, *An Introduction to Madhva Vedanta*, Ashgate 2003, Preface)

Sarma makes the point also voiced by John Hick, that the Advaitists represent a doctrine which Hinduism has for a long time been moving away from, since *Advaita* is by some centuries the predecessor of Madhva. That would not amount to an argument against it for traditionalists like Guénon and Schuon, however. With their lack of belief in progress, they would say that the older doctrine was the more true, but when it came to choosing their own religious traditions, they both converted from Christianity to Islam, a religion which began six hundred years after Christianity, so the older doctrine was not the truer one in that instance. This implies that the motive at work in this was really expediency, and not a doctrine linking value to its position in time, especially as there was a need to appeal to Europeans who were but little attracted to religious orthodoxy as such.

The usual ideas of integrity are not entirely appropriate here, however, because the kind of logic peculiar to the idealist mind is also a major factor. Firstly, Guénon and Schuon undoubtedly believed that if people were to believe that a whole sacred tradition was dedicated to a monistic idea of God and salvation, it would be for their spiritual good. Secondly, they believed in consequence that this must give them a right to speak as though it were in fact the case that 'Hinduism' meant 'Shankara'. They may not have noticed that they were tacitly adopting utilitarian conceptions of ethics and truth, for which the end justifies the means, a common result with idealists, which occurs as though worldly reality were taking revenge on them for aiming too high above it.

Their use of strategic misrepresentation is foreshadowed by Plato's advocacy of the 'noble lie,' (Rep. Bk.III, 414b), but Plato was at least frank about it. He thought that those with power had a right to lie, while their subordinates did not. The fact that Guénon and Schuon were both converts to Islam, for which it is always permissible to be economical with the truth if it is believed to be for a worthy purpose, very probably affected their behavior in this connection. That they could have acted in this way indicates strongly that they felt that the case for monistic spirituality, especially in the context of orthodoxy, was not a very strong or accessible one, and that it therefore had to be supplemented by some extraordinary means, and hence the consistently-suggested idea of an orthodox monist tradition.

But the problem their doctrine has with orthodoxy is far from accidental, as the issue of creation has shown, and attempts to annex or colonize religious truth in the name of *Advaita* reveal a kind of impudence which traditionalists are wont to see in the works of the moderns. If, as appears from the above, this doctrine does indeed comprise an unusually subtle way of idolizing the created, sufficient reason should be seen for the criticisms which follow, at least by those to whom religious orthodoxy is a major issue.

2

Non-Dualism
and its Presuppositions

Comparisons With Other Systems

Any attempts to criticize a position like that of non-dualism may arouse doubts as to whether comparisons with modern philosophy could have any relevance for it in any case, not least among those for whom non-dualism is a welcome alternative to a materialistic culture which has no time for metaphysics. For many, it is unfortunately almost the only alternative to the dominant kinds of modern thought. But while there may be much in both linguistic philosophy and non-dualistic thought which is mutually exclusive, it is not true that they have nothing in common, because that would only be the case if Non-Dualism made no theoretical claims for its own position and was solely a form of mysticism. It gives a central role to the intellect, and so implicitly to reason as well.

In case this comparison between non-dualism and modern linguistic philosophy should still look like a confusion of categories, one major issue on which they coincide is that of the soul, or rather its elimination. For the purposes of *Advaita*, the soul is either ignored or taken as part of the natural life along with the body, while the followers of Wittgenstein deny the soul by denying the reality of private language, and believe their own interior lives to be non-existent. Since that would make the soul a nullity, these two systems are doctrinally close to one another on an issue of fundamental importance, in which case comparisons between them can be relevant and enlightening.

A further point of contact is the mystical passion of Wittgenstein, the founder of linguistic philosophy, which is manifest in a dominant subjectivity going to extremes in reaction against the excessive objectivism of science. Consequently, some instructive comparisons between them are possible in the general context of cultic thought, in which one also finds Darwinism and Freudianism as ideologies. In this field, therefore, some observations about linguistic philosophy made by Ernest Gellner have a wider relevance:

> Gellner examines both the movement's ideas and what he takes to be the intellectual sleight-of-hand by means of which they are expounded. He shows that key ideas are never stated, rather insinuated by attacking opposed ideas, and that there is systematic denial of all attempts by outsiders to state these ideas.

> Those who were attracted by these ideas (of linguistic philosophy)

> were not savoring them as but one set of ideas amongst others.... No; this was all-embracing, this was a final fulfilment, or a new dawn, or indeed both at once. (see Ernest Gellner, *Words and Things*, Preface, pxv, Routledge Classics, and ibid., Introduction, p2)

These two aspects of the subject are closely linked, comprising on the one hand, a desire for one's ideas to be more oracular by appearing to emerge from a higher source, open to examination only by a select few, and on the other hand a desire for ideas which are important enough to occupy a privileged place in relation to all others. The latter preference is perfectly legitimate, since the ability to order ideas according to priority is a normal part of the pursuit of truth. The preferential selection of certain ideas which give a unity and a coherence to one's worldview, is, in itself a sign of intelligence, but if these ideas are defended to the extent of putting them beyond critical study by not allowing the most essential among them to be examined, we must suspect that there is in fact some 'sleight-of-hand' involved, possibly because of doubts as to whether the whole position would be defensible if openly stated.

The converse of this attitude to ideas is the way in which Plato was not afraid to engage with criticisms of the Theory of Forms, on which his philosophy rested. The alternative to this is always a recourse to arbitrary power, since that alone could spread and uphold ideas which are intrinsically dubious. The oracular and the irrational, if held with enough determination, thus lead inevitably to tyranny and violence, which is an additional reason why cultic thought like that of non-dualism should be critically examined.

Neither non-dualism nor linguistic philosophy has any intrinsic relation to religious orthodoxy, despite the claims made for non-dualism, whose real effect on doctrines is one of dissolution and relativism, because of its commitment to universal illusion. Even in Hinduism, where it originates, it is only one school of doctrine, one which resulted from Shankara's attempt to adapt Hinduism to Buddhism, despite the fact that according to Hindu doctrine Buddhism was heresy. This adaptation has in any case been disputed by the Vedantists of later times. As for all the other major traditions, it does not appear explicitly at all.

Moreover, such doubts about the universal orthodoxy which has been claimed for non-dualism are reinforced by the difficulty in showing that it must remain ultimately separate from monism. The residual duality it allows is really only a metaphysical dead-end, and its inclusion is owing mainly to social and cultural considerations. The support it offers to orthodox beliefs is more symbolic than concrete, but since the heterodox nature of monism is generally recognized, that term is avoided. Moreover, non-dualistic thought is, to say the least, generically monistic, rather as persons of French, German, and Slavonic race are generically speaking Caucasian. Because of this similarity, much can be said which is relevant equally for monism and non-dualism.

Some Basic Presuppositions

Although to some minds its truth appears to be almost too nearly self-evident to need any supporting ideas, the monistic and non-dualistic ideas of God and creation can be shown to depend on a set of presuppositions, in much the same way as anything in mainstream philosophy. Ideally, such presuppositions should take the form of self-evident axioms, or they should at least be convincing in their own right, but in the present case they are much more contestable than that. Four of the main ones are as follows:

(1) That all determination is negation. (This was first formulated explicitly by Spinoza.)
(2) That the individual self is its ego and nothing else.
(3) That God as personal Creator and God as Absolute are objectively separable realities.
(4) That the individual self and its intellectual faculty are likewise existentially or objectively separable.

These are a few of the fine points on which the monistic form of religion turns. It is not exceptional in depending on premises as such, since all coherent systems of belief have them, but their problematic aspect lies rather in their content. When these ideas are examined, it would be well to consider whether we would still assent to them if they appeared without relation to an existing spiritual agenda, or whether they would find only a provisional credence for the sake of argument.

While 1) is true as a particular aspect of determination, it is just as untrue of the condition of determination taken as a whole. If determination was literally and univocally a negation, it would have no content, and there would be no determined things to be known. In reality, every determination is intrinsically an affirmation as well, whether it be a question of form, color, quantity or relation, even though it also involves extrinsic negations. In other words, there can be no simple equation of determination with negation, and that subverts the effectiveness of this axiom.

There is a sense in which the determination 'green' is a negation, in that the choice of green for a given purpose must mean a refusal of yellow, purple, brown, pink, and so on. But there is a confusion here between the intrinsic, or observer-independent reality, and the extrinsic, or observer-dependent reality. In itself, 'green' is a quality which simply is, without affirming or denying anything. Its function as a negation comes from its use by an agent external to it, whence the observer-dependent aspect of this function.

However, this aspect or function of negation depends on the fact no color can combine with any other and remain itself, just as no shape can combine with others without losing something essential. Conversely, the most real Being of all must, (it is supposed), have no determinations, because it could have no limitations or negations. This assumption comes from a further presupposition, according to which, the Highest Reality would consist solely of affirmations, i.e., all Yang and no Yin. This conception is by definition one-sided, and therefore opposed to the all-comprehending totality which alone could suffice for absolute indetermination. Affirmation and negation are not separable here, but are equal parts of reality like Plato's circles of the Same and the Different. To think otherwise, and to take the Absolute to be either univocally positive or negative, or either purely one or purely multiple, would be to reduce it to the level of the phenomenal distinctions it is supposed to transcend.

The second presupposition is that the individual self is solely its ego, because the ego is obviously determined as such, and is therefore clearly a negation according to the first of the above presuppositions. It is doubly a negation because it is understood in the modern manner, which results from a view of the self common to both Cartesian and Empiricist philosophies. It is thus conceived as being nothing more than the flow of conscious phenomena pertaining to it, and not to a soul or substance containing the consciousness. If, on the other hand, the ego is the manifestation of a self which is in reality the soul, as nearly all traditions teach, it means that the individual person is not purely and simply finite, but has a degree of infinity, through having a place in the order of spirits. Consequently, the possibilities of the real self correspond to those of the universe, and it is able to know God to some degree. This amounts to much more of an affirmation than a negation. Even what it has by way of negation is by no means incompatible with perfection, since, from a Christian point of view, it can be redeemed. For non-dualists, the soul's intellectual faculty cannot be part of the individual person, because for them it is God as such, and not a transcendental which shares the Divine attributes. This assumption is necessary for the monistic idea of identification with God, which must not include the deification of the physical person, as that would mean Pantheism, which non-dualists do their best to deny. The idea that the 'divine spark' in the soul is God, and not simply a faculty which shares in the Divine attributes, is thus essential for the non-dualist doctrine.

In practice, the working of the intellectual faculty blends seamlessly with the working of one's ancillary faculties, or one could not be a whole person. That means that if the intellect was God, everything else would have to be God as well, and we would have classic Pantheism after all. The denial of Pantheism in this context is therefore self-contradictory, however necessary it may be for professions of orthodoxy.

If these issues are passed over unnoticed, monistic religion can have a considerable psychological power, especially when the self is taken to be solely the ego, when that nervous bundle of desires, fears and aversions appears to be all we are as individuals. As for presuppositions 3) and 4), they are clearly too dubious to be held for their own sake (and that without proof), and the more plainly they are stated, the more dubious they appear to be. Their acceptance is owing much more to the ideological programme of monism than to any merits of their own.

Where things are objectively separable, it can be seen where and how they have objective limits in relation to one another, and these limits must be limits of being and not just of function. Such limits are as foreign to what we know of God as of the soul. This could, in theory, be taught by revelation, but the monotheistic religions never teach any such idea, although there is a text in the Upanishads which expresses a duality in the self by means of the image of two birds in a tree, one of which eats the fruit on the tree, while the other one just watches. But to take that so literally as to make the self into two different things is to misunderstand one of the basic functions of language. By the same token, any argument for the actual separability of the soul and its intellectual faculty would serve to prove that memory, reason, imagination, feeling and sensory-awareness were all separable entities as well. In this case, there would be no point in supposing the existence of a self, and there would then be nothing in which or to which God could ever be manifest.

To return to the principle that 'all determination is negation,' this idea bears within itself the further presupposition that there is no negation in God. But knowledge of God in the light of the Via Negativa implies that in God there are all degrees of negation as well as all degrees of affirmation, corresponding to all possibilities. Negation is a necessary part of reality as we know it, and to deny it to God as Absolute would be to deny the total and plenary reality that the Source must have. Thus 'all determination is negation,' questionable as it is, further commits us to a presupposition which contradicts the real indetermination of the Absolute by making the latter something specific. On this basis, a more complete set of presuppositions for Non-Dualism would be as follows:

(1) The Absolute is pure unity, undetermined in an explicit sense, without including degrees and negations of determination.

(2) All determination is negation.

(3) God as Person and Creator, and God as Absolute, are two separate realities.

(4) The Individual self and its intellectual faculty are likewise separable realities.

(5) The individual person is solely his ego, and his ego is solely its conscious contents.

(6) The intellectual faculty is not just divine, but is actually God.

A direct consequence of the above, if taken as axioms, is that the perfection possible for man must be the same as the perfection proper to God, since the individual self would have no identity as a member of the class of spiritual beings. This conclusion is clearly necessary for Non-Dualism, and so follows closely from the above. The list of presuppositions is not exhaustive in any case, since it can also be shown to be necessary for Non-Dualism that man be able to know how all the realities known to him form a unity, such that man's knowledge of them could not ultimately be said to differ from that of God. Otherwise, God would have to be reckoned to be free to define the last ends of life in ways which owed nothing to the criteria of conceptual economy and elegance which governs man's intellectual constructions.

One final assumption required by non-dualism is that the Many are absolutely dependent on the One, while the One itself is in no way dependent. This axiom too is not fit for purpose because the One does in some sense depend on the Many, if only for its causal power. This issue is discussed further in Chapter 7.

All the presuppositions considered above are contestable, such that none of them has any true self-evidence, and the certainty of a system cannot be any greater than that of the least certain of its premises. It may be argued that this is to approach the idea from the wrong direction, and that it is rather the presuppositions which depend on the monistic conception of God and salvation, on the grounds that that conception has a self-evidence which makes it logically independent. Its proponents often take it that way, which is why they avoid philosophical preambles about axioms, and are willing to believe that 'all is one' is self-evident both as premise and conclusion—nevertheless, they still have to explain why this truth, if such it is, gives rise to such doubtful consequences as the ones listed above.

However, if this dictum is taken to mean (as it logically could be), that moral evil, untruth, and ugliness are just as much parts of reality as their opposites, the result would be a naturalistic pantheism, and the only transcendent reality would be just the unimaginable vastness of the scale of the real. But non-dualists want to retain the Divine transcendence, however, and so they reject naturalistic forms of pantheism. In this case, the 'all is one' idea depends on the assumption that all negative realities can be consigned to the realm of illusion, but even that does not really solve the problem because we then need to know whether this illusion forms part of the 'all one' or not. If it did, it would conflict with the transcendental perfection, and if it did not, there would be a duality, not a oneness. This is why the idea of world-illusion cannot guarantee the truth of the idea that all is one, if the oneness is understood as a oneness of being. This problem with the illusion idea applies just as much when the world itself is conceived as illusion, and in this case there is the additional problem that it means a God whose perfection did not include power, since there would be nothing for power to effect in the absence of real world. Such a conception is also a denial of the Platonic idea that perfection necessarily implies self-communication and self-propagation, in a way which corresponds to the Christian doctrine that God is love.

The Moral Argument

The truth which is usually felt to be implicit in Monism or Non-Dualism is not metaphysical so much as moral. It connects effectively with something which is essential to all forms of morality, something which integrates the values of social relations with the realm of principles. Morality as such opposes the preference-for-self common to fallen humanity, a preference which always creates an imbalance between the value we give our own interests and the value we give to those of others. The fact that others may treat oneself in just the same way is usually felt to justify this position, although in fact it does not. What is wrong in principle must remain so, regardless of circumstances. Even though preference for self is not always wrong, since there are many cases where it is easier to do some real good to oneself than to anybody else, it serves in a general way to distinguish the non-moral.

Apart from cases of enlightened self-interest, however, it is clear that the more value we allow to ourselves in relation to others, the more harmful and even criminal our behavior will be, since this self-valuation must mean an assumed right to sacrifice the interests of others to our own. Conversely, if we improved morally to the point of being perfectly just, we should allow exactly the same value to ourselves as to others. But justice alone is not the height of virtue, because there is the possibility of allowing more value to others than to oneself, even to sacrificing one's life for them. The ideal of self-sacrifice points therefore to the final extreme of allowing oneself no value at all, and all value to others, and that, presumably, must coincide with perfection. Such would be the last word in perfection, if morality were the only system of value.

Monistic religion translates this moral crux into a metaphysics, and thereby provides the reason why monists think that perfection must lie in the disappearance of the individual self in God; that would be the most inward and essential achievement of the virtue of self-sacrifice which is the summit of self-denying morality. At this point, preference-for-other would not only eliminate the preference-for-self which is the assumed to be basis of all moral wrong and intellectual delusion, but would finally make it impossible, by denying the reality of the self as such. Here is the source of the moral strength which many people find in monistic religion, and which other kinds of person find in Marxism.

Nevertheless, this idea of perfection still misses the mark because of a factual untruth, namely, the assumption that one's own self must be without value in relation to other selves. If this were factually true, it would apply to all selves, and there would be no value anywhere, and the very idea of value would have no basis. Morality would serve to relate only the worthless to the worthless, and this could not be rectified by the idea of the Absolute, because the Absolute does not enter into relationship with anything else. The fallacy involved here ought to be called the Great Inductive Fallacy, because it involves a progression, in which successive reductions in the value assigned to the self result in corresponding increases in one's virtue, while its final step subverts the whole scheme and makes it meaningless. Such is the result of making a relativity into an absolute.

This kind of fallacy can best be illustrated by a story about somebody who has used computers for many years, and has noticed how they have grown steadily smaller with time. He collects facts and figures about this, and plots a graph of Size against Time, and the graph is clearly going down. He then extends the graph to where it crosses over the Time axis, revealing the point which shows the year at which computers must disappear altogether! And why not? After all, computers have always worked as well and even better after every reduction in size, so on this basis they will work best of all when they are reduced to nothing.

The fact that this kind of thinking can easily be seen to be foolish is owing only to the fact that it concerns practical matters most people are familiar with; but when it concerns the universal values and the higher abstractions, this kind of mistake easily passes unnoticed. It is the mistake made by monists and non-dualists, and the sense of standing on moral high ground is satisfying enough to discourage any attempts to look very closely at the validity of this position.

The Mentally Separable

In connection with the question as to whether the intellectual faculty can be separated 'physically' or existentially from the soul, and not just conceptually, the question should be considered in the context of a number of examples of the physically inseparable as follows: Color and extension, which are clearly separable for the mind, even though in physical reality one can never have an extended thing without color, nor a colored one without extension. Similarly, there is a circle and its center; a musical note and its pitch; a stone and its solidity; the two sides of an equation; the woof and warp of a fabric; matter and energy; a thing known and the act of knowing it; a syllogism and its conclusion; salt and its salty flavour; subject and object; height and depth; cause and effect. Rather less obviously, there is the will to continue to live in this world and in the next as well, because there are no arguments against personal immortality which could not serve equally well to justify suicide.

All these things are conceptually separable, but in no other way, whereas there is another class of pairs which are separable physically as well as conceptually: Body and soul; humanity and divinity; nature and grace; chemical elements in compounds and mixtures; liquid and solid; parent and child; work and reward; male and female; religion and philosophy; water and alcohol; stars and planets; light and darkness, food and drink. These examples belong in the most numerous category, one which is only too easy to add to. In such cases as these, at least two distinct substances can be discerned fairly easily, but is that the case with soul and intellect? In such cases, we must also have some idea as to what the supposedly separable entities would be like if and when separated, which is hardly possible in this instance. And yet this concerns realities at the center of our being and experience; in this case, what chance is there of seeing some such dichotomy in God, whom we have never even seen? Such is a further reason why presuppositions (4) and (5) concerning separability are of no use as axioms.

The Single Subject Idea of Identity

While this topic looks like a digression, it serves to elaborate the modern unspiritual idea of the person, the deficiencies of which lead some people to adopt non-dualism as a way of rectifying them. However, this rectification boils down to a replacement of the soul with a transcendental Self or *Nous*, which has no intelligible relation to it. Thus there is apparently an objective basis for the non-dualist fission of the personality, thanks in no small way to materialistic ideas of the self.

In his book *A Parliament of Souls*, Stephen Clark explains some things about the 'single subject' idea of identity which show it to be a glissade down to an idea of the self which is purely and simply materialistic, however little its proponents may wish to be identified as materialists. In the case of soul and body, what is involved is a combination of a material and publicly-perceptible element, and a subtle one. Conversely, the 'single subject' school of thought maintains that there is no objective or intrinsic distinction between these two elements, and it holds that the individual person can be understood as a compound of these two things which could only differ by aspect and by function. But in such cases, where one element is subtle and the other is gross, the removal of the distinction between them really means only the elimination of the subtle element. In other words, the objective reality of the subtle element depends on its having a separate reality. For example, in the case of a wire and the electric current flowing through it, a denial of the separate nature of the electricity simply reduces this combination to the wire alone.

Distinctions of this kind are a matter of routine for philosophy, so why should philosophers who are not materialists think it worthwhile to argue for the 'single subject' idea? Partly this is owing to a desire to keep in step with fashion, which is always an issue where academic careers are at stake, and partly it is owing to an inclination to materialism which one wishes to conceal because of moral embarrassments about it.

Clark further argues (ibid., pp149–150), that the exclusion of souls and psychical causes from the objective world means that everything — and everyone — must eventually be passive material open to direct manipulation, since the soul is the only basis for self-direction and determination from within.

Consequently, this denial of the soul serves as an ideology for a lust for power over nature and over other persons. In effect, it would mean that nature must be open to rape, and people subject to external control, and justifiably so, if externals are all there are. That this position, where it claims to be scientific, is riddled with contradictions is shown from the fact that theoretical physicists like Schrödinger tend to deny a world separate from the mind and the choices of the observer, while at the same time neuropsychologists and molecular biologists, oblivious of this, believe themselves to be reducing the human mind and will to a purely physical reality as popularly understood:

... people seem to have no difficulty in believing both that there is a world discoverable by scientific investigation that is the real cause and context of human evolution and invention, *and* that it is merely superstitious to suppose that how-the-world-is could be specified at all apart from human thought. (Ibid.)

The contradiction here is blatant, but it is typical of modern thought, and follows inevitably from the denial of the spiritual soul of the individual; if we deny the psycho-physical duality of the person, it exists just the same, but now in a supposed single substance where their properties are mixed up in a contradictory manner which is opaque to the understanding and to self-knowledge. Those who are blind to this fail to see that, as Clark puts it:

If matter is only a 'logical construction' it ought to have better manners than to roll like Juggernaut over the human aspirations and logic which constituted it.

To further illustrate the modern incomprehension of body and soul, the same author quotes Shankara concerning the presence of the *Nous* along with the physical being of the person, although what this text says does not make any sense of the fact that they both make up one and the same person, or even that they are related at all. The prevailing modern philosophy denies both sides of this Shankaran teaching. On the one hand, it denies the absolute nature of the *Nous* or Self and merges it with man's physical and subjective being, and on the other it denies that the individual person is just a compound of organic matter. The defiance of logic is all too clear here, and its cause lies in a desire to preserve the idea that there is meaning and value in persons while at the same time denying anything of an objectively spiritual nature in them. This is equally true whether the spiritual principle is conceived as something integrated with the embodied person, or whether it is conceived as something present with, but not really part of, the person, as according to Shankara.

The Multiple Aspect of the Soul

In the same book, Clark continues this discussion of the self on the basis of the non-dualistic conception of it, even though this contradicts the objective distinction of soul and body made hitherto. This is done because of a belief that the separation of the spiritual or intellectual principle from both the soul and the rest of the personality is supported by the traditional conception of the four parts of man, represented by the Ox, the Lion, the Man, and the Eagle.

This is a duality which makes that of soul and body almost ineffectual. The Eagle is said to represent the *Nous* or intellectual principle which judges and corrects the other three, and so cannot be part of them. The Lion and the Ox respectively represent two of the three principles of the soul according to Plato, these being the 'irascible' part, which was represented as residing in the upper chest, and the 'desiring' part, residing in the lower abdomen. The part or function called the 'irascible', or the Lion, communicates between the reasoning and intellectual part and the irrational 'desiring' part, ensuring the unity of the person, because it has properties adapted to both of them. At the same time, this unity of the person is directly realized in the 'Man', who symbolizes the will of the whole person, and this entity symbolizes the sum-total of the effects of the other three in any given person.

Thus the most reasonable interpretation is that all four of these principles inhere in one and the same soul or substance so that they do after all constitute one person. The fact that the 'Eagle', is in a different category from the other three, as it transcends the psycho-physical individuality, is not enough to make it into a separate being, and sacred tradition does not say this, even though it be a universal reality localized in man. It is enough that the soul should have a part or function which participates in the universal nature of the *Nous*, just as it also has another part which participates in the functions of the body, i.e. the 'Ox'. Even more clearly, the soul has functions which are peculiar to it as such, notably the reasoning faculty and moral sentiment. Either the 'Eagle' or the 'Man' can be the highest principle of the four, depending on one's point of view, because the former is highest according to the Chain of Being, owing to its union with intellect, whereas the 'Man' can be taken to be the highest inasmuch as he holds the balance among the other three as manifest in the individual person.

Elsewhere, (*Self and Spirit*, Chapter 3), I have described this fourfold constitution of man as given by Fabre D'Olivet, which answers precisely to the Ox, Lion, Man, and Eagle, in a way which accounts for the personal unity. In the image he uses, which represents man's inner life by three inter-penetrating spheres contained in a fourth one, the first is specifically the consciousness of the body, and is concerned with sensation and instinct. This sphere, represented by the 'Ox', develops up to the center of the second sphere, the 'Animic,' which is that of soul as such, not determined directly by either body or intellect.

This second one is also referred to as the 'Lion'. It develops up to the center of the third one, the Intellective sphere. The development of the latter from its own center symbolizes the truly intellectual possibilities, whereas the region common to this sphere and the Animic symbolizes the level of human reason and rationality. In any given person, there is no necessity for the second 'sphere' to expand far enough to activate the intellective center, and in many or most persons it does not, even though it realizes rationality by union with the lower part of the third 'sphere' below its center. In any case, the fourth and ruling sphere, that of the 'Man', is the container of the first three, so that it, far from breaking with the unity of the self, rather guarantees it and perfects it.

This symbolic analysis of the soul's functions is not therefore to be understood crudely either as a combination of four different things or as a combination of three having a fourth one not really part of it. In particular, this is because the Intellective sphere or 'Eagle' is not Intellect or *Nous* as such, (or intellectual error would be impossible), but is rather the part or function of the soul which can interact directly with Intellect itself. This is the part of the soul I have referred to as the 'divine spark' or synteresis, and it is the distinguishing feature of the rational soul as distinct from the irrational kind.

This conception of the soul's nature is thus a dynamical and interactive development of Plato's tripartite soul, and it expresses the complexity-in-unity of the person, while accounting for the possibilities of both truth and error equally. Conversely, the conception of persons as containing a part which was not effectively a part of them is the kind of idea one would expect from cultures which discovered the distinction between soul and body at an early date, but without developing it from the half-mythical form in which it was first conceived. In this case, the conception of the person would remain in the form of an unintelligible relationship between a divine being and mere matter.

Conclusion

What has been argued concerning the self and its supposed divisibility does not extend to a duality of *Nous* and the physical person, since this one would be too extreme for either member to have anything in common with the other, in which case there could be no relationship between them. Nevertheless, it is just such a relation of the unrelatable which is comprised in presupposition (5). This kind of duality is typical of what results unintentionally from monistic doctrines, where it is assumed that one side of a relation can be cut free so as to become an independent reality by itself. Then there is the 'single subject' conception which is an easy target or straw man for the kind of self-transcendence conceived of by non-dualism. Thirdly, there is the psycho-physical dualism which does not oppose the unity of the person, since it does not require two substantial unities, because it means a duality of natures subject to a single unity, the cause of which is the soul.

Given this relative duality, the unity of the person is participated by the body, and through this dependent relation the body remains recognizably the same through the constant turnover of its material content as long as life and its union with the soul lasts. The four-fold conception of the soul, illustrated by the Tetramorphs, reflects the idea of self as microcosm, according to which the individual being comprehends the whole chain of being from the body to the reflective consciousness which represents the world. So much is requisite for the traditional idea of the person as a substance which contains the ego and its conscious states, and is not merely a stream of ego-phenomena, and is the equivalent in its own way of the grand total of being. This is the traditional conception which is not compatible with presupposition (6), for which the individual self and its intellectual faculty must be two separable entities.

At the same time, the modern single-subject idea of identity is self-contradictory inasmuch as it tries to confer on an organic entity a value which could only belong to a transcendental and immortal substance. Subject to this idea, the attributes which are physical and the ones which are psychical exist as ever, but now as an incoherent mixture in a single mode of being. There is in reality no one kind of substance to which these disparate attributes could belong on the same basis or by equal right. However, those who reject psycho-physical dualism may well be unable to find any escape from presupposition (6) if they will not locate the intellectual faculty in the soul. If so, it would be a good reason why monism and non-dualism find a ready acceptance in many minds which are first shaped by modern reductionist fashions of thought, and then seek dubious alternatives to it.

Concerning presupposition (4), applying to the divine nature, it should be related to what was said about the Mentally Separable. If God as Creator really was separate from God as Absolute, it would mean that the world was caused by a demiurge who was in most respects finite. Even if it is said that this demiurge must be caused by the Absolute, so that the world would indirectly proceed from the very highest order of the real, there still could not be any causal relationships between the Absolute and anything which is finite in any way. Only if God as Absolute and God as Person or Creator are one being can this causal hiatus be avoided.

Were the world created by a demiurge with no intelligible

relation to the Absolute, the result would be much the same as the Manichaean conception of an evil universe which wholly obscures the true God who had no part in its creation. That would reduce salvation to a union of the divine spark in the person with the God hidden by the world. Everything else would be evil *per se* and therefore outside salvation. This would make moral quality, sacrifices and sacramental worship irrelevant, besides excluding salvation of any personal kind.

Where the Absolute is concerned, as in presupposition (1), the short answer is that it could not be the Absolute if it were specifically affirmative by nature, any more than if it were specifically negative; the Absolute must be both equally and neither equally. Failing this, it would be a determined entity, and therefore part of the order of phenomena. In this case, presupposition (3), besides being dubious in itself, would fail in its purpose of excluding determination from the Absolute, even if it were not flawed. Such are some of the main ideas on which monistic religion is tacitly founded, and it is not hard to see why these ideas are hardly ever referred to by non-dualists. Whatever can be claimed for them comes nowhere near the profound certainty claimed for non-dualism itself, and this disparity is a major objection to that certainty.

3

Ignotum per Ignotius

Knowing the Knower

The fallacy of *ignotum per ignotius*, that is to say, of an unknown thing supposedly being made known by means of some other unknown thing is one which can enter unnoticed into all kinds of explanation. Genuine explanations relate the unknown factor to one which is already understood, while the more superficial ones relate it to something familiar, though not well understood. Unfortunately, familiarity can be confused with understanding, and in such cases, things can appear to be understood when they are not. In some cases of explanation, the thing to be explained is shown to be a mere appearance, or a disguise for a more substantial reality. The apparent flatness of the earth, for example, is explained away by the way in which a spherical body appears to an observer situated at a point on its surface. This explanation is effective since we already know what a sphere is and what its properties are.

In more abstract realms, this kind of eliminative explanation is used in monistic philosophies to explain away the apparent multiplicity of the world as an illusory manifestation of what is really a single reality. In such cases, the single true reality behind the appearances is typically equated with consciousness, or at least with consciousness developed to its furthest limits, and no one ever doubts that we know what consciousness is. The individual self would then be seen as a transient phenomenon in the unreal world of appearances, and the distinction between objective and subjective reality would disappear. However, this kind of explanation also eliminates the self-reflective and self-cognitive functions of consciousness along with the individual self, and with them, the possibility of consciousness' ability to explain itself.

The monistic development of consciousness aims at a state of awareness without self-awareness, which is taken to be an ideal despite the fact that a non-self-aware consciousness is in any case the normal condition of nearly all forms of animal life. In a more relative way, it is also manifest in large sections of mankind in which people were or are aware of themselves more as members of races or tribes than as individuals. Insofar as we can understand past cultures, it appears that large numbers of ordinary people in the last few millennia had little awareness of their own egos, not through any spiritual practice, but simply through ignorance. And yet, despite such facts, monists and non-dualists look to this twilight zone of consciousness as though it were the embodiment of some fine ideal.

While taking this view of consciousness, they ignore the fact that self-aware consciousness is the highest kind of consciousness in this world, and regard it as a burden instead, and envy what they take to be the unreflecting peace of the backward parts of mankind among whom tribalism rules. This outlook has a problem with the fact that the self-aware principle is necessarily dualistic, because the awareness-of-awareness is an irreducible duality, and different in kind from the simple awareness of objects in the outside world. It may appear that, even though the self-aware mind is at a high level of development, it must after all be a spiritual dead-end, if the final goal is unity. Must it not yield at last to reduction, and to a simplicity which is more real than it? In reality, the faculty of self-reflection points in a very different direction.

We are concretely aware of the outside world, and equally concretely aware of that awareness. These two levels of awareness are clearly a matter of experience. But theoretically, we could also be aware that we are aware that we are aware, and so on, to yet higher degrees. What if these higher orders of self-awareness could become as concretely real as the one we already possess? In that case, the path of spiritual advance would move into ever greater complexity, not into reduction. The fact that man has a self-aware consciousness, even if only one degree of it, confirms the belief that he belongs in the order of spirits. The fact that he has only the first degree of spiritual being would also be supported by the traditional doctrine that the human state is the lowest member of the order of spirits.

In this case, the angels would differ from us by the possession of such extra dimensions of self-awareness naturally, just as man is distinguished from the animals by his single degree of self-awareness. This being so, it would profoundly affect what we believe about man's relation to God: if we compare this relation with the growth in awareness which occurs with the successive changes in our relation to our parents from childhood to maturity, these stages would represent the higher degrees of self-reflection possessed by superhuman orders of being. The most complete relation to God ever given to a human being would thus be the greatest possible for the most limited species among those which have self-aware consciousness, represented by our childhood relation to our parents in the above comparison.

One objection to the conception of ever-higher orders of self-awareness or self-reflection is that it would only serve to reinforce personal limitations by means of a progression into ever-greater degrees of self-centeredness and self-sufficiency. The answer to this is both surprising and instructive, because it is counter-intuitive. Firstly, the degree of self-awareness which we have now does not, as such, make anyone self-centered unless it is corrupted. On the contrary, it makes one aware of self-centeredness as such, so that it can be corrected. Conversely, if we were to judge the behavior of animals by human moral standards, overlooking the inappropriateness of this for the sake of argument, we would have to judge them to be completely self-centered. Being in this negative moral condition is therefore possible with a near-complete lack of self-awareness. Only self-reflection can correct faults like self-centeredness. It would therefore follow that higher degrees of self-reflection should make possible so many higher degrees of unselfishness at the same time. The higher the order of self, therefore, the less relevant is the issue of being either egoistic or altruistic.

The Scale of Being

The importance of this conception of a hierarchy of beings with successively higher orders of awareness can be seen from the fact that it gives real content to a vista of higher being which would not be possible for systems which have no place for individual self-awareness. Consequently, there need be no fear that arguments against non-dualism and monism might be merely arguments for a lower or more limited idea of ultimate reality. On the contrary, on this basis, it would rather be the monistic schools of thought which can be seen to have the more limited option, that of confining the whole range of higher reality to the human state.

This is why the usual result of not understanding the possibilities of the super-human is an over-estimate of the human state, even in minds which have a deep commitment to self-transcendence. For example, E.F.Schumacher (in his *Guide for the Perplexed*) appears to think that when human self-awareness is fully developed, there could not be any higher order of possibilities. He conceives the scale of being in the natural world as ascending through the levels of Matter, Life, Consciousness, and Self-aware Consciousness, in the inorganic, vegetable, animal and human levels of being. Each one of the last three includes those which precede it: vegetative life includes matter; conscious or animal life includes the vegetative and material elements; and self-aware or human life includes the material, vegetative, and conscious elements. This ascending order points to others above the human level as man's is above the animal level, but this conclusion is not drawn by Schumacher.

Without the higher orders of self-awareness, it can be easy to ignore the significance of the degree of it which man has, which is why non-dualists see nothing strange about seeing awareness without self-awareness as an ideal, and not as the limitation it really is. They may argue that the un-self-aware consciousness they seek is at a vastly higher level than any example of it in the natural world, but this would still not answer the objection. The fact that the loss of self-awareness was supposedly compensated by a transference to a higher state of being would do nothing to raise the intrinsic value of the un-self-aware state. A lower reality would be consigned to a higher place, as though it were an advantage to go from being men on earth to being animals in Heaven.

The idea of an un-self-aware Heaven would be an apt way of drawing attention to the unadmitted humanism which tacitly controls much modern non-personal spirituality. Not least among the paradoxes which follow from this is its dismissive treatment of consciousness as merely a manifestation of the individuality on the one hand, while its spiritual system consists of developments of consciousness which are meant to eliminate the individual. The fact that there can be no source or vehicle for consciousness other than individual persons is disregarded, along with whatever else would obstruct monistic sublation.

Self-awareness marks out the individual as a spiritual being, or at least a being with spiritual potentialities, since it transcends natural phenomena without being the Absolute. It is not part of anything in this world, since it is a whole in which the whole of reality is reflected, the *capax universi* of the Scholastics. Such is the significance of the self's self-reflective core, or the *sakshi* as it is called in the dualistic Vedanta. This was perceived in particular by Madhva, the third of the three greatest Vedantins, and he used it in his refutation of Shankara's monism.

Nevertheless, numerous attempts are made by some monists or non-dualists to show that the individual self can be completely sublated, so that there would no longer be any individual subject of experience. If this were the case, it would free this kind of doctrine from the accusation that it must mean merely a solipsistic reduction of everything to oneself. A good example of this is to be found in the writings of Alphonse Levée who wrote as 'A Monk of the West' (see *Christianity and the Doctrine of Non-Dualism*), who sought to exclude the possibility of solipsism in this way, but without realizing that the supposed process of sublation must still take place within an individual soul which cannot cease to be what it is by reason of what occurs within it.

What this author says in this connection makes it clear that the elimination of the self-aware principle is logically necessary for the goal of non-dualism. If, nevertheless, superhuman states are indeed characterized by higher degrees of self-reflection for the reasons given above, all doctrines of monistic sublation must ultimately be a spiritual dead-end.

What is Consciousness?

Colin McGinn has revived a longstanding controversy as to whether human consciousness can know what it is (*The Problem of Consciousness*, Blackwell 2004). This is highly relevant, because the negative conclusion he reaches can only mean that the ideal of an absolute consciousness could not be real for human beings. It appears that for consciousness to be able to explain itself, it would have to do something it has never done before, and not in the trivial sense of an eye seeing something it had not seen before, but rather in the manner of an eye hearing something; in other words it would have to do something in a different category from what it had done hitherto.

The possibility of consciousness explaining itself does not appear to be self-contradictory, but can it be shown to be worth taking seriously? It will be said that a robot could be made to investigate itself, that is, detect and record certain of its properties, but that is not the same as a machine explaining what it is. For one thing, it is only a 'machine' for human machine-users, not for itself, so a machine would be the last thing to be able to unravel the meaning of 'machine'. The machine *qua* machine is in fact a product of the intentionality of its users, just as a social event like a party or a board meeting is what it is owing to the intentionality of those present. This applies to the deep difference between consciousness investigating its various conscious activities and investigating itself as such. Since it is not a machine, it may somehow be able to make such a study, even though it has not done so hitherto, but it is much more likely that this could only be done for us by another kind of being altogether. Since this involves self-knowledge of the most essential kind (even though the essence of consciousness is not the same as the essence of the human state), it is not affected by the conditions of life as they have been altered by technology. This being so, it must have been equally possible for rationally-conscious beings for hundreds of thousands of years, and yet it appears never to have been achieved. By way of comparison, supposing it were claimed that human beings would one day have eyes that could see inside themselves as well as outside: that would be impossible because it would be self-contradictory in terms of biology and optics; all the parts inside an eyeball are directed to what is outside. It is highly probable that the mental vision of self-explanatory consciousness may be constructed in a manner analogous to this. The belief that it is designed to act upon everything but itself is expressed in a Sufi proverb: 'As a sword cannot cut itself, and a finger cannot touch its own tip, so mind cannot see itself.'

This is apparently the verdict of traditional wisdom in general, excepting the school of *Advaita*. Supposing consciousness could explain what it was: would that not mean that it coincided with God? It would if the precondition of self-explanation was that of being self-caused and self-existent. In this case all outside agency and outside inputs would be wholly excluded, and therefore complete self-explanation would follow directly. In reality, it is only too obvious that human beings are not self-caused or self-existent, whence any self-explanatory awareness they might possibly have could not be self-generated, but would have to be implanted in them from outside. In this connection, Aquinas argues that this kind of self-knowledge is in reality peculiar to God, where he says that

> From the fact that God is intelligent it follows that His act of understanding is His essence.' (*Summa Contra Gentiles*, vol. 1, chap. 45, [1]).... Also the divine essence is through itself perfectly intelligible, as is clear from what we have said. Since therefore, the divine intellect and the divine essence

are one, it is evident from what we have said that God understands Himself perfectly. (Ibid., bk. 1, chap. 47, [4])

This cannot apply to man, inasmuch as the essence of human consciousness is not the same as the essence of the human state; we *have* consciousness, but it is not what we are.

Similarly, in the same chapter, Aquinas says that:

The operation of the intellect will be more perfect as the intelligible object is more perfect. But the most perfect intelligible object is the divine essence, since it is the most perfect and the first truth. (Ibid., [6])

These ideas concerning God's self-knowledge should now be compared with what Aquinas says about the human soul's ability to understand itself. To begin with, he quotes St.Augustine who appears to say that in fact it can know itself through itself:

Just as the mind gathers knowledge of bodily things through the bodily senses, so does it obtain knowledge of incorporeal things through itself. And so, it knows itself through itself, since it is incorporeal. (*SCG.* vol. 3, chap. 46, [1], quoted from *De Trinitate*, bk. IX, chap. 3)

However, the qualification to this is stated as follows:

Now it cannot be said that it understands what it is, through itself. For a cognitive potency becomes an actual knower by the fact that there is present in it that whereby the knowing is accomplished.... But the soul is always actually present to itself, never merely potentially or habitually. So if the soul knows itself through itself, in the sense of what it is, it will always actually understand what it is. And this is plainly false.' (Ibid., [2])

Were it otherwise, nobody would even need to be a philosopher or a theologian in order to enjoy this degree of self-knowledge, and this is obviously untrue in view of all the conflicting attempts which have been made to explain man's identity. What Augustine really meant about self-knowledge can be seen where he says:

> Let not the mind, therefore, seek itself as though it were absent, but let it take care to discern itself as present. Let it not know itself as though it did not know itself, but (know) how to distinguish itself from that which it knows to be another thing.' (*De Trinitate*, bk. X, chap. 9)

This implies that the mind can know what it is negatively, that is, by knowing itself to be different from things it does know. To go from knowing *that* it is to knowing *what* it is, it would have to seek its own nature 'as though it were absent,' as Augustine puts it, which is apparently impossible. This is in fact the conclusion drawn by Aquinas:

> And so, according to Augustine's meaning, our mind knows itself through itself, insofar as it knows concerning itself that it is. Indeed, from the fact that it perceives that it acts it perceives that it is. Of course, it acts through itself, and so, through itself it knows concerning itself that it is. (*SCG.*, vol. 3, chap. 46, [8])

The question of the inability of human consciousness to say *what* it is has implications for man's knowledge of God. Mind does not have to know what it is in order to have some kinds of knowledge of God, at least where this arises within the scope of dualistic doctrine. However, where knowledge of God is taken to be total and absolute, as in Advaitic religion, the mind's ability to know itself becomes an issue. The closed ring of 'realization' cannot really be closed if the instrument or vehicle of the identity is not knowable to itself. There is even something self-contradictory about a supposedly absolute knowledge of God residing in an entity which cannot explain itself to itself. It does not matter that the sense of individual selfhood may have been all but eliminated by mental disciplines and techniques, because the absence of self-explanation cannot be atoned for by the suppression of what needed explanation, any more than a disease is cured by killing the patient.

Besides, the resultant condition of the non-dualist sage could still be merely that of an individual self in a severely contracted state, and not something outside that state. There is no possibility of deciding this question by appeal to experience, since it concerns an alleged experience which is by definition non-dual and non-conceptual. There are therefore no criteria by which it could be communicated, shared or verified.

Experience Without Content

Spiritual experience is of unique importance in connection with monistic types of religion because its theoretical basis alone is not adequate, even for those who believe in it. Nevertheless, if any two Advaitists (or Buddhists) were to claim that they have been through the same experience, they would have no way of confirming it, since it was by definition non-dual and non-conceptual, and therefore in no way expressible. This is made clear by Paul Williams (*The Unexpected Way*, p67, T&T Clark Ltd., London 2002) as follows:

> If two people say that they have each had an experience of X and that it was non-dual, nonconceptual and inexpressible, they precisely have said nothing as such about either X or the experience of X. The experience of X has no content. Thus they cannot say that both experiences were of the same thing. That would be a contradiction.

If this were not enough, the Absolute with which non-dualists aim to identify is believed by them to be without attributes or qualities, in which case, one must believe that they have had an incommunicable experience of something about which nothing could be said in any case. There are of course innumerable natural experiences which words alone cannot convey, even though their content is clear and specific, but when there is no specific content, the result is not so much the unknown conveyed by the unknown as the unknowable by the unknown.

Consequently, alleged experiences of this kind cannot justify the belief that they are the essence of any one religion, let alone of all religions, as Guénon and Schuon believed. What is believed in this way is therefore an example of a subjective religious belief which cannot connect with an objective conception of the real. One consequence of its being true would be that the revealed form of a religion could not reveal the essence of that religion. That non-dualists think this to be the case is shown by their application of such metaphors as the 'shell' and the 'kernel' to express the difference between form and essence in religion. This metaphor is question-begging because it presupposes that the form and the essence of a religion are two separate things, loosely fitted together. This could not be possible according to Platonic thought, where the so-called shell would necessarily be an instantiation of the essence, just as with body and soul. In this case, the essence by itself must comprise the shell to a higher power.

None of the universal religions has taught that its essence was non-dual experience, and that everything else about them was rind or shell, even though their aim was always union with God as a union of real persons. Likewise, none of them has taught that the essence of consciousness could be detached from the personality and could thus live a separated life.

Humanly, however, such beliefs often go together with a passionate advocacy of religious orthodoxy, as in the case of Guénon himself. There is an incoherence here, in that it is a spiritual way for which everything depends on individual mystical experiences, while at the same time the nature and content of these experiences is completely unverifiable, and not accidentally unverifiable, but from the very principles held by this form of religion itself.

These principles follow Shankara's doctrine that the supreme reality is the Nirguna Brahman, who has no attributes. In God there must no doubt be a reality which is beyond expression in terms of attributes or qualities, along with all that is so expressible. But where it is a question of a reality which is *solely* without attributes, one cannot escape the question as to why it should be named at all. To divide the Divine nature between Brahman (with attributes) and the Absolute (without attributes) is in any case considered blasphemous by Hindus who follow Vedantists other than Shankara. (see Eric Lott, *Vedantic Approaches to God*, chap. 8, p121) Logically, what has no attributes must be beyond the scope of consciousness, while in monistic religion there is no alternative to consciousness and personal experience. Even if one were simply to claim that consciousness was an absolute in itself, that would involve an insoluble problem of proving that there was no other reality beyond it.

In the present state of philosophy and science, consciousness has next to no prospect of being able to explain what it is, either in the reductive manner of materialism, or in terms of itself alone. The huge advances in scientific knowledge have failed to bring this self-explanation the tiniest bit nearer, and its apparent impossibility for the human mind contrasts with its reality as a Divine attribute, as explained in the previous section. This state of affairs could not be so if non-dualism were true, nor if the human level of self-consciousness were the highest one. From this it would be rational to conclude that human consciousness is in fact a created thing, which is to say that its cause lies outside itself. This being so, Advaitist attempts to transcend God would be as hopeless as trying to lift oneself by one's shoe laces.

Whatever the followers of Shankara were to do, it would still be done before God, to whom they would be accountable for it, as with anyone else. Even where one's life was in all other respects a continuous example of virtue, the pursuit of an evident impossibility like the above must be a problem when justifications have to be found for it, except in cases of invincible ignorance. This conclusion follows from the conception of the soul as the locus of a unique representation of the world, in which attempts at self-transcendence of this kind must be made. (See *Self and Spirit*, chaps. 1 & 2)

On this basis, the soul contains its own form not merely of the material world, but of the psychical and spiritual worlds as well.

It is thus the theatre of all spiritual experiences, whether they are valid or not, and therefore not liable to be subsumed in them.

Reality Above Intellect

Non-dualism derives support from the doctrine taught by the Neo-Platonic philosophers that the highest function of the soul is above even the intellect. However, they made this higher function the medium whereby the soul can communicate with the Divinity, rather than sublating itself. By the standard of pure unity, the intellect falls short of the highest level because its nature is that of a duality of knower and known within a unity. Such is the traditional doctrine which monism and non-dualism distort where they take this highest function of the soul to be identical with the One or the Nous, when in reality it is part of the soul, with which it interacts with the pure unity of the One. It is thus the summit, so to speak, of the personal microcosm, participating in the higher realities in the manner appropriate to its own nature.

Consequently, non-dualism could only be true if this faculty could break free from the rest of the personality and live a separate life in a state of identity with the objective *Nous* or Absolute. In any case this is impossible because the soul is not an assembly of parts like a body, even though it is a unity ruling a plurality of powers. If it could undergo any such separation, the result would mean destruction for what was separated as much as for what was left behind. When it is realized that the unity of the soul cannot literally be disrupted, and that therefore all experience is by definition intra-psychic, non-dualistic mystical experiences must be private activities in the 'inner space' of certain souls, and this is precisely a consequence of their being created spirits.

Even if it is accepted that non-dualist teachings are correct descriptions of things which actually happen in certain souls, the fact that this interior change can transform the life of a given person is no proof that it must be a model for others, let alone an insight into the nature of reality as a whole. How many persons claiming to have monistic or non-dualistic illumination would there have to be before their testimony amounted to an argument or tentative proof that they had the highest truth? They are in any case far less numerous than those who believe in alien abductions, besides which there is always the problem with non-dual experiences from what was indicated above by Paul Williams.

Thus the monistic idea of reality is founded on a hypothetical experience which, if real, would comprise a one-way progression from the many to the One. The belief that reality as such must be monistic on the basis of some such experience is a good example of a kind of thinking which is unable or unwilling to go beyond subjectivity. The implicit belief that reality itself must be monistic or non-dual because some people claim to have experiences of this kind reveals a massive confusion between subject and object. Where ideas of God are concerned, it appears in an unawareness of the difference between God as such, and God as experienced by certain persons. This position is known to modern philosophy under the heading of 'verificationism', so-called because it equates the truth of statements with our means of verifying them without reference to any objective conditions to which they would be relative.

Where this thinking is applied to past events, these events are equated with what we can remember of them, despite the fact that they cannot be verifiable in this way because they transcend our memories of them; what has happened remains so, regardless of how well or badly we remember it. What would make something true, regardless of whether we have access to it or not, and our personal experiences of it, are quite different things, whereas verificationism conflates them with its subjectivist point of view. Such also is the position of monism and non-dualism. As Colin McGinn has expressed it (*The Making of a Philosopher*, chap. 4),

Thus I know what it would be for there to be a table in the next room, since I have a conception of physical objects in objective space, and I also know what kind of evidence would make me assert this, namely the experience of seeing such a table. Why conflate these two pieces of knowledge? Only, it seems, to insist that the former knowledge be reducible to the latter; but that is just to presuppose antirealism (or verificationism) from the start.

In a spiritual context, the conflation just referred to by McGinn in the above is also precisely the conflation of the non-dualist mystic with his God; the principle is the same in either case.

The same author continues:

The general point here is that it is wrong to confuse reality itself with our ways of knowing it. Reality is one thing; our knowledge of it is another. The past is not the same as our memories of it; physical objects are not the same as the sensory states we have when we perceive them; other people's minds are not the same as the behavior we use to infer things about them; the future is not the same as the current indications of how it will turn out; elementary particles are not the same as the meter readings that signal their presence; and so on.

Significantly enough, there is just one realm where the verificationist idea of reality *is* valid, namely, that of fiction: what was written about Sherlock Holmes, for example, and the character himself coincide completely, since he and Conan Doyle's images of him are one and the same. Thus the fictional character really is subject to the verificationist test of reality. In the theological context, this shows what the followers of Shankara are doing with the ideas of God and of the Absolute. Once they are equated with an alleged experience, the result would be to empty belief in God of objective reality, since that meaning would be wholly in the subjective grasp of certain individuals. Such a God and such a religion would, of course, be absolutely irrefutable, even if in the dubious sense of the word which appears in modern thought, (which fully explains the confidence and sense of spiritual power which appears in its advocates), but its irrefragable content is certain only by being tautological: the known has no criterion but the knower, and vice-versa.

Consciousness and Finitude

The question of consciousness being able (or not) to explain itself is manifested in quite down-to-earth ways. For example, no one knows why or how their own conscious processes can function with sufficient continuity and reliability to complete whatever statement they are making, or any other rational purpose. Why anyone's wits continue to function at all for even the briefest purpose was never known even to a Plotinus. One knows only that when one wills one's mind to do something it usually happens, just as one's foot goes forward when that is willed. Similarly, no one knows how their minds come to grasp the truth about things they previously did not understand. A certain effort was made in that direction, but that is always anything but a guarantee that the required understanding will arise. No one, in other words, can guarantee that they will understand any given thing that interests them, and this is the same for the most intelligent minds as much as for the least, and neither is this affected by differences in moral virtue.

Clearly an absolute consciousness could not be subject to any such contingency, whether in regard to its own continuity or in regard to its ability to understand. This is the issue which Plato and Augustine resolved by the idea of the illumination from God or the Form of the Good, which acts as the bond between intelligences and their intelligible objects. If the intelligence must converse with God, whether it intends to do so or not, in order to fulfil its function, it could not claim divinity for itself without self-contradiction.

In the *Meno* dialogue, Plato found that he could not explain what virtue is, not particular virtues, but virtue as such. Since then, the religions have had comparable problems with explaining what holiness is, or with explaining the one thing needful which it is imperative that we do. (Christians can equate this knowledge with the imitation of Christ, but that is still a pragmatic answer which does not explain virtue in Christ or in oneself.) This difficulty has no doubt exacerbated disputes over heresy. The problem here is not the same thing as an inability to explain consciousness, but there is an obvious relation between them; something of the most essential nature to our being is mysteriously opaque to us. When we say 'explain' in this context, it must be understood as 'explain non-reductively,' because reductive explanations are little better than denials of the reality of what they purport to explain. On this level, consciousness would be nothing but the behavior of brain cells, and virtue and holiness would be just an extension of the herd instinct. These things merely underline the conclusion that a consciousness explaining itself by means of itself non-reductively boils down to a way of defining God, since only absolute aseity could ensure such a thing.

Another aspect of the creaturely nature of human consciousness can be seen in the fact that no human mind is able to concentrate on more than one thing at a time. This has nothing to do with the power or intelligence of any particular mind, since it is universal. This would be no problem for an absolute consciousness of course, and an ability to concentrate equally on at least a small number of different things would not be a problem for a consciousness which was still far short of absoluteness. That even the heights of mystical experience do not raise anyone above this issue is clearly manifest in the fact that monistic mystical sages nearly always have to isolate themselves from direct contact with the world and its activities in order to preserve and consolidate their unitive vision. No being with absolute consciousness could ever need such precautions.

This is very much part of the related issue of awareness without self-awareness so much sought by non-dualists. Here again, a superhuman consciousness would have no difficulty with combining the most extreme degree of awareness with the most extreme degree of self-awareness, even though it were far short of divinity.

Dangers of Impersonal Mysticism

Those who are attracted by such beliefs usually cannot resist equating the non-dual state with some preconceived idea of what they think it must be like. The mere fact of its verbal expression must give rise to a mental formation which is radically adverse to common sense. What one takes for truth in this way can only give rise to a belief that normal experience is illusory, with the inner conflicts that that gives rise to. Where this involves the belief that human consciousness is in principle if not in fact absolute, a special danger results precisely from its lack of any power of self-explanation.

In normal life, this deficiency is simply a harmless limitation which one can easily ignore unless one is a philosopher. It is a privation or relativity which it shares with everything else in creation, whether it be material or subtle. But once the question of absoluteness arises, however tacitly, this privation ceases to be merely something that could be made good from elsewhere, since there could no longer be an 'elsewhere' for an absolute reality. In this case, the privation or 'reality deficit' must itself be made absolute along with the consciousness itself. Consequently, one has no alternative but to identify with this negation, since a personal God is excluded along with any other reality outside one's consciousness. The positive function of consciousness cannot balance this because all it can do is focus one's mind on the negation.

To believe oneself to be committed to a void like this is a more than adequate cause for depressive mental illness, which is most likely to affect those whose minds are healthy and logically serious enough to react against irrationalities imposed on them. People can get caught in this way because consciousness is one of the very few things which is spiritual and comprehensive enough by nature for one to be able to conceive of absolutizing it without a sense of absurdity. It can be tacitly made into a God without any immediate problems, as long as the idolatry remains unrecognized. Those who can stabilize this condition and seem to live healthily on it do so because they are able to avoid mental contact with the 'absolute void' which their doctrine logically implies in the midst of their supposedly absolute consciousness.

This is usually because of mental defenses which keep one firmly joined to the world of common sense reality, no matter what one believes theoretically. The mind can have its own equivalent of partitions and fire screens. This can appear in persons who understand the world very well, and are talented and resourceful in dealing with it and using it. The mind-destroying identification with negation is thus blocked by a prior identification with the world. On the other hand, less extraverted people, who nevertheless have essentially healthy minds are more seriously at risk. They may well be among those whose energies cannot be spread so widely, and so must live closer to the flaws at the center of their world-view. The problems of such persons are compounded where they are more than usually logically-minded, because they would not be able cheerfully to march past deep problems in the way that a more worldly kind of mind can.

These issues are relevant in today's world because the traditional injunction 'Know thyself' is so often taken over by those who believe that the more deeply the self is known, the more absolute and unlimited it will be found to be. This not only involves taking the mind to be inherently separate from its embodied individuality, which is all too obviously limited, but it also requires us to ignore the ways in which our conscious nature itself can be seen to be limited as such. Contrary to such teachings, the price of self-knowledge remains, as in the purely psychological field, realism.

4

Descartes & Shankara: A Revealing Parallel

A Perennial Issue

In the realm of traditional wisdom, the idea of comparing Descartes and Shankara has rarely if ever arisen, because one of them is taken to be a paradigm of traditional orthodoxy, while the other is perceived to be the founder of the modern individualistic speculation which first deformed traditional truths and then attacked them. For Guénon and Schuon, Shankara's monistic doctrine was the very essence of tradition, and a basis for the interpretation of most other doctrines, even those which showed no connection with it. But a question remains as to how far Shankara was handing on an existing tradition, and how far he was an innovator. In the eighth and ninth centuries AD, Hinduism was under pressure to defend itself from Buddhism, and I shall argue that he produced a Vedantic idea of salvation which was nominally opposed to that of Buddhism while being substantively the same as it. The true Self of the Advaitins is in any case subjectively convertible with the no-self of Buddhism in a way which presents no psychological difficulty.

The means whereby Shankara arrived at his doctrine are discernible from criticisms made of it in later centuries, and much will depend on the validity of the method he used. It appears that he made a radical change in the way in which the individual self or *atman* was understood, one which made it easily reducible or sublatable to the one and only true reality by reducing it to a phenomenon. Since this took place in the context of Indian thought, it would be made easier to understand if it could be linked to a corresponding change made in Western philosophy, and in fact there is a change of precisely this kind in the philosophy of Descartes.

What Descartes did with the Scholastic idea of the soul will make it clear that there is a universal issue here, which is liable to arise in traditions which are otherwise completely unrelated. The fact that it did not lead Descartes to either materialism or monism was owing much more to the constraints of religious orthodoxy in his time than to the nature of his idea.

A further reason for introducing Descartes' thought in this context is the fact that for the dualistic or *Dvaita* Vedanta, the self-reflective principle in the soul, on which the *cogito* argument depends, has always been considered to be a fundamental objection to monistic spirituality. This is because it is not merely a phenomenon, despite being part of the individual, because self-reflectivity is transcendental and world-defining by nature. Such an entity would be outside the natural order, and therefore not liable to be sublated. This issue is separate from the one just referred to, that of the reduction of the self to its conscious contents, however, but both are highly relevant in regard to the validity of the monistic *Advaita* doctrine. Since it is negatively relevant to *Advaita* thought, I will introduce the self-reflective principle with a summary of the *cogito* argument which is founded on it, beginning with its impact on secular society.

To modern minds, the idea of a spiritual role for the *cogito* argument and its ontological basis may seem very strange, in view of the effects it is known to have had on modern thought, and from thence to modern values. It can appear as malefic, though it enshrines an idea which enhances the active powers of the self. The individual mind is conceived as a self-luminous center, surrounded by a world which is problematical, deceptive, and thus open to being re-ordered by the lucid mind which has a privileged position in relation to it. Even if everything outside were an illusion, the mind would still know itself and its innate ideas. The ideological support this gives to individualism is clear enough, and it is doubtful whether this idea of the self has ever been given up by any of those who verbally reject Cartesian philosophy. It is simply too attractive. Modern writers never doubt that they have privileged access to their own subjective condition, while modern science and State officialdom tend more and more to see the world as passive material for endless interventions from minds which have no relations to it except those of their own choosing. All these assumptions are typically Cartesian.

This enhanced power for the individual reasoning mind, supposedly free of binding relations to God or man, is derivable from the Cartesian conception of the self. Here again, it is one thing for critics to deny the reality of, say, innate ideas, and quite another to give up the intellectual self-sufficiency which would be reasonable if there were innate ideas. The decay of intellectual culture in modern times is thus visible in the professedly anti-Cartesian culture where individuals still assert their right to engage with the world and society as though they were outside of it, independently of any principle or authority which might dictate any obligations to them or limit their right to judge. This is an obvious source of social disorder; it means that what is affirmed in practice no longer reflects what is held in theory.

If a rootless individualism is the cause of secularized society, individualism is in turn based on the idea of the self associated with Descartes, whether those concerned realize that or not. But the question still remains, is this idea simply a falsehood, or is it a truth which is open to abuse? The former option is accepted by some traditionalists who equate individuality itself with sin and delusion, but traditional wisdom itself does not support this. The basis of the *cogito* argument in the soul appears both in the works of St. Augustine and in the interpretations of the Vedanta made by Madhva, which will be considered later.

The *Cogito* in Tradition

The original form of the *cogito* argument was presented by Augustine in a number of places in his works, and it is his unique contribution to the conception of personality. He wanted the truth to be established in a way which would be proof against attacks by sceptics, and this was also the motive for Descartes's version of it, of course. The latter's 'method of doubt' was meant to be purely provisional, but in fact it entangled minds which were too much open to doubt in any case. Against this, Augustine had made it clear that doubt itself is only possible on the basis of an implicit certainty:

> Everyone who knows that he has doubts knows with certainty that something is true, namely, that he doubts. He is certain, therefore, about a truth. Therefore everyone who doubts whether there be such a thing as the truth has at least a truth to set a limit to his doubt. (*True Religion*, xxix, 72–73)

It should be noted that this kind of argument is independent of the imagination, and of any imaginary pictures of the self which may derive from its internal dialogue. It therefore does not involve any attempt to reify something subjective. The union of being and knowing is independent of more relative conditions, and Augustine makes this explicit elsewhere:

> I know without any fantastical imagination that I am myself, and this I know and love. I fear not the Academic arguments on these truths, that say, 'What if you err?' If I err, I am. For he that has no being cannot err, and therefore mine error proves my being.' (*City of God*, vol. 1, bk, xi, chap. xxvi, J.M. Dent & Sons, London, 1967)

The words 'If I err, I am,' are an obvious precursor to 'I think, therefore I am.' But for Augustine, the 'I am' was inseparable from 'I live,' because that is not affected by the question as to whether we are awake or dreaming:

> But he who is certain about the knowledge of his own life does not say of it: 'I know that I am awake,' but 'I know that I live,' whether he, therefore, sleeps or whether he is awake, he lives. He cannot be deceived in his knowledge of this

even by dreams, because to sleep and see in dreams is characteristic of one who lives. (*The Trinity*, bk. xv, chap. 12, §21,
The Catholic University of America Press, Inc., Washing-
ton, DC, 1963)

In relation to the question of sublation, it should be noted
that the above arguments show the self-cognitive principle to be
unaffected either by sense-related faculties such as imagination,
or by the difference between being awake or dreaming. In this
case, it could not be sublated into anything in the course of life
or nature, although Shankara's doctrine requires that it should
be. This involves the essential connection between knowing and
being which underlies all metaphysical knowledge, and sets it
apart from cultural fabrications. They are, besides, two of the
three universal miracles, as Schuon calls them, that is to say,
being, knowledge, and life, and their intrinsic union can be
known in the self-reflective function of the soul. Such is the traditional conception which Descartes took over for purposes of
his own, and he was probably the first major thinker since
Augustine to do this. However, he changed its use so as to
emphasize the autonomy of the thinker while depriving the
thinker of a true substance, as will be shown later.

Descartes begins from the position that there is nothing in
the outside world which could not be experienced in a dream.
But this problem pointed to its own solution:

> But immediately upon this I observed that, whilst I thus
> wished to think that all was false, it was absolutely neces-
> sary that I, who thus thought, should be somewhat; and as I
> observed that this truth I think, hence I am, was so certain
> and of such evidence that no ground of doubt, however
> extravagant, could be alleged by the sceptics capable of
> shaking it.... (*Discourse on Method*, part iv, J.M. Dent & Sons,
> London 1957, John Veitch, tr.)

An indication of the direction in which this idea is being
taken can be seen in some further statements in the same place:

I thence concluded that I was a substance whose whole essence or nature consists only in thinking, and which, that it may exist, has no need of place, nor is dependent on any material thing; so that 'I', that is to say the mind by which I am what I am, is wholly distinct from the body.... (Ibid.)

There is an obvious parallel here between this formulation and the total disjunction between the Self and the body taught by the Advaitists. In either case, there is a deeply impoverished idea of the individual self. It is besides linked to Descartes' controversial contention that the mind knows itself more readily and effectively than it can know anything in the outside world. In fact it does not follow that what is known from within must always be better known than something known from without. Granted that knowledge from within is in principle deeper by nature, it can still be frustrated by false assumptions and emotional blockages, whereas the external mode of knowledge can be clearer, especially as the conditions for it are simpler.

Although the *cogito* argument has often been challenged in modern times, it remains an essential part of traditional metaphysics. It is denied only by philosophies which are created to satisfy a desire that philosophical thought should engage only with words and not things. This tendency is in any case a means of saving scepticism and of excluding belief in God. H.M. Bracken maintains that the *cogito* argument is also an effective answer to the sceptical challenge based on the fact that, because we have to use a criterion in order to judge a proposition to be true, the truth of the criterion has to be proved in the same way, and so on ad infinitum. (See H.M. Bracken, *Descartes*, p 46, One World, Oxford, 2002) In answer to this problem, the *cogito* argument unites the true proposition 'I am' with its criterion 'I think' in a seamless whole which requires no further support. Though he does not say so directly, this is true in this case because being and knowing belong in the primal triad of Being, Life, and Intellect, which is central to Platonic thought.

More generally, the *cogito* is valid because anything which purports to be objective can turn out to be otherwise, but subjective experience as such is always necessarily what it appears to be, even if we do not know how it is caused. (See Bryan Magee, *Confessions of a Philosopher*, pp 94–98) Consequently, conclusions based on the mere fact that we have subjective experiences must needs be true. This is why the *cogito* can only be disputed by the kind of verbalistic thinking for which words relate only to other words and not things.

I have dwelt on the subject of the *cogito* argument, not just because of its importance in the Christian tradition, but because it is equally important in that of Hinduism. In the works of Madhva, the third of the great interpreters of the Vedanta, the faculties of the soul are described under three headings, namely, *Indriyas, Manas, Sakshi*. Of these, the *Sakshi* is the central self-reflective faculty which is the objective basis for the *cogito* argument:

> The *Sakshi*, internal witness, is the most important compo-
> nent of Madhvacarya's epistemology. Perceptual cognition
> has several layers, and the *sakshi* is the innermost one. The
> *indriyas* are at the outermost layer, the *manas* is in the mid-
> dle, and the *Sakshi* is at the core.... The *Sakshi* serves an
> identical purpose to that of the *cogito* argument in Madh-
> vacarya's epistemology as the experience and source of
> absolute certainty and awareness that there is a knower. (*An
> Introduction to Madhva Vedanta*, p 28, Deepak Sarma, Ashgate,
> Aldershot, 2003)

The importance of this, 'the basic level of reflective conscious-ness,' (ibid.) results from its being both individual and yet not part of the individual's sensory phenomena. As such, its individual nature is beyond the reach of encroachment, and for Madhva this makes it the basis of a real self and immortal soul. Sarma points out the parallel case that, for Descartes, also, 'self-reflection and thought, at the very least, proves that there is a knower' (ibid., p 28). Consequently, the *Sakshi* is also understood as the basis for absolute certainty in *Dvaita* Vedanta. Being self-reflective, or converted to itself as Platonists would say, the *Sakshi* is said by Madhva to be '*svaprakasa*, self-luminous and self-validat-

ing,' and therefore independent of any other validating principle. Although it is without *dosha* or defect, it can still err if given
wrong information by its attendant faculties, such as *manas*. Such
is the key to the Madhva realism, and its validity has the same
basis as that of the Cartesian *cogito*.

Soul Without Substance

What Descartes gives with one hand, he takes away with the
other, however, because as soon as the existence of the self is
demonstrated, he equates it with things which the Scholastics
would have called its accidents. Here, he directly opposes
Aquinas, who argues that the souls are individual substances
which determine the nature of the whole person, independently
of the conscious phenomena of thoughts and sensations they
may entertain. For Aquinas it is their being which comes first:

> Mind is the form of man's body. Active things must have
> forms by which they act; . . , now the soul is what makes our
> body live; so the soul is the primary source of all those
> activities that differentiate different levels of life. (*Summa
> Theologiae* 76, 1, p111, T. McDermott ed.)

In this passage, the word 'mind' is used instead of 'soul',
despite the fact that the soul is the more comprehensive reality.

Here, as elsewhere, he asserts that mind or soul is united to its
body, not just as its mover, but as its 'form', that is, its immaterial
type and causal principle. Having set aside a number of materialistic explanations of our mental life, he concludes that:

> it remains that the human soul is an intellectual substance
> united to the body as its form.' (*SCG.*, vol. ii, chap. 68, [2])

The fact that the form is detachable or 'subsistent' as Aquinas
calls it, does not prevent it from being able to communicate
its own being to the material of the body, in a way which answers
to both Aristotelian and Platonic ideas of the Forms at the same
time. The soul is said to be 'an actuation of body,' and its

receptiveness to all Forms without being determined by any of them means it cannot have any material nature. This is the basis of its mental activity:

> The human soul, however, because it is a source of mental activity, must itself subsist, even though it is not in a body. (*Summa Theologiae*, 75, 2, p109, T. McDermott, ed.)

Far from consisting in mental events, therefore, the soul is the source of them, but contrary to this, Descartes drastically simplifies the idea of the soul, such that it would indeed be purely and simply its thoughts; the substance would not *have* the accidents, it would rather *be* them. In this case, it must cease to have any specific identity, or be able to impart any to the body:

> As Descartes puts it later on in the Second Meditation, 'I am, I exist — that is certain: but for how long? For as long as I am thinking. (John Cottingham, *Descartes*, p36)

The reductionist tendency in this is perfectly clear, since the very idea that there should be a thinker to think the thoughts is implicitly denied. Now the way is open for modern reductionism which denies the reality of personal identity in the name of a supposed economy of hypotheses. Descartes himself does not draw that kind of conclusion, even though rather illogically. Hume, who also equated the self with its 'ideas,' made that definition the direct grounds for a complete denial of personal identity (see *Treatise*, bk I, part IV, section VI). Granted the initial assumption, one cannot fault the logic in this, and it is also a live issue in Vedantic interpretation, as will appear later.

Commenting on what Descartes says in the *Second Meditation*, H.M. Bracken says:

> Descartes next seeks to find out *what* he is. Answer: he is a being whose whole essence is thinking.' (H.M. Bracken, *Descartes*, chap. 3, p32, One World, Oxford, 2002)

This is followed in *Meditation II* by a detailed comparison of the self with a piece of beeswax, and the changes it undergoes on being melted. Almost the only thing the different states of the wax have in common is their occupancy of the same part of space. The wax is seen to be constituted by a series of different phenomena, ranging from all-solid to all-liquid, and this is the model we are offered for the mind or soul. The continuing substance in which the accidents inhere is marginalized if not actually denied. Thus by this comparison the soul or thinking self is its sequence of thoughts purely and simply. This is confirmed by Cottingham where he says:

> In his Synopsis to the *Meditations*, Descartes specifically refers to the problem of how it is supposed to follow from the fact that he is not aware of anything except thinking as belonging to himself, that nothing else does in fact belong to his nature.' (*Descartes*, pp 112–113)

This is followed by a quotation from the *Meditations* where Descartes confirms that his view of the soul in this context came from his experience:

> So the sense of the passage was that I was aware of nothing at all that I knew belonged to my essence except that I was a thinking thing . . , (ibid.), [i.e., a disincarnate self].

Finally, this transition to a non-substantial self is also confirmed by Zeno Vendler:

> He no longer views the soul as the 'form' of the body, pays only lip service to the 'faculties' of intellect and will, and, by using the respectable disguise of Suarez' modes, effectively *identifies the sequence of thoughts with the mind itself* [my italics]. (Zeno Vendler, *Res Cogitans*, chap. viii, p 183. Cornell University Press, Ithaca and London.)

This view of the soul reveals a deep conflict with the enhanced role of mind and consciousness enshrined in the *cogito* argument. Why should so much be conferred upon something so apparently devoid of any specific identity? Vendler points out that Descartes' reductionist ideas of mind and soul could still be fitted into the traditional doctrine according to which the soul was said to be the '*subjectum inhaesionis*' of all its accidents, not the least of these being its acts of thought. In itself, according to this traditional conception, 'it remains distinct from all these operations, which are nothing but actualizations of the soul's faculties (intellect and will) which themselves are really distinct from the substance.' (ibid., p184)

In this case,

> As the essence of the fiddler, as such, is defined in terms of fiddling, yet the acts of fiddling are distinct from the fiddler, so the essence of the thinker is defined in terms of thinking, yet the acts of thinking are distinct from the thinker. Needless to say, this is not what Descartes means. (ibid.)

It was possible to fit the Cartesian conception into the orthodox doctrine because it affirmed things which would only be seen to conflict with it if and when the 'nothing but' condition was made clear. As a rule, it was not. Thus Descartes set the scene for the reductionism of modern philosophy, and by making the soul so superficial a reality opened the door to both materialism and monistic mysticism. No doubt this can explain why Frenchmen in particular, educated in Cartesian thought, can become deeply converted to the non-dualistic thought of Shankara if they lose their Christian faith.

Shankara's Reduction of Atman.

Reference to Shankara in this context is doubly appropriate inasmuch as it can be shown that his monistic doctrine was arrived at by a process like that of Descartes' treatment of the Scholastic treatment of the soul. What he did can be inferred from the arguments used against him by later interpreters of Vedanta, notably Ramanuja, in the eleventh and twelfth centuries. Unlike Shankara, Ramanuja taught that the individual natures of different selves was a metaphysical reality which endured even 'into *moksha* or final liberation.' (Julius Lipner, *The Face of Truth*, chap. 3, p49, SUNY, New York, 1986)

For Ramanuja, the relation between the individual *atman* and its consciousness was far from being one of identity. His idea of it was comparable to the Scholastic idea of the soul, for which it is a substance in which conscious acts are products of its faculties. Likewise, he held that consciousness was an act of illumination of substance which was caused by the existence of that substance. It thus manifests objects to its own substrate. He made comparisons between the *atman* and a lamp, because of this self-luminous quality, which clearly corresponds to the self-reflective power manifested from the *sakshi*, as Madhva understood it. This is what Shankara and his followers denied, with their idea that the *atman* and its conscious content could be identified without remainder in much the same way as was done by Descartes.

Since this point is of special importance, it will be best to resolve a possible misunderstanding about it before going further. The idea that the self is solely its flow of conscious contents is obviously part of Buddhist doctrine, in which case Shankara must surely have argued against it, not for it. However, he only argued against it so as to assert the existence of an individual self which was as much a part of the phenomenal world as its contents, as will be shown later. In addition to this, he argued for a pure Subject which was one and universal, and in no sense part of any individual as such. This was because Shankara thought that the objective, empirical self and the self as pure subject were two separate things, although they can be shown to be two modes of awareness within one and the same self or soul.

Given the above qualification, therefore, it is true to say that Shankara's doctrine does not differ significantly from that of Buddhism in regard to the reality of the person as such, but only differs in regard to a pure subject which is treated as separate from individual selves. According to J. Lipner, Ramanuja opposes this non-dualist position with the idea that:

the *atman* and consciousness cannot be identified without remainder. In the final analysis, this is what the Advaitin does, and in the process is dissolved not only the distinction between the conscious subject, the knowing act, and the object known, but also the plurality of selves, in an infinite, homogeneous non-individualized expanse of Knowing (*Jnaptimatra*): a position clearly calculated to strike a mortal blow at the root of theistic religion.' (Julius Lipner, ibid., p52)

This Cartesian-type reduction is also stated as clearly as possible by Ramana Maharshi, a twentieth-century follower of Shankara, as follows:

The mind is a unique power (*shakti*) in the *Atman*, whereby thoughts occur to one. On scrutiny as to what remains after eliminating all thoughts, it will be found that *there is no such thing as mind* apart from thought. So then, thoughts themselves constitute the mind [my italics].' (*The Collected Works of Ramana Maharshi*, chap. 2, p40. Arthur Osborne, ed., Rider & Co., London, 1959)

The above text leads on to a discussion of the question 'Who am I?' which must be capable of innumerable different answers if the individual mind was no more than its thoughts. If these thoughts should be centered on the Divine Self, then, there would be nothing to prevent its being the same as the latter. This shows how essential the reduction of the soul or *atman* to its contents is to the mystical monism of Shankara. It is clear that the philosophical method used here is just as empiricistic as that of Hume in 'Of Personal Identity' (*Treatise*, ibid.)

For Hume, there could be no self because it could not be found among its 'ideas', no one idea having any intrinsic precedence over any others. The assumption made here, and shared by the Advaitists, is that what the self cannot see, handle, taste, and so on, cannot exist. If that were valid, only empiricism could be true, and all forms of metaphysics would be utterly false, not least the Advaitist variety, and yet the latter is widely regarded as a metaphysics of the greatest profundity. In this case, *Advaita, qua* metaphysics, is self-contradictory.

Besides its negative implications for theistic religion, this

position is also anti-intellectual, because it undermines the possibility of rational proof. In effect, Shankara extended Plato's
conception of instantiations as inferior copies of Forms to
include not merely the physical world, but the soul, the intellect, the Forms themselves, and indeed everything but the Absolute itself. This assimilation of the knower and the known on a
phenomenal level is the same in principle as the reduction of
everything to natural phenomena made by Darwinism, for all
that the latter has no spiritual pretensions.

It should be remembered that Plato based his idea of defec-
tive instantiations on their component of matter, which was
never fully mastered by Form. But Shankara extends the realm
of instantiation to spiritual realities which by definition are not
material, unless, of course, one is a materialist. The soul and the
intellect are thus merged with the natural world which they
serve to make known. Consequently, Eric Lott (*Vedantic
Approaches to God*, Macmillan 1980), is justified in referring to
Shankara's system as 'absolute monism'.

If mind is denied the independent status that follows from its
self-reflective principle, for the purpose of making it open to
sublation, the grounds of reasoned argument are thereby sub-
verted. There would, besides, be no source for generalizations—
not least those of *Advaita*—since that also resides in the soul's
self-reflective principle. The lack of direct argument for both
monism and non-dualism results also from the fact that argument as such requires that the assertion of a truth must be supported by a criterion which is already admitted to be true or
very probably so. Now if the statement for which truth is
claimed was 'Only one thing is real,' we could not have any real
criterion by which to support it, if it were true, as only like can
support like. This is why monistic thought shows a lack of dia-
lectic which has to be supplied by dogmatism. Despite its claim
in the abstract, that there is but one real substance, there is
ambiguity as to what kind of substance is intended. By what criterion could it be identified?

The power of self-reflection appears not to be sublatable or
reducible to anything else because it is both outside phenomena

and is the center of a representation of the world in which such transformative changes as sublation are contained. This relation of container and content cannot be annulled by experiences, even if they are such as to suppress self-awareness for a time, since the containing subject belongs to a different order of being from that of that of the contents. I say 'for a time,' because the resumption of the same individual identity is just as necessary for the knowledge of monistic experience as of any other kind, a fact which Ramanuja examines at length, as will be shown. In addition to its relation to the *atman* or soul as container, any given experience is relative on another level to the ones which preceded it and to those which succeed it in the same person, because it is necessarily part of the history of one person's representation of the world.

Ramanuja and Self-Awareness

To confirm the transcendence of the individual self over its conscious contents, Ramanuja argues from the typical effects of self-awareness, distinguishing the recognizing subject from the objects of his awareness. (see Lipner, ibid., pp52–53) According to Lipner, he maintains that the permanence of the producer of the conscious acts is as directly perceived as are the particular movements of pleasure, pain, change, and so forth, with which consciousness is concerned. When one recognizes something after not having seen it for a time, it is clear that the 'I' has continued unchanged through all the conscious processes which have occurred from the first experience to the latest repetition of it by which the first is remembered:

> If it were accepted that selfhood derived from the momentary consciousness [of separate acts], recognition [of the form] 'On one day this was seen by me and on the next day I saw it again,' could not take place, for it is not possible for something cognized by one to be recognized by another. (Lipner, ibid., p53)

Lipner also points out that the above arguments serve equally well to establish the plurality of individual selves, since the faculty of memory is irreducibly individual and private. This plurality was of course something Shankara sought to disprove. His identification of the *atman* with its states of consciousness is interpreted non-monistically by Ramanuja as merely a kind of shorthand by which one expresses the fact that consciousness is the self's determinative property. In this case it would be harmless, just as Descartes' reduction of the soul to its thoughts can be harmless as long as one can pass over the 'nothing but' status it had for Descartes. This free mode of expression is universal without being taken literally: when one designates a man in ordinary speech by his occupation we do not mean to say he is merely a fragment of that occupation or profession, and nothing else.

But this is in effect precisely what the *Advaita* school actually intends to do in relation to the individual self and its conscious contents: what we experience as individual consciousness 'is not the real thing, but a reflection, an imitation in the cognitive apparatus of the real thing.' Instead of being an autonomous and self-illumined reality it is merely 'a non-conscious product of prakriti called the 'internal organ' (*antahkarana*), sometimes the 'ego' (*ahamkara*, literally 'I-maker'). (Lipner, ibid., p54)

For Ramanuja, this is to assimilate consciousness to the materiality of the body, and so to suppress the most fundamental distinction of soul and body. In Platonic terms, it would reduce mind to the level of an instantiation of a Form in matter, which would make it an object without inwardness. This would even be self-contradictory, because one could not explain how an entity without inwardness could frame conceptions of this kind. Who or what knows that it is merely material? Here again we encounter the reductionism which is a part of monistic and non-dualistic thought. While it would be appropriate for empiricism, it is incongruous for a system which claims a deep spiritual wisdom for itself. The denial of separate selves is a consequence of a denial of the spirituality of the individual soul, which would explain why this kind of mysticism is easily acceptable by those who have little or no religious belief, and who do not think beyond common sense materialism or the single subject idea of the self.

A point of fundamental importance here is that all acts of consciousness directed to external objects involve a simultaneous conscious act directed toward the knower himself. In this case, the phenomenal element is joined indissolubly to the trans-phenomenal, which Ramanuja describes as 'self-luminous.' The spirituality of the individual self can thus be ascertained without any need to assimilate it to anything else:

> Here Ramanuja is affirming, it is true, that every [transitive] conscious act is stretched between, so to speak, a subjective pole, the knower (the I), and an objective pole, the not-I. But what makes his statement momentous is that he is claiming more than this for the transitive act of awareness. He speaks of the 'evident knower' in it, of the knower's being self-luminous. He says in fact that in such acts the self is aware not only of the outside object, the not-I, made manifest to it by consciousness, but that it is also aware, *at the same time*, at least implicitly, *of itself*. (Lipner, ibid., p56)

A reality of this subtlety, which combines both center and periphery, is one which comprehends even the processes of sublation, and is not comprehended by them. Those who fail to appreciate this are liable to do so because their consciousness is dominated by sensation rather than by reflection, and they exemplify in a practical way the kind of consciousness which empiricist philosophers take for a norm. The latter are at least more consistent in not supposing their system contains anything spiritual or divine. Contrary to this, the upshot of the above arguments is that human self-reflective consciousness is supernatural, even though the word is not used as such. At the same time, this does not equal divinity, because the self-reflective faculty can err, owing to its dependence on other faculties for its data and premises.

Another problem of consciousness, when it is supposed to be able to ascend beyond the heavens, is the problem discussed in

Chapter 3, that it is unable to explain itself, or say what it is. Conversely, a self-caused and absolutely self-existent being would not suffer any such basic obscurity, and that indicates strongly that human consciousness is in fact a creature, even though it is a created spirit. This inability to explain itself is equally a challenge to materialists and advaitists: to the former because it reveals a frontier with mystery, and to the latter because it does not allow us to assume it into Divinity. Materialism and *Advaita* are theoretically opposites, but on the psychological level, the difference is much less clear-cut.

In the light of the above, it can be seen that the non-dualist equivalent of the Holy Grail must be a state of awareness without self-awareness, in defiance of the fact that self-aware consciousness is the highest kind of consciousness, and of its self-luminous property as taught by Ramanuja. To deny this is to commit oneself to something which one could not know to be real even if it were real.

'Thou Art That' and Other Dicta

Adherents of monistic religion usually believe that their doctrine is divinely-revealed, because it appears to be supported by scriptural texts, the best-known of which is taken from the Upanishads:

> In that which is the subtle essence, all that exists has its self. That is the true, that is the Self, and thou, Svetaketu, art That. (see *The Perennial Philosophy*, chap. 1 by Aldous Huxley, Chatto and Windus Ltd., London 1957).

It is thought that the assertion 'Thou art That' is a revealed confirmation of the belief that all individual selves are literally identical with the Divine, and vice-versa. In this case, monism would have to be the essence of all traditional doctrine, as expressed here with directness and simplicity. Yet those who think in this way would never take the statement 'You are a teacher' to mean 'You are solely an instance of an act of teaching something.' It is only common sense that such a statement is only an abbreviated way of saying 'You are a being among whose functions is that of teaching.' In short, identity statements in literal form are constantly used for making attributions.

Consequently, it is easy to see that the above text states that the 'subtle essence' of all things is in each one of us (as it would have to be), such that it must reside among all our other attributes. Implicitly, it can be said that one *is* this essence, therefore, but this identity is not reversible, i.e. this essence is *not* oneself.

Another dictum of this kind, one quoted by Schuon, is 'God became man, that man might become God.' Here again, it is a statement which can only support monism or non-dualism if it is given a rigidly literal interpretation, which in fact it cannot have. 'God became man' taken literally would have to mean that God disappeared and was replaced by a human being, which is no more conceivable than its counterpart, namely, that of a human being disappearing and being replaced by God.

To instance a different kind of traditional dictum, Scripture also says 'God is love', rather as each one of us is love insofar as love determines our behavior, while at the same time it is impossible to say that love is ourselves or God. Besides that, Christ utters an identification of himself with a vine, a statement which not even non-dualists would think of taking literally.

The Ideology of Reduction.

Finally, some consideration ought to be given to the reasons why Advaitists feel they have a right to deny the validity of individual spirituality and the plurality of real selves. This belief results from their idea of the Absolute, which for them is pure and undifferentiated unity, despite the fact that this would make it one of a pair of opposites with the world of multiplicity. In this case, its nature would be determined negatively by the nature of the world. Being thus an extreme of simple unity, as opposed to complexity and division, it would be part of the system which embraces both these extremes, and thus relative.

Shankara is a prominent exponent of the idea that 'all determination is negation,' and accordingly he makes much use of the idea of *upadhi* or limitation, when relating things to the Absolute. Thus it would be impossible for anything to differ in any way from the Absolute, except by reason of some defect, arbitrary limitation, or distortion. This includes the individual soul, which has a mode of reality subject to all the conditions of 'name and form,' and this is taken to be enough to ensure its ultimate unreality. Lott quotes from Shankara as follows:

> Similarly by this limiting finite connection . . . the gods, different species, individuals, men, animals, spirits, and so on, the Self assumes [as it were] those particular names and forms (*nama-rupa*). The difference between these things, therefore, is due to the difference of the limiting conditions and to nothing else. For all the Upanishads conclude that there is 'One only, without a second.' (*Vedantic Approaches to God*, chap. 5, p 44)

The last sentence of this quotation, if meant as an argument, is just a *non-sequitur*, because Christians, Moslems and Jews, who believe in a real creation, also believe that God is 'one only, without a second.' In other words, Shankara's monistic conclusion from this text must be held to begin with, if one is to elicit it from the text. It follows from this text that the Self or Absolute must have a specific nature of pure indetermination, by which it is qualitatively distinguished, and that is precisely an *upadhi*, which should make it less than real for consistent Advaitists.

This purely indeterminate nature is clearly contrary to that of the true Absolute, in which all determination and all indetermination are comprised in a way which transcends all our specific concepts. This has serious consequences for the moral and intellectual impact of non-dualism, because its idea of the Absolute is inherently opposed to the complex nature of finite beings. At the opposite pole from the benign Creator who saw that the creation was good, this idea of divinity is thus necessarily antagonistic to creation, since it is opposed by nature to everything but itself. Such a divinity could not be related to created beings apart from being the occasional cause of their elimination. Psychologically, that means that the non-dualist doctrine is a rationale for a war, not so much against evil and untruth, but against everything that appears to be different from the Absolute. This conflict is liable to spill over into the political realm because many of those who are most moved by this kind of doctrine are not likely to be swayed by human considerations, which they will take to be less than real. At the very least, they will be opposed to theistic religion insofar as it is taken to be more than a *darshana*, or a provisional means, while being allies to it insofar as it is necessary as a source of potential converts to their kind of religion.

In relation to Christianity, Shankara's doctrine excludes the possibility of the divine *Logos*, except as a *darshana*, because the *Logos* has properties other than those of the Absolute. This issue, in relation to other Christian doctrines such as the Incarnation, the Eucharist, and the Resurrection, makes the opposition between non-dualism and Christianity more extreme than with most other religions. The doctrine of the Trinity alone is particularly apt to exclude a wholly simple idea of the Absolute, and that is only consistent with a God who is the source and preserver of created natures, and not their negation.

This conflict results directly from belief in a deity which has no attributes. While showing that such a belief is far from representative of Hinduism, Eric Lott confirms that the Advaitist doctrine is that:

> Brahman-with-qualities (saguna) must be replaced by Brahman-without-qualities (nirguna). And only in this way can the perfect identity of the inner self and the supreme Self be maintained. To the theist, on the other hand, this whole method appeared blasphemous, not only because it 'robbed' the supreme Person of qualities essential to his being, but more specifically because it reduced his transcendent supremacy in relation to the individual self . . . and it was the knowledge of the self's dependence on this supremacy that

he declared as the only means to ultimate liberation. (*Vedantic Approaches to God*, chap. 8, p 121)

In any case, this also involves the negation of any spiritual role for the creative principle in mankind, since it could not reflect the highest reality. Yet the fact remains that *Advaita* is still the doctrine with which Hinduism is popularly identified in the West, as it has been for a hundred years or more.

In Guénon's time, this was considered acceptable by European scholarship, as witness F. Max Müller's *Theosophy or Psychological Religion* (The Gifford Lectures in 1892, Longmans, Green & Co., London 1903), in which it is taken for granted that God and the soul really mean the same thing. Nevertheless, Guénon must have known that the Hindu tradition did not really consist of a succession of disciples of Shankara, but he equated Hinduism with *Advaita* in his writings just the same—and extended this identification to most other traditions as well. However, in the light of the foregoing, we have suitable means of judging this question. In short, the correspondence which can be seen between Shankara and an anti-traditional thinker like Descartes on a major issue should suffice to counteract belief in an idea of traditional wisdom which depends on a form of reductionism.

5

Knowledge, Reality, and Tradition

An Attempted Merger

A particularly important case for the assimilation of Catholic doctrine to that of Advaita Vedanta has been made by Alphonse Levée, an author who wrote *Christianity and the Doctrine of Non-Dualism*, under the name of 'A Monk of the West' (Sophia Perennis, 2004). Most of the arguments offered in this book have now already been considered, except where it is proposed that they could serve equally well in a Christian context. If this book is justified, it would mean that Advaita Vedanta was what Christianity was really all about, despite the appearances. The general ideas of truth and reality assumed by the author are controversial, and in view of their importance, I will consider them first.

Denial of the Supernatural

It appears that the Catholic idea of the supernatural cannot be reconciled with monistic teachings, and our author seeks a way to discredit it. The problem with the supernatural is that it has a correlation with the natural, rather as with the potter and the clay, or at least it implies some kind of relationship between them. That in turn is tied to the conception that the created world is real in its own way, whereas the Shankaran-Vedantist version of the supernatural is one which places it outside any relation to anything else. For that reason, it is referred to as the 'supra-natural' by Levée, so that it will not be confused with the supernatural. This change is justified on the grounds that 'Since Truth is transcendent, and things considered 'in themselves' are not truly real because all their reality is in God, all knowledge that we can have of these (created) things will never be anything but the knowledge of an illusion.' To confirm this point, he also says

> All human knowledge, whether scientific or philosophical, is rooted in sensible or psychic experience. (Ibid., p76)

The latter point shows that he gives no room to Platonic ideas, since Plato and Plotinus affirmed above all else that the Forms were above the level of sensible and mental phenomena, and this conception is no small part of traditional wisdom. Besides, what is said in the above quotation implies that there is nothing between God and matter, and that even this matter is only an illusion. Where he affirms that 'only the Infinite is absolutely real,' (ibid.), this can only serve his purpose if the Infinite is conceived in a simplistic manner, where there is no idea of an infinite consisting of both infinite and finite together.

However, he then proceeds to undermine the idea of the supernatural as such, by reference to its origins in Western philosophy as they appear to him:

> Now it is quite well known, though all the consequences are seldom drawn, that the viewpoint of philosophy ... is an essentially 'profane' point of view, exclusive to a late period of the Hellenic world, and that it does not have its exact equivalent in other civilizations, where the very idea that there could be an independent knowledge and reality can only be deemed a proof of ignorance and incomprehension. (ibid., p77)

These words express the point of view of Guénon precisely, with the idea that 'an independent knowledge and reality' could only be the result of 'ignorance and incomprehension.' There is no attempt to consider what religious doctrines would mean to people whose minds were never trained to think; it is assumed that this ability will always exist, whether anyone understands the art of acquiring it or not. The most obvious answer to this is that without independent knowledge there would have been no Guénonian reaction against modernity in the first place.

If we were to agree that philosophy is to be of no account in relation to doctrines, and that the distinction between the natural and the supernatural was created by philosophical thought in late Hellenic culture, we might have some right to set it aside in favour of an Advaitist alternative, namely, the 'supra-natural'. However, this depends on our acceptance of the confident assertion that there cannot be an independent knowledge and reality, as though it were self-evident. This is obviously not self-evident, and if we may leave aside the question of an independent reality until later, we must first ask what a *dependent* knowledge would be like if there were such a thing. In reality, the very expression is an oxymoron, because it would not be knowledge at all, but opinion, and dictated opinion at that.

Knowledge and Opinion

The essence of knowledge lies in an act of self-activation, which cannot be anything but independent and individual. This is manifest from the fact that, as opposed to knowledge, opinions and beliefs can be shared directly, as well as imparted by rote, or suggestion, or imitation. But if they are ever to develop into knowledge, it has to be by means of an internal act which must be all one's own. This transition is in effect like that from a picture of a reality to the reality itself, as Zeno Vendler explains it (see *Res Cogitans*, chap. v, Cornell University Press). In this book, it is also shown that one always has to have causes for believing something, whereas knowing something is an achievement which is its own explanation and justification, and so one can only ask how it is achieved, not why. This property of knowledge is spiritually pivotal because it means that the rational soul is capable of being determined by a kind of causality fundamentally different from the natural causality which acts on our physical and psychical being.

It is ironic that the passionate pursuit of truth and wisdom so well exemplified by Guénon should lead one of his followers to a denial of its legitimacy, but something like this always happens when the truth is presumed to be known definitively; it gets reduced to an object. This is also the case when truth is conceived in a manner out of all relation to anyone who actually knows it, as though the latter were unnecessary. We are not offered any resolution of these conflicting needs: on the one hand, a passion for truth, and on the other a desire for a culture which makes the ingestion of traditional beliefs almost unavoidable. Our author has identified Guénon's ideas with the latter option, whether or not this was true to Guénon's intentions.

The occasional cause of the above notion is in this instance the need to sideline the Catholic idea of the supernatural, which could be done if the idea of the supernatural (the correlate of the natural), really is only an artificial conception taught by philosophers in the late Hellenistic period. Conversely, if it were an ultimate reality, it would rule out monism. But if in fact philosophy was really nothing more than an activity of the profane mentality, it would be safe to believe that the distinction of natural and supernatural was of no importance.

Levée, like Guénon, will not face the fact that even philosophers must hit upon the truth now and again, if only by good luck, and even more to the point, the fact that Catholics are supposed to believe that the Church has the Holy Spirit whereby to identify valid ideas, whatever their origin. If that is being denied here, it is hard to see how this book can be an honest attempt to make a true reconciliation between the two traditions.

This issue is of particular importance for Catholics, because the ideas of the natural and the supernatural are the basis of their belief in the Eucharist, as well as in the qualities of sanctification, and the miraculous. I have argued elsewhere that the distinction of natural and supernatural cannot always be precise because there are some realities which partake of both at once, since otherwise the chain of being would be incomplete, but that is worlds away from denying the distinction in itself, as Levée effectively does, owing to his desire to give pride of place to the idea of the supra-natural, which allows no positive meaning for the natural. Much more is involved in this than terminology, as the supra-natural cannot impart anything to the natural because there is no mediating conception of the *Logos* in Advaitist thought; higher and lower realities are not related at all, and revelation could not come into the world from the highest source.

Independent Reality

Independent knowledge and independent reality appear to imply one another, and so if there was any reason to object to the one, there would be as much reason to object to the other. As with independent knowledge, we need to ask what a non-independent reality would be, if we could identify such a thing. Here again, the answer is near at hand: it would not be a natural reality, but a culturally-contrived one. In the West, we draw a firm line between the objective and the subjective, but the Guénonian doctrine as interpreted by our author seeks to suppress the distinction between them, presumably because it is a duality and therefore not consistent with monistic ideas. This adds to the difficulty of judging the truth of non-dualism, since it does not recognize the normal assumptions about objectivity.

It is the more surprising that the idea of an 'independent reality' should also be attacked, because Christianity accepts it, at least as long as this does not mean 'independent of God'. Conversely, the world of illusion taught by *Advaita* really is independent of God or the Absolute, since by its principles the Divine can have no relations. This, then, is not the independence our author has in mind. Rather, it must be an independence of collective subjectivity, especially where it appears in tradition. However, taken to an extreme, this would reverse the relation between the world and man's representation of it, or at least it would amount to a denial that mental representation had to have an objective basis. In that case, it would not be representation, but a self-sufficient reality to which there was no alternative.

Without nature's independence, our minds could not be influenced by anything but other human minds. In that sense, then, independent reality would be excluded, but to what purpose? The nearest approach to this condition in practice is to be found among people who live at a low cultural level, that is to say, in barbarism. Under such conditions there is hardly any room for the idea of natural causality, because the idea of causality is mixed up with the effects of human wills and the work of nature spirits, and reality is 'humanized' in the worst possible way.

The Christian idea of God, as understood from revelation, would not be meaningful or credible except in relation to the objective or 'independent' world-order. This duality of God and nature is another of the dualities which Advaitists cannot accept, even though it exists primarily for human minds, without meaning that God is *intrinsically* matched with anything. According to the teachings held by our author, the very fact of God's being even conceptually in a relationship must detract from His true reality. But this rejection of dualities only makes it so much the more strange that according to the same non-dualist teachings, the essential Subject in all conscious beings is held to be Divine, despite the fact that Subject and Object are a natural bipolar phenomenon, neither of them having any meaning without the other, like male and female or cause and effect. What kind of divinity is it which is fated to be one half of a polar relation with phenomena?

The subject is intrinsically bound to the object far more rigorously than God is to nature, since the subject-object relation does not result from human points of view. Nevertheless, non-dualists or Advaitists object to the relation of God and nature as conflicting with their ideal of unity, although this does not seem to show any deep understanding of the ideas of subject and object and their relation. If they were not both natural, created things, they would each have as much and as little reason to be regarded as divine.

To misunderstand the subject is thus to misunderstand the object, there including the meaning of such permanent realities as the sun and moon, eclipses, the tides, the seasons, the rainbow. However, realities of this kind give rise to truths of an extra-confessional and spiritually neutral kind, with which spiritual truths may be compared. They raise awareness of a non-human world in which the practice of religion goes on along-side those of arts and crafts, politics, and so forth, but such truths are not acceptable to Advaitists, because their idea of real-ity is literally acosmic. That is no exaggeration, and whatever may be said for or against it, it is enough to make the Christian idea of the Incarnation meaningless, since the reality of the Incarnation requires the reality of nature.

On this basis, the doctrine expounded by Levée approaches a position where one sees reality as a cultural artefact. In this way, it bears a peculiar resemblance to post-modernism, in which words similarly have a meaning and a reality which makes them independent of any outside world. Thus the consequence of rejecting an 'independent reality' is language independent of reality, whether one is a profound monist or a post-modernist. Extremes can meet, of course, possibly even those of tradition and anti-tradition, but there is too little reason to accept Levée's doctrine as traditional, especially as the Hindu tradition as a whole has moved away from it. In any case, what can be seen here in either case is a conviction that reduction is the key to deeper truth; that if we arrive at one principle instead of two, the remaining one will inherit what pertained to the other, along with its own. In short, both independent knowledge and reality must be valid if objectivity differs from subjectivity.

Non-Dualism or Monism?

Where Levée quotes a text from St. Bernard, (ibid., p13), it is in support of the idea that creation adds nothing to the sum total of being, because it is supposed to be possessed wholly by God. On page 14 he says explicitly:

> there is no more being (singular) if creation is included than if it is excluded.

This is to ignore the possibility that there could be possibili-ties of being external to God which could not be realized in God as God. Only if this were the case, could there be a real creation, the probability of which cannot be less than one in two, as pointed out in Chapter 1. Although God's existence is perfectly self-sufficient in principle, God cannot be morally self-sufficient in relation to a world, once He has created it. This is the possibility of a freely-chosen necessity, which cuts across the simple dichotomy of Free and Unfree. According to Neoplatonic principles, not only God, but each order of creation has possibilities which it can only realize outside itself, so that each is the proximate cause of the next one below it. For Plato, the Good always goes beyond itself, and that can only mean creation.

At the same time, there is the more familiar consideration that finite being is necessarily infinitely more than nothing, in which case it cannot be equated with nothing, as it would have to be if it really added nothing to the real. If God could not multiply being, in what would His omnipotence consist? Only in the production of a real creation could it be realized. A 'creation' which did not constitute an addition to the sum of being must be quite rigorously nothing. As if to underline this implication, Levée adds:

> In reality, the created *esse* is the property of God in a two-fold sense. First, not only as related to past origin, but at present.' (Ibid., p15)

In other words, only God can rightly be the possessor of the *esse* of each and every being, which is to say once again that there is no being other than that of God, despite the fact that, for Christians, this is something for God to decide. There is no reason why this should not be Monism purely and simply, so why do we need to qualify it as 'Non-dualism'? If there cannot be any reality other than the God of monism, there can be no argument, only constant reiteration, which continues as follows:

> Being properly pertains to God, *suum ipsius, et omnium esse*: it does not belong to me to be who I am; he who I am is not I; I am not what I am. The renowned divine 'definition' of Exodus will have been recognized, but as inverted. The 'world', of course, can only see alienation and scandal in this

doctrine, and this is natural, *because it is precisely the alienation of the true man which constitutes the 'world' as such.* (Ibid., p16)

The option of pantheism has already been excluded by our author, but it reappears here despite his intentions. The above text can imply that everything which is said about God is convertible to ourselves. To place all reality rigorously in God and to exclude it from everything else points to the pantheist conclusion that everything is God. If we *were* somehow excluding God, by what would that be done? If the word 'illusion' is used, there would have to be real persons to suffer the illusion, but if no such reality can be allowed to anything but God, the above text can only mean that nothing could exclude God.

Levée brings together the ideas of world-illusion and absolute dependence where he states that:

> The illusory or entirely dependent character of his existence, having no other being of its own than this dependence. (Ibid., p 20.)

Dependence can have different meanings, however, for example, we are dependent on our parents for our having been born at all, but that reveals nothing as to how dependent or not we are on them today. Where the dependence is on God, the issue is made more complicated by the fact that in the religious life, one is assimilating the divine nature. God is by definition absolutely independent in His being, in which case every assimilation of the divine nature must mean a corresponding degree of independence. Consequently, the absolute dependence of which Levée speaks would apply most appropriately to persons with no God and no religion. This must mean that if Christians were to remain absolutely dependent, as our author supposes, they would in that case be absolutely *different* from God, and therefore absolutely unassimilable to Him. This is a conclusion that the mystically-inclined are not likely to be able to live with. Thus the non-dualist idea of total dependence defeats the ideal of union with God and creates a permanent duality.

However, the intention behind such teachings is rather that our sense of God will be much increased, and therefore our choices for the morally good and the self-denying as well. As long as we believe ourselves to be really nothing or perhaps quasi-beings, we will be most likely to have the faith and virtue we need, but this will only happen if religious habits of mind survive here. A quasi-being, as I indicated in connection with the nature of non-dualism in Chapter 1, is always in a state of aimless change and transformation. It is aimless because it is wholly subject to outside forces, and because there is no substantive nature or quality to resist such change. Every change it undergoes undoes the last one, so that it can never change in the sense of acquiring a new nature or function. It is the last degree of reality, on the edge of conceptual thought, which can be reached only by 'a kind of bastard reasoning' as Plotinus put it.

This conception of identity is unlikely to motivate anyone, spiritually or otherwise, but it follows from the non-dualist idea of what we are. When the alternatives are only those of God or nothing, there is no point in expecting those on the 'nothing' side of the issue to feel involved, since they would be beyond the possibilities of either gain or loss.

God and the World.

These observations about the divine and the human apply to the very existence of our ideas of God and the world. Levée states without argument that God and the world are a duality which exists only from the point of view of the ego. As such, they are merely a part of the realm of relativities which Advaitist doctrine is intended to transcend. Above and quite separate from the duality of the Creator and the world, Advaitists believe that there is the undetermined Absolute, and this is what they want to identify with. This is the identification which could only be possible if consciousness and the soul in which it arises were not created. Our author reserves this identification for an impersonal consciousness, while denying that it could be possible for anything recognizable as the individual person, whom he thinks of as an unreal observer of an unreal world, and whom he describes as follows:

> that impossible *ego*, a pseudo-aseity appearing between the 'world' and 'God' as their common *limit*, point of incidence of the uncreated Ray on the 'surface of the waters'. Entirely relative to the *ego* and arising from its point of view, 'God' and 'the world' are no less illusory insofar as they exclude and limit one another by their very opposition. How could they be 'real', *since the real is identical to the Infinite: Satyam Jnanam Anantam Brahmah*? (Ibid., p 98.)

Here again, we see the familiar assumption that God-as-Creator, i.e., the God with determined attributes, and God-as-Absolute are two separate realities, an assumption which results from the fact that human minds find it hard to grasp the unity of these aspects of divinity. Their separation is assumed without argument, even though it is a denial of what is felt instinctively about the infinity of God, that it must comprise the essence of all realities, and not just those in a single category. The infinite presented here is mainly like a mathematician's abstraction, conceived purely and simply as the negation of anything having determined aspects or properties. This is no doubt part of ultimate reality, but the assumption that it is a reality separate from the Creator seems to rest on nothing more than ideology.

The next point of importance here is the statement in the above quotation that 'God' and 'the world' are no less illusory insofar as they exclude and limit one another....' This statement shows that Levée thinks of God as an entity which is of essentially the same nature as that of the world, since God and the world could only 'exclude and limit' one another if God was somehow a finite and physical entity like the world, since only like can exclude like. It is surprising that anyone writing on theology could ignore the fact that there can be no such symmetry between God and the world, if only because God is the world's Creator. But in the above text, God and the world are obviously thought of as a corresponding pair like land and sea, or topsoil and subsoil.

The text quoted reveals an indifference to the doctrinal issues which are central to Christianity, such as the difference between the created and the uncreated. This is explicable if caused by a subjectivism which does not recognize itself. Just as God and the Absolute can appear as separate entities for psychological purposes, so it is easy to imagine God and the world as a symmetrical duality, but these subjective assumptions are taken as being objective realities. In other words, Levée ignores the difference between what God and the world are in themselves, and what they can seem to be in common sense thought. This conflation of objective and subjective is rather like that of assuming that some famous public figure really was *per se* no more than what one has heard of them through newspapers and newsreels. That would be a common and popular kind of mistake, which also appears in the attitude of those who presume a doctrine to be false because they find it hard to understand.

It is therefore all the more strange that this tendency to confuse our limitations with objective reality should occur in connection with something which is above all a cult of transcendent consciousness. There is no necessity for it, since we all have the intellectual faculty for thinking outside our subjectivities, but it may not be used without the moral qualities of goodwill toward truth and a freedom from preconceived ideas. With a more open attitude, it is not hard to see that we do not have a right to say that God as Person and as Absolute must be objectively separate. Similarly, we would not have a right to think that God and the world must exclude one another because we found it hard to understand their real relation. A comparison with modern science is relevant here, where we are told by physicists that light is both a wave motion and a stream of particles. It is hard to see how it could be both of these things at once, but no scientist thinks that that means we can say that light is two separate things.

Returning to the idea that God and the world are just a duality on the level of relativities, which we must transcend by identifying with an Absolute which is above both of them, it should be noted that this conception fails in its purpose because the alleged duality of God and the world is only a duality under one aspect, since one member of it is the Creator of the other, rather like the light of the sun and the light of the moon. That removes all symmetry from them in objective fact, even though they can appear as symmetrical to careless thought. To say that they limit one another could only be literally possible if they were both creatures or both Creators.

Finally, the idea that God and the world can only exist for the ego, as though they were somehow affiliated to it, is stated as though it were self-evident that the ego could produce only false representations of reality. However, the doctrine of non-dualism also depends on the ego's powers of representing the world, as do all other systems, so if the ego can only falsify reality, non-dualism itself must be as false as all the ego's other productions. We also need the ego in order to formulate arguments against the ego as such, since it is the operative part of the personality with which it relates to the outside world. If the ego signifies the manifest activity of the soul, the ego must be as necessary for a doctrine which denies the reality of the ego as in one which affirms it. Mystical doctrines do not think or believe themselves, but depend on individual sources of consciousness.

Some would say that this was because the ego is inherently self-contradictory, because its nature is to affirm itself as a center of reference, while knowing that innumerable other egos are doing the same thing. A center is by definition unique, so to claim to be one center among others must be self-contradictory. Frithjof Schuon criticizes the idea of the ego on this basis, which is strange in view of the fact that his thought makes the fullest use of the idea of the 'relatively absolute,' in connection with the diversity of different revelations and traditions. If his reasoning about the ego were valid, therefore, he would have had to conclude that all the traditions were false and self-contradictory, because they all claim to be the whole and exclusive truth.

In reality, the claim to be a center of reference, or even an absolute, whether made by a religion or by any person's ego, is logically perfectly in order as long as this claim is not specified as absolutely unique. This is supported by another comparison used by Schuon (see *Stations of Wisdom*), where these relative absolutes result from the fact that there are relative infinites, as where the length of a line can be infinite just as much as the area of an infinite surface. Given only that the idea of the ego is without inherent contradictions, therefore, the non-dual objections to it fail for the reason just given, that the ego itself would have to be the source of its own refutation: were the ego a pseudo-reality, this refutation would be a pseudo-refutation, and if it were a true reality, the refutation would be a denial of known facts.

Before leaving the subject of the ego, it should be noted that in a number of places our author calls it a 'pseudo-aseity', as in the last passage quoted, and he assumes this to be true of the ego as such, and not just a certain kind of ego. If we take this idea of a pseudo-aseity as an insight into the spiritual disease of modern man, it is unquestionably correct, but unfortunately Levée expects his readers to take it for granted that this truth about the profane ego is such that no other alternative but that of non-dualism could suffice to correct it. But this is a *non-sequitur*. False aseity does not mean that the true aseity must be that of God alone, because man can find grace and so live as to realize the true aseity of his immortal soul. Such is the Christian idea of the way in which the divine aseity is to be shared by mankind, and it is diametrically opposed to the monistic vision of irredeemable futility for which eradication is the only solution.

Explanation of Illusion.

It is pointed out (ibid., p57) that the mistake made in the rope-and-serpent example cannot be a matter of pure imagination, since there is in fact a real rope. The illusion is simply that of thinking there is a serpent when in fact 'there never was a serpent.' This is the basic pattern of illusion which causes us to take the world for a reality, we are told, when the reality is Brahma who is being experienced in a false perception. Here, the conclusion is clearly monistic: we cannot now use the idea of subjectivism to account for the difference between the perceived world and reality itself, *because the subject himself is not real.* It is argued that the subject must be unreal as such because 'there is nothing outside the Infinite'; if what is seen to be other-than-Brahma is no more real than the appearance of a serpent imposed on a rope, it would have to be nothing, of course, being in effect an illusion suffered by an illusion.

These ideas all assume that we know so much about Brahma that we can know that we are perceiving the world as other than He, just as we can learn our mistake when we confuse one other person for another. In reality, there is scarcely a single thing about Brahma that anyone knows at first-hand, so that in this case there is no basis for the alleged illusion. One can confuse one person with another when one has been equally able to perceive them both, but one cannot confuse somebody with an object which one cannot perceive at all, and yet that is precisely what Levée is saying we do, when we supposedly confuse Brahma with the outside world.

To return to the rope-and-serpent example, it should be obvious that it only makes its point because we have knowledge of both ropes and serpents equally, and the differences between them; two different knowns can always be confused, but where only one term of an alleged confusion is known to us, it is absurd to call it an illusion; the ideas of illusion and confusion are relational by nature, if they mean anything.

The case is very similar in regard to the argument that there can be nothing outside the Infinite. Who knows so much about the Infinite that he can tell us whether we are outside the Infinite, or inside it, or somewhere in between? One could only argue in this way if one is unconsciously thinking of the Infinite as though it were a phenomenal reality like the visible Church, which one could be a member of, or not. In this case, the statement that there can be nothing outside the Infinite would be merely a re-statement of the old dogmatic belief that there could be no salvation outside the Church, but now presented in the guise of philosophy. But it tells us nothing about the real Infinite.

On the other hand, the statement that there can be nothing

outside the Infinite can be taken as a tautology, with no consequences for matters of fact. In this case, it would not prevent
anyone from believing the exact opposite of what Levée is arguing for. Having nothing outside it is indeed all part of the definition of the Infinite, but its all-comprehensiveness might more
reasonably be expected to enhance the reality of manifest
beings, rather than negating it.

In spite of this, we are told that the creature is not really nothing, because it is in fact nothing but a projection of God, as if
that did not mean the same thing:

> The doctrine of non-dualism does not annihilate the crea-
> ture as such any more than it deifies him. It simply asserts
> that the creature is entirely a projection or an expression of
> the Divine Reality and that it is nothing in and for itself.
> 'The entire universe is but the effect of *Brahma*, unique real-
> ity. That is its veritable substance and the world does not
> exist independently of That. (Ibid., p57)

This does not distinguish non-dualism from monism, because
one cannot call something a 'projection' or an 'expression' of the
Divine Reality unless one is able to say in and for whom or what
these projections and expressions are taking place; if they take
place in God, as is suggested by 'and God saw that it was good,'
they would be realities, being real in and for God, but in this
case God would not be exclusively real. On the other hand, if
they were to take place in persons or things which were themselves similarly projections and expressions, they would in
effect be nothing. In this case, God would be exclusively real,
and there would be no alternative to monism. The former alternative is appropriate for a God who is omniscient, whereas the
conception of Brahma we are offered here does not appear to
have this attribute, and what He does not know cannot be supposed to be real in any way.

This supposed absence of knowledge of the creation in God
can be explained on the basis that God is being equated with the
Divine Essence, which has no relation with anything else, as
with the One as understood by Plotinus. But in reality God is

one being, and the Essence cannot be detached and treated as though it were a separate reality, like Nirguna Brahman. Since to do this would be to reify an analyzing operation of abstract thought, a well-known philosophical confusion, it is rather strange that it should appear as a defining feature in a system of spiritual wisdom which repudiates philosophy.

There is in addition the question as to *by whom* or *by what* these expressions and projections are made. If by *Brahma*, they must have a share in the divine reality, and so be creatures, since it would be by particular acts of the divine will that they were conceived and projected into being. If, however, they are spontaneous phenomena with no part in the divine, they would be truly nothing. The answer given to this dilemma is that 'The relation of creation is non-reciprocal, that is to say it is real only from the side of the creature.' (Ibid., p22)

This answer expresses precisely the 'one-way' relation which exists by definition between a Form and its instantiations, since the Form is in no way affected by how many there may be of the latter, or by their fate. But this very fact shows how inappropriate such a relation would be for God and creation. It would mean a god who was not omniscient, being unaware of the creation, whereas God is by nature capable of an incomparably greater knowledge of the creatures than they could have of Him. In view of this fact, Levée's conception of this relation looks perverse. In the *Genesis* account of creation, God is completely aware of every thing which is created, and if this were replaced by something like Dawkins' 'Blind Watchmaker', there could be no question of religious orthodoxy.

This view of creation is used in support of the idea that: 'There is no more *being* if creation is included than if it is excluded.' (Ibid., p22) This is reaffirmed later (ibid., p60), where he repeats the idea that creation adds no being to God. But at the same time, it is affirmed that 'creation is really distinct from the Creator,' even though it comprises no additional being. But if creation has no being of its own, by what does it differ from its Creator? Only by being nothing, apparently. In this case, the doctrine would in effect be monism.

To affirm the distinction between God and creation while denying any being to one side of this distinction must be meaningless unless it is just a platitude that God is different from nothing. Since, in this context, 'God is different from creation' contains nothing that is not stated in: 'God is different from nothing,' they must in fact be the same statement. The distinction between creation and nothing in this case is not enough to allow room for the distinction between monism and non-dualism, which is asserted because of a desire to keep the discussion within the domain of religious orthodoxy. This desire not to fall foul of orthodoxy was equally an issue in India in the eighth century, when Shankara concealed an essentially monist conception behind the minor concession of non-dualism.

Here is a clear example of a peculiarity of religious thought, according to which one is free to affirm in the concrete what one denies in the abstract. (Stephen Clark has drawn attention to this; see *A Parliament of Souls*.) In this case, monism is verbally denied while one affirms any number of things which would be true if monism was. Instead of saying that creation is nothing, Levée accordingly says that it adds no being to reality as a whole, just as Eckhart does. We are expected to assume that 'adding nothing' must mean 'being nothing', but this is not so. The Second Person of the Trinity adds nothing to the First, and neither does the Third Person add anything to the First and Second, because all three Persons are equal. Each has an infinity of being and reality while adding nothing to the others. (This is an argument suggested to me by Stratford Caldecott, author of *Secret Fire* and *The Seven Sacraments*)

A more mundane comparison can be seen in the process of publication: when someone writes a book and submits the manuscript and gets it published, the printed copies clearly add nothing to the author's book, but who would imagine that this meant that the printed copies were nothing? There is a standard problem of logical reversibility here: if in fact the printed books really were nothing, then they would of course add nothing to the original text. But this relation cannot be reversed, because it does not follow that something which 'adds nothing' to something else is nothing in itself; it just may or may not be. If the Persons of the Trinity do not add anything to one another, then, it need not detract in any way from the reality of creation should it add nothing to the being of God.

Our author makes use of the teaching that all realities are first of all ideas in the mind of God (ibid. p. 14), so that we may presume that created entities are insignificant or unreal. This idea could be orthodox if it were not presented as a complete account of the relation between God and creation. This can be seen from the way in which this issue is treated by Kallistos Ware:

> From all eternity God saw each one of us as an idea or thought in his divine mind, and for each one from all eternity he has a special and distinctive plan. We have always existed for him; creation signifies that at a certain point in time we begin to exist also for ourselves. (*The Orthodox Way*, Mowbrays, London and Oxford, 1979, chap. 3, p56)

The great difference here is where the connection to creation is made. It is clear from the above that if our reality was solely that of ideas in God's mind, creation would not only have been unnecessary, but would conflict with what God really wanted. Thus the created being, referred to dismissively by Levée as 'the ego' would then have no purpose but to disappear, and this is enough to show that the non-dualist doctrine is in deep conflict with the idea of creation, for all the claims to orthodoxy made for it here.

To return to the question of nomenclature, and the presentation of monism as non-dualism, it is usual for a negative term to include more than does the positive which it negates. If the population of a town was described as 'non-European', it could be made up of numerous non-European races; where living organisms are described as 'non-human', they could be animal, insect, or vegetable; where people are said to be 'non-Christian', they could have any number of other religions, or none. But the negative term 'non-dual' is an exception to this rule, since its only realistic meaning is simply pure unity. Nevertheless, the comforting sense of compromise suggested by the negative term corresponds to the vestigial reality it allows to the world.

But no matter whether one speaks of monism or non-dualism, the theological affirmations behind them are close enough: namely, that if God exists, either there is nothing else, or nothing else has any existence worthy of the name. If this is true, God has not taught it through any revealed religion, not even in Hinduism outside its *Advaita* school. Religious minds in all traditions have always held the exact opposite of the above. Since the doctrine of creation, taken literally at least, obviously contradicts the idea that God's existence must be exclusive, monistic thinkers are bound to try to empty creation of meaning, without denying it outright.

Thus Levée never says in so many words that God's existence negates that of everything else, but what he does say points to no other conclusion. Here again the question raised before in connection with idolatry is relevant: if the intellect and its speculations, along with consciousness in general, is inherently part of creation, its attempt to transcend the Creator-creature distinction must confuse a creature with the Creator. In other words, consciousness would have to function as though it were external to creation in order to make the monistic point. These arguments can therefore only be compelling for those who can think that creation consists solely of material things, while consciousness was inherently part of God.

Infinite and Finite

The affirmation 'there can be nothing outside the Infinite' can only be taken to confirm the monist doctrine as long as the word 'outside' is ambiguous. If 'outside' were taken to mean 'different from,' there would be no reason why there should be any objection to anything being 'outside' the Infinite, and in fact this would be the natural condition for finite things. If it were taken to mean 'exclusive of', however, this could only mean that the Infinite was one term in relation to some finite entity, in which case it could not be the Infinite. An Infinite existing competitively with other beings is an absurdity, as only like competes with like, but some such belief is necessary for the non-dualistic position.

However, this idea is modified (ibid., p60), where Levée states that the Infinite comprehends everything, while adding that 'we must avoid the too common error or misunderstanding of conceiving the Infinite as a totality formed by the addition of parts.' He adds that the Infinite is without parts and that *'the finite is not part of the Infinite.'* If this were unilaterally the case, it would be right to claim that the Infinite must rigorously exclude the finite, and that the latter must therefore be nothing. In this case, the infinite would indeed be a hostile competitor with everything else, but how does one prove that it is without parts? Having parts and having no parts are both phenomenal distinctions, and they are not alternatives which can be imposed on the Infinite.

Despite this problem he goes on to use an argument which reveals a failure to think beyond the finite, namely the argument that if the Infinite really was made up of parts, it must cease to be Infinite as soon as one of them was removed; and if this part were to be replaced, the sum total would still be finite, because finites cannot make an Infinite, any more than many zeros can make a finite. This argument assumes the exact opposite of the concept which really defines the Infinite, i.e., that it remains what it is despite the removal of any number of finite parts; only thus does it differ fundamentally from the finite.

Thus the supposedly composite idea of the Infinite is tacitly treated as though it were in reality finite, and so it is proved that it would have to be finite by a tautology. On this basis, we are offered the conclusion that the Infinite must therefore be without parts. But in reality, it is as mistaken to say it is univocally partless as it is to say it consists of parts, because both of these alternatives by themselves belong to the realm of opposites. It cannot be defined in terms of any properties which would make up one side of a pair of opposites, because it must by definition transcend all such distinctions. Both pure unity and diversity are there, but not in the mutually exclusive way in which they appear in nature.

Since the Infinite thus cannot be identified with any specific nature, it cannot exist in an exclusive or competitive relation with anything, and in that case it cannot serve Levée's purpose of negating finite realities as realities. This obviates one of the most frequently used arguments for non-dualism, and undermines the certainty claimed for it.

Where the above question is related to causality (ibid., p63), it is asserted that because the Infinite alone has aseity (is self-caused), the finite must be illusory. But if in fact the finite has its cause in the Infinite, it would have a real, even though derivative, necessity, in which case it could not be illusory. It could only be illusory if it were uncaused, either by the Infinite or by itself, but to say that this kind of uncaused nature is illusory is almost a statement of the obvious. Besides, if the finite (and all the relative orders of infinity) really were uncaused by the Infinite, it would follow that the Infinite did not cause anything, any more than the material principle in Platonism, and that would make it as ineffectual as some finite things. In other words, the unreality of the finite indirectly implies the unreality of the Infinite. These two modes of reality cannot be separated and treated singly in a vacuum, except for an artificial kind of abstract thinking or philosophism, which is the last thing Guénon wanted.

The Ephemeral and the Unreal.

However, another kind of reason why the finite is said to be unreal is given as well:

> It is man himself who puts himself in fetters because, in his ignorance, he views as real things which have only an ephemeral existence. (Ibid., p64)

The real, he adds, is not opposed so much to the illusory as to the ephemeral, this criterion being a typical feature of Advaitist thought: 'unreal' is taken to be synonymous with 'does not last very long.' But by what do we judge certain things to be ephemeral? By sense-perception alone. This reveals a contradiction in Advaitist thought which I have previously indicated, (chap. 5, pp96–97 of *Self and Spirit*), where this doctrine requires us to take sense-perception as though it were the absolute truth, and moreover in the context of a metaphysical doctrine which must by definition transcend the senses. One cannot have it both ways: if the senses give us the ultimate truth, metaphysical knowledge would be meaningless, since it could only duplicate what would be known anyway, if it were possible at all. Conversely, if metaphysical knowledge is real knowledge, we would have no reason to trust the senses, let alone take their contents as a kind of revelation.

Natural entities are perceived to come and go, of course, and where they come from and where they go to seems to be a mystery. But everything depends on whether these sensory appearances mean that the entities are ephemeral *in themselves*, or whether it is only our perceptions of them which are ephemeral. This distinction is fundamental to our knowledge of the outside world, and it has to be learned in the course of natural development. Babies in the first few months of life never distinguish the real from what they perceive, this being shown by the fact that they will not try to look for anything when it has been covered up, as they assume that it no longer exists when it can no longer be seen. Later on, it is learned that things go on existing while we cannot see them, even though common sense still assumes that they have completely ceased to exist once they are known to be in the past.

But the latter assumption is not much more rational than the former, because the fact that our senses relate only to the present moment does not in itself confer any greater reality on the present. The supposed non-existence of things past is thus a result of our limitations, just as much as the apparent non-existence of things which are physically concealed at the present time. Consequently, the Advaitist position that things are unreal because we soon cease to perceive them for one reason or another results from an unsophisticated idea of the relation of perception to reality, involving an equation of objective reality with our sense data.

Monism bases itself on this apparent transience of all things, even though this transience involves a self-contradiction, namely an assertion that 'X exists' followed by an assertion that 'X does not exist.' The sources of these statements are separated

by an interval of time, but by what right do we confer an exclusive truth on one side of the contradiction when there are
equally good grounds for believing both of them? The answer is
psychological: we grant truth to the latter case—the negative
one—because our thinking is egocentric. The fact that 'X does
not exist in relation to our senses' is unthinkingly equated with
'X does not exist' shows how subjective this thinking is. In reality, whatever is, and is determined by a specific place and a specific time, is unalterable with a mathematical rigor. It could only
'cease to exist' in an extension of its being which lay outside
every place-time combination where it had existed hitherto.
There is no apparent reason why even the passage of infinite
time should undo the lock formed by the combination of place
and time in their unseen dimension. Things cannot be treated as
unreal just because we cannot perceive them all the time,
despite all our common sense materialism.

A truly metaphysical account of the sense world would not
only relate perceptible objects to their archetypal causes, but
would also extend to the possibility that all apparently changing
things are permanent in a dimension of their own, such that
their motions and changes result from the motion of our limited perception along that dimension. (For a full development
of this idea, see *Living Time*, by Maurice Nicoll, and chapter 9 of
Self and Spirit by R. Bolton.) In that case, the ephemeral nature of
sensory things would have no implications against their intrinsic reality, and the Advaitist system would be deprived of its
main reason for treating them as illusory. This limited idea of
reality includes the grossly one-sided conception of the individual self in its world as a tiny object inside an enormous one,
since that too comes from an uncritical acceptance of sense-
perception.

In monistic thinking, this unreality of the world is felt to be
necessary in order to make room, so to speak, for God, as
though God and the world were two things of the same or similar kind, as they easily can be in casual thinking. For some
minds, however, the idea of the mutual exclusion of God and
the world is justified by its being an effective antidote to

worldly-mindedness and the false equilibrium of natural life. Its practical value appears to be independent of theoretical considerations, but in this instance one is correcting one kind of unbalance with another, in a way which suggests a utilitarian theory of ethics. This is not what Christianity means by faith, moreover, since the equation of all reality with God is a denial of man's free will in relation to God. Although such a doctrine is theoretically monistic, it is practically dualistic, since it opens a door to Manichaeism, as can be seen from a text which is quoted from Eckhart, which states that all creatures are pure nothingness (*purum nihil*), and in the same place this idea is linked at once to the teaching that 'evil has no being,' (ibid., p74) pointing clearly to the third part of the syllogism which would be 'creatures are evil'.

In the above text, 'creatures', 'nothing', and 'evil' are interchangeable terms, or at least we are not offered any criteria for distinguishing them. As if to escape the Manichaean conclusion, our author emphasizes the aspect of 'nothing' so as to eliminate evil as such, as where he goes on to state that:

> That which has no being is nothingness,' and 'he who would add the entire world to God would have nothing more than if he had God alone. (Ibid., p74)

This line of escape from Manichaeism only moves us from one pitfall to another, however, since the denial of any reality in creation is a repetition of what was said previously where everything was equated with God. The two alternatives here are either that the world is evil, hence Manichaeism, or the world is nothing and hence everything is God.

This is the crux from which non-dualism is intended to offer an escape, with the idea that something other than God exists in some indefinable way. But for what purpose could there be such a quasi-reality? (By 'purpose' I mean intrinsic purpose, not the dialectical or ideological purposes which human beings create.) Could it be for the glory of God? But God could not be glorified by a next-to-nothing. For its happiness? But it does not have the modicum of real being necessary for that. Could its purpose be the final, completing element in a scale of real being which descends from God down to true nothing? But that would imply the Great Chain of Being, with all the degrees of real being apart from God, which non-dualism must exclude.

Absolute or Nothing

A document of Vatican II is quoted (ibid., p74) where it says: 'the creature without the Creator evaporates,' in support of the belief that creatures are nothing. At first sight, this could be taken to mean support for *Advaita* from Christian doctrine, but in reality it does not, since it presupposes a conditional reality for creation, not unreality. This point could only be missed by minds which equate being and reality with absolute and self-caused being, as though there could be no other, and as though there were no degrees of reality between absolute self-existence at one extreme and the quasi-existence of the material principle at the other. The idea of degrees of being includes that of degrees of self-existence, since self-causation is under no necessity to be absolutely unique. Only on this basis could there be immortal souls, which are nearly always excluded from discussion in works on non-dualism. Instead, one is offered a dichotomy which polarizes everything between absolute self-existence and the fringes of nonentity.

Theologically, this dichotomy means a refusal to contemplate any manner of diffusion of the Divine attributes among the countless possible relative beings. This is in accordance with a belief in a Divinity which was neither willing nor able to communicate or impart anything of itself. Such a God could not conceivably be God as believed in by Christians, since he could not be either good or omnipotent. Simply by being the sole possessor of reality, such a being, if believed in, could serve only to drain meaning and reality from everything else, which is the opposite of what is involved in the idea of a creator. It is stated that things in themselves are unreal because their reality is in God, as though their presence in the Divine knowledge gave rise to nothing else. In reality, this presence in God means the exact opposite: they have an ultimate causal basis, and therefore their objective and created existences cannot be illusory.

There is of course an aspect of the Divine nature which is in no way concerned with creation, and Scotus Eriugena accordingly saw God as 'the uncreated which creates' as well as 'the uncreated which does not create.' Obviously, the non-dualist position would be secure if God were exclusively the latter of these two, or if it were a separate being, and superior to 'the uncreated which creates', but to think of God in this way is to suppose that God is in actual fact divided according to the distinctions that the human mind has to make in order to think about God. This would indeed be a case of man making a God in his own image. The truth that the role of being the Creator does not account for the entirety of the Divine nature is misunderstood to mean that there are two Gods, and that the one which is worshipped in exoteric religion is the subordinate one.

The non-dualist doctrine supposes that we really can have knowledge of God, and that when we do so, we are not deceived by any kind of illusion, despite the fact that our ability to know about God is inseparable from our ability to know about anything else. Man's ability to know is one thing, no matter how material or spiritual its content may be, and yet Levée says that human knowledge, 'whether scientific or philosophical, is rooted in sensible and psychic experience,' as if this did not apply to his own doctrine of non-dualism.

We are told in the same place (ibid., p76) that human knowledge is 'radically incapable of making us know the real Truth,' because, not being the same as God, it must be a kind of illusion.

The fact that this must mean that non-dualism also must be a kind of illusion shows clearly how this doctrine is one of a well-known class of doctrines and theories which all have the common feature of needing to be magically exempt from the constraints they apply to all rival ideas. For example, Darwinism as an ideology must be exempt from its reductive explanation of man's higher faculties if the reasoning powers of its advocates are to be capable of proving evolution. Similarly with Freudianism as an ideology. It may explain all other kinds of thought in terms of the irrational, but its own reasoning must be founded on a rock if it is not to be just one more expression of irrationality. The same applies to Marxism. The kind of self-contradiction peculiar to such doctrines is always compensated by what Ken Wilber calls 'the narcissistic move', the affirmation that one's own position must be well founded unlike all the others, simply because it is one's own.

In addition to this weakness, *Advaita* also has a tautological way of thinking about God and the world, as where it is assumed that we all know so much about God that we can know for a fact that we are not experiencing God in any given situation. Yet this conclusion follows only from the professed denial that we are teaching plain pantheism. In reality, no one knows so much about God, and the reality branded as 'illusion' may contain countless glimpses of God, despite the illusory elements it may contain as well.

Levée's idea of man's relation or disrelation rather, to God is the same as that of Guénon in this respect. For Guénon, man was sealed immovably within his own level of being, beyond any possibility of personal relation to God, so that his only possibility of escape from this condition was through a relationship with some master and teacher who actually was divine. Similarly, for Levée we are all totally enclosed in a realm of pure illusion from whence one could escape by only the most extreme means, so extreme that they would eliminate anything which could be said to have escaped. If true, this would mean that most of the traditional religions would be full of false doctrines. Such must be the case inasmuch as this doctrine requires the assumption of a God who is neither willing nor able to allow any personal relation between himself and his creatures.

This view of man and God teaches nothing about theology, but it inculcates a nightmarish idea of reality which might well inspire a frantic desire to escape which could be diverted into religious channels. Theologically, it would correspond to a greatly intensified idea of our fallen state; we should be so utterly and fatally fallen that only the strongest remedy could serve for so strong a disease. But this is in stark contradiction with the traditional idea of the role of the intellect in the spiritual life, which is manifest as much in Plotinus as in Aquinas. If our fallenness is so extreme (and what Levée says about human knowledge in the above bears this out), there would be no point in trusting the light of the intellect, and therefore no point in following a contemplative way of salvation. By a strange irony, this *impasse* is much the same as the one that results from the belief that we are products of Darwinian evolution, as its implications for the status of human intelligence are much the same.

Given this assumption that the human mind is as much a product of illusion as the senses, what would the Guénonian idea of tradition amount to? Levée's answer to this appears in what he says against the idea of there being any such thing as 'independent truth and reality,' where the only option left is a blind adherence to inherited cultural norms and formulae, as though they did not need to be understood. This has been considered already, where the function of independence as the basis of truth was pointed out.

Problems of the Self

According to Levée, as with other monists, 'Who am I?' is a real question, even though this reveals an idea of the self in which the ego is almost pathologically separated from the soul. An average common sense idea of the self is assumed, and at the same time discounted because the soul is ignored by non-dualism as much as by common sense materialism. The question as to 'who' one is apart from the ego is then a mystery.

In the light of the complete personality, this question is in the same tautological category as 'Who wrote Beethoven's Ninth Symphony?' or 'What is in this bag of apples?' If 'I' ask or say something, I know by definition who does it, unless my faculties are overcome by drugs, alcohol or sleep. The question 'Who am I?' is also one of a kind which would exclude the ability to understand any answer to it if it were really necessary to ask it. Any such answer, coming from without, could only be a piece of hearsay, and therefore utterly unlike the self's knowledge of itself.

In this respect, it differs completely from the question *'What am I?'* because one can rationally ask what manner of a being one is. The whole of philosophy consists more or less directly of answers to this question. In this case the knowledge of who one is can be connected with other realities that were hitherto unsuspected. But if one could rationally not know who one was, there would be nothing for answers to connect with, and one would be as well satisfied with nonsensical answers as with anything else. The 'who' question is something that can only be asked by way of a denial of something self-evident. In such cases, this denial has the strategic purpose of transplanting the center of self-evidence.

This is because the intuition of a self-evident identity is an integral part of consciousness. When this identity is denied in its natural location, it must therefore appear somewhere else, usually somewhere of one's own choosing. Such a change is perfectly within the scope of auto-suggestion, at least for those whose way of life is simple enough. Under such conditions, one can enter into the role of 'pure subject' to the extent of identifying with it, and then the function of self-identity which is denied can be rediscovered in the state which is thus chosen.

Nevertheless, there is no true identity here, but rather an option determined by one's individual will, even though it may feel like something supra-personal if persisted in long enough. The individual voluntary agent is always the central reality, not least where it works at denying itself, and therefore all attempts to evacuate the contents of the individuality must fail because the central one among them, the will, must remain. This is why identities which result from the willed displacement of the natural identity are more correctly called options or roles, rather than objective identities. The displaced identity can of course be transferred to an idea which one equates with God or transcendence, but this too is a role adopted by one's own volition, and thus still dependent on the latter.

As if to forestall this objection, Levée expresses Christian orthodoxy by denying and deploring the more common ideas of identification with God as a voluntary process, by asking 'What have I, myself, to do with such an identity? How does it concern *me*?' He adds that the answer he offers will, at first glance, be 'necessarily disappointing and a little ambiguous.' (Ibid. pp 83–84)

However, the disclaimer made here concerns only the way in which the identification is understood, not the thing itself. We are told to reject the common sense idea that it is something the individual might decide to do on his own initiative, because orthodoxy excludes the idea of any such initiative by man, while allowing the idea of it as proceeding from God. This, however, is a false dichotomy, because God's initiative can effect nothing without the concurrence of man's will, which must be applied in the first place. The need for a denial of man's will is said to result from the illusory nature of the individual self, its real identity being quite different from what it appears to be to one-self and others. Leon Bloy is quoted in confirmation of this as follows:

> It is the most common of illusions to believe that one really is what one seems to be, and this universal illusion is cor-roborated throughout life by an ongoing deception of all our faculties. Nothing less than death is necessary to teach us that we are always deceived. (Ibid., p 86)

That one's real identity is different from what it appears to be for external observation could only be a discovery for persons who were so identified with their physical egos as to be unaware that they had souls at all. Yet this immersion in materialism is now presented as a precondition for a life of spiritual realization far above popular orthodoxy, although it is really not a precon-dition for anything except a rediscovery of one's full natural personality.

But whether the initiative is from the will of God or from the will of man, the non-dual idea of identification depends on the idea that there is an 'I-subject' which is separate from the 'me-object', as F. Copleston calls them, but there is no reason to admit this, for, as Copleston says,

> The fact that in self-consciousness the self functions as subject does not prove that there is in the human being a distinct entity, hidden away inside, which can be identified as the real self, the self as object being relegated to the realm of mere appearance. To be sure, the self as object is appearance in the sense that it is the self as appearing to a subject. But to say this is to say that the self appears to itself. In other words, *the distinction between I-subject and the me-object lies within the self,* insofar as the self is self-conscious or aware of itself. *The distinction arises in self-consciousness.* (Frederick Copleston, *The self and the One,* chap. 8, pp176–177, my italics)

The polarization between a known-but-unreal self and unknown-but-real self is therefore at best a figure of speech to illustrate the ways in which the self or soul does not know itself, and at worst an invention to make it appear that there is a factual basis for the monistic world view. There is at least a psychologically sound method here, because the more one's known identity is equated with the ego or 'me-object' the more it can be made to appear insignificant and dubious, and the more open one will be to alternative identities, like the one conceived by Levée. The fact that the modern mentality has no more idea as to what God is than it has of personal identity means that there are correspondingly more minds receptive to doctrinal suggestions of any kind. The spiritual level of modern mankind as a whole has reached a very low level, as any student of traditional wisdom might be expected to know, and to represent the modern spiritual vacuum as a seedbed of a new age of spirituality far above what has been known in recent centuries is to ignore the nature of the real world as it nears the end of its dark cycle.

Soul and Atman

Levée says that *Atman* should be translated as 'self', not as soul, because in that way no particular object is signified. (The very word 'soul' is too risky for non-dualism.) But if God also should be the archetype of the soul, this should mean that the 'self' he speaks of in preference to the soul would be just an abstraction. Like Schuon, he assumes that the 'I' 'implies not just the existence but the exclusion of other 'I's. A solid object excludes other such objects from the space it occupies, it is true, but does that apply to individual persons? Where it does, it could only be because of an attitude of mutual hostility among them, and not because of their mere existence, which asserts nothing. The Three Persons of the Trinity are one as well as three, in which case it is strange that a Christian should think that persons are inherently exclusive.

We are told that if the 'I' is taken to mean the individual person formed by the union of body and soul, we would be merely equating the person with the ego (ibid., p89). 'The individual is falsely identified with the person,' although this could only be true if the individual ego was something completely different from the true person, and this is the lay dogma which the non-dualist argument keeps revolving around. The individual ego is obviously not the whole person, but it is just as obviously not *other than* the whole person, no matter how subordinate it may be to the latter.

In support of this idea that non-dualism means an impassable gulf between the real self and the perceptible self, a text is quoted to the effect that souls in a state of celestial beatitude do not behave like independent beings external to one another. Instead, their individual natures are to a large extent merged, like the parts of the body. This is not Christian, because the other side of the picture is given by the Scholastic conception of the angels, for which each angel differs from the others as one species differs from another. But that is not considered. Instead, to emphasize the insignificance of the finite self, Shankara is then quoted as teaching that the ego is engendered by the Self (although for Christians it is created by God), which amounts to a reiteration of the assumption that the true self and the ego are existentially separate things.

One assumption behind this is that the individual self is *ipso facto* limited, in which case it must be separate from the true self, which is beyond limitation. Such are the views on personality which are also constantly expressed by Guénon who, like Levée, assumes them, as though they were self-evident. If the individuality really was nothing more than a creature like a shellfish, incapable of radical development, there would then be nothing to obstruct the conclusion that there was but one spiritual reality behind all the phenomenal detritus. The circular reasoning here is not hard to see: there is but one spiritual reality, and therefore individual selves are unreal and irredeemable; and individual selves are unreal and irredeemable, and therefore there is but one spiritual reality.

The belief that the individual self is inherently limited and therefore necessarily unspiritual is also closely linked to a one-sided conception of the Godhead as having no distinctions. In this case, individual selves would in any case be unreal because of their distinct natures. However, if that were the whole truth about the Divine, it would amount to the distinction of being *purely* undifferentiated. The whole truth of the ultimately real is rather the sum total of all differentiation and all undifferentiation, but in that case the Divine nature is of no use as a standard by which to deny spiritual meaning to individual selves.

The idea of salvation would have no meaning unless the individual being participated in the endless possibilities of the whole personality. The realization of such possibilities by the whole person is enough to explain the apparent loss of individual distinctions in Heaven, for the more souls are spiritually realized, the more inclusive they each must become, and therefore the more they have in common. As they ascend the scale of being, they comprehend in themselves more and more of the possibilities which were separate and mutually exclusive on lower levels of being. In this case, the question as to whether those in Heaven are more or less individual is irrelevant. On this basis, one could not equate the ego with 'the illusion of aseity,' (ibid., p90) because its participation in the whole being implies that it participates in the immortality, or relative aseity, of the soul.

The Christian idea of sanctification implies that all parts of the self can by grace increasingly participate in the spiritual nature. In paradigm cases, this participation has been manifest in saints whose bodies have remained incorrupt after death. If sanctification can change the nature of the body to this extent, how much more the soul? As if to exclude this possibility and to confirm once more that non-dualism depends on there being an insoluble dichotomy between the physical self which was born, and the intellective self with its timeless intuitions, Levée quotes Maritain at some length (ibid., pp91–92). Maritain speaks of a 'lived contradiction' between two contrary certitudes, that of the thinking being who has always existed and the personality in which it acts. The former had an existence in God before receiving a temporal existence and personality.

There is nothing out of the ordinary here, since anyone who knows that two twos make four knows that this has always been true and always will be, unlike one's individual existence. Some part of our being is thus intrinsically spiritual, as few people have ever bothered to deny, but to conclude that the individual self must needs perish everlastingly while the intellect goes to monistic Heaven reveals an instinctive disregard for the Christian idea of salvation in Levée and possibly in Maritain as well, which lies too deep to be penetrated by any amount of Catholic faith and practices. The ultimate dichotomy they believe in makes nonsense of the Hypostatic Union of natures in Christ, and therefore of Christianity itself.

The manifest intention behind the form of doctrine surveyed here is to reserve salvation for an intellective principle which could not conceivably need it, and to deny salvation to the natural personality precisely because it does need salvation. This is, among other things, a denial of what distinguishes Christianity from paganism. All this is in accordance with the ideas in Guénon's *Initiation and Spiritual Realization*, where there is at least no attempt to align them with religious orthodoxy. While I would not claim that no more could be said for non-dualism than what has been considered here, the claim that non-dualism is compatible with Christianity is not open to anyone with a care for orthodoxy. One cannot reasonably argue that Levee *knew* that the *Advaita* doctrine was the truth and not just a matter of belief, because he must have been aware that the greatest minds in the Catholic tradition knew that it was *not* true, i.e., that they knew things which, if truly known, would mean that non-dualism was not true. If it is objected that Catholic doctrine does not mean what it appears to say in this context, there would be no reason to suppose that the *Advaita* doctrine does so either. While Catholic doctrine could be a spiritual phenomenon for which non-dualism is the correct explanation, the exact opposite is possible here as well: non-dualism can be explained on Catholic terms, as is shown by the Church's condemnations of Amaury and Eckhart.

It is consequently incredible that a supposed reconciliation of Christianity with *Advaita* Vedanta should have been published *cum permissu superiorum*, especially as this reconciliation assumes that all religions mean the same thing, and by the author's own admission, that this means the elimination of both God and man.

6

Body, Soul, and *Advaita*

The Body's Significance

The case for the relation of body and soul according to the criteria of Theism follows from the Christian idea of the body's significance for the personality, whereas Advaitists would
eliminate duality by denying any such meaning or purpose to
the body. In this connection, I shall take some examples from
the writings of Ramana Maharshi, who has expressed non-dualist ideas about the body in a clear and forthright manner. A further reason for questioning these teachings comes from the fact
that neither here nor in other Advaitist teachings is there a hint
that the body's real nature might differ profoundly from what it
appears to be for untutored common sense.

This would not matter, but for the fact that teachings of this
kind are commonly taken to be deeply esoteric, perhaps more so
than any others. If this were the case, they would have to include
the truths that whatever once is, is for ever, and that this applies
to every psycho-corporeal state of the person from birth; these
things would have to be included because their implications for
personal identity and immortality are very great. If all our states
of being are permanent in their own places, one's real body
would be immensely extended and undying, while the only
thing that died would be the last and least temporal extension of
the true body. The fact that this esoteric truth is never hinted at
is a good indication that monistic religion need not challenge
the world-view of minds dominated by sense perception, who
do not understand that it is only an error of egocentric thinking

to equate 'no longer accessible for me' with 'no longer exists'.

For the followers of Shankara, any kind of identification with the body, whether understood by common sense or by any other way, is the depth of delusion:

> He who, forgetting his real nature, mistakes this body for the Self, gets attached to it, and cherishes it, and by so doing becomes a murderer of the Self. (*The Collected works of Ramana Maharshi*, Arthur Osborne ed., Rider & Co., London 1969, p 135)

This obviously excludes Christianity, since Christ's use of the words 'This is my body....' to His disciples at the Last Supper can only mean that Christ saw a very deep identity between Himself and His body. But according to Advaitists, this could be done only by those who are subject to delusion. So Christ must have been either deluded or knowingly not telling the truth about a matter of vital importance. In this case He could not have been divine, which makes a major problem for those who believe that all religions are one.

A very similar idea of the transcendence of the Self in regard to the body is quoted by Alphonse Levée (see Chapter 5) with the intention of showing that Christianity and Advaita Vedanta are compatible:

> I no longer have any more relation with the body than the ether has with a passing cloud. How can these states of waking, dream and deep sleep, these attributes of the body, touch me? (*Christianity and the Doctrine of Non-Dualism*, chap. 5, p 98, Sophia Perennis, Hillsdale, 2004)

If such statements about the irrelevance of the body were true, one would not be able to specify which body one was talking about; conversely, where one can do so, it could only be by virtue of a relationship to the body which was supposed to have ceased. Thus for example we do not see why we should claim to be free from the gravitational force of a planet orbiting about a star in another galaxy, or that we are free from the boiling point of liquid krypton, since we do not doubt that this is so. One must be consciously related to one's body in order to deny any relation to it. Non-dualists also remain aware of the difference between what others would call 'their own' bodies and the bodies of other people, even though their principles would not allow any awareness of this difference. The resolution of this problem depends on the soul, because monistic statements would not be possible unless the disembodied 'I' and the body it claims exemption from were both parts of the conscious contents of one and the same soul. Only in the soul can they be connected in a system in which ideas of mutual relation and disrelation may arise.

Although they are poles apart on the theoretical nature of the self, Christians and Advaitists can equally well be able to cope with life and use their world constructively. And yet one or the other must be profoundly wrong, even though without apparent disadvantage. This fact testifies to the autonomy of consciousness which results from each soul containing its own unique representation of the universe. From this it would follow that a general theory of reality, once adopted, will alter the manner in which the world is perceived, giving rise to a selective treatment of the outside world, one which brings the individual mostly into contact with the realities to which his ideas apply, and very little with others.

However, this does not mean relativism, because representation is far from being creation, despite all its creative elements. Some representations will be very true to the nature of objective reality, while others will be much less so. This apparent elasticity of the real is necessary as a condition for freewill. In most cases, death alone could upset the soul's self-created representation of the world, if what it takes for reality is reasonably self-consistent.

Who Makes the Mistake?

Consequently, the test of truth here must be theoretical and logical, rather that experiential. The Advaitist teaching misses the point that identification with the body need only be a delusion when it is *exclusive*. To say that any identification with the body is delusion because it is so in the exclusive case is really just bad logic. Unless there was some degree of inherent identity, I could not conceivably think of my body as being 'mine' in any way at all. I could just as well regard my clothing and other external objects as 'my' body. The transcendence of the 'Self' in relation to the body, which the Advaitists believe in, makes its relation to the body completely inexplicable. Neither can it explain who or what it is that performs the deluded identification with the body. If it were the 'Self' which did so, that would refute the perfection which they attribute to it by definition; conversely, if it is something of a lower nature, an organ of consciousness inseparable from the body, its identification with the body would be reasonable, even on monistic terms.

So, then, who or what is deluded? It can only be either the Self, which can have no right to be deluded, or something of a lower nature which would belong by definition to the realm of delusion. The idea of the co-presence of these things in the immortal soul is excluded, because the soul is both individual and transcendental, and thus a counterpart to the Divine, which can have no counterpart according to Shankara's doctrine. To ignore the soul is as great a delusion as an exclusive identification with the body by the mind. Given the soul as the theatre of individual consciousness, there is a basis for a continuous chain of connection between the Self or, better, the *synteresis* (συντηρεσις, the substantive of συντηρεω, 'I watch closely, keep safe') of the soul, and its subordinate faculties down to the body.

On this basis, a *relative* identification between the 'higher' and 'lower' principles in the person would not only not be deluded, but would rather be a fundamental truth.

According to a principle of Proclus, the highest principle alone is the cause of the lowest entity in the whole structure of causation, because only its causal power can extend down to the most extreme instance. This would imply a special relationship, (though anything but an actual identification), between the *Nous* and the body, which does not involve the *Nous* itself, because the *synteresis* is the function of the soul which interacts with the *Nous*. This is the *Nous* as manifest in the individual person. By its nature, it is next in order of being to God, but it is not God as such, as taught in Advaitic doctrine which denies divine transcendence by making the Divine present in the self *as such*. Conversely, in the person according to Theistic doctrine there is a range of realities corresponding to that of the Great Chain of Being, from whence comes man's attribute of being potentially a microcosm, and actually so to some degree or other. Individuals differ inasmuch as the *Nous* in each is manifest in a unique mode which is expressed by the orientation of his or her will.

This implies that the reality comprised in the 'divine spark' is too great to be able to manifest itself in any finite number of individuals. The body is a necessary part of this unique personality, but no such positive a view of the body is taken by traditions which do not accept the uniqueness of each person. For example, Ramana Maharshi, in making clear the Advaitist idea of body and spirit as taught first by Shankara, says:

> So you too reject this inert, impure body, and realize the pure and eternal Self of wisdom. Give no more thought to the body. Who would care to take back what he had vomited? (Ibid., p161)

This reflects a belief that the body is incapable of spiritualization, or of participating in a spiritual mode of being. There is a salvation of a kind for the 'Self', but it is conceived solely as a kind of escape, like that of a sailor from a sinking ship, because its relation to the body is regarded as being just as contingent and external as that of sailor and ship. This is not the same as the Christian idea of salvation, which is one of transformation, not of elimination, and the separation of the soul from the body in death is only a preliminary to its rejoining the risen body.

Similarly, (ibid., p164) he refers to 'the body, which is unreal, and a figment of illusion,' and says that 'the I am the body idea' is the reason why one is affected by bad *karma*, and furthermore:

> The 'I am the body' idea is the seed of all sorrow. Therefore just as you do not identify yourself with your shadow body, image body, dream body, or the body that you have in your

imagination, cease also to associate the Self in any way with the body of skin, flesh, or bones. Make every effort to root out this error and, holding fast to the knowledge of Reality as absolute Brahman, *destroy the mind* (my italics) and obtain supreme peace.' (Ibid., p141)

The injunction to destroy the mind carries the implication that, as long as the mind works at all, it must present an opposing idea of reality, not by a malfunction, but merely by being what it is. This could only mean that we were made with something which was designed to deceive us, but by what kind of a God? This would mean that there could be no such thing as moral responsibility, and in any case, we have nothing other than this deluded mind with which to decide to reject this mind. There is besides an obvious rational deduction in the contention that the body is of no account because:

the gross body was created out of food. It is the sheath of food. Compounded of skin, blood, flesh, fat, marrow, excreta and urine, it is most filthy. It has no existence before or after death, but appears between them.' (Ibid., p141)

In this way it is made clear that the Self is in the body and the individual personality without there being any inherent unity between them. The body is not produced or determined by any causal principle in the soul or self; not being the Form of the body, the Self is not manifest as anything spiritual. In relation to the Self as conceived by Ramana Maharshi, the physical self has no more relevance than the dirt on a window pane has to what is seen through it. In terms of the previous comparison, the monistic idea of salvation would mean that when the ship is destroyed, the sailor swims ashore, where he is able to resume his life without having to be a sailor any more. But on what grounds must we believe that the individual person is made up of such unrelated things? We are expected to find it easily believable without need of argument.

A Conceptually Simple Absolute

One reason for the disjunction between the Self and what we normally mean by the self lies in the undifferentiated and quality-less nature which monistic doctrine ascribes to the Self:

> Just as milk is uniformly white, though drawn from cows of different colors, so also Realization is uniform for all persons of whatever denominations.' (Ibid., p109)

Nearly everything most Advaitists say about their Absolute indicates that they too conceive it as purely simple and non-conceptual by nature. This is the concept of the Absolute which I have elsewhere said to be self-contradictory, on account of its having but a single specific nature, purely negative in form, just as though it were a Cartesian clear and distinct idea. (see Chapter 4, last section.) However, it still would be true to say that a purely undetermined entity cannot conceivably have any relations with anything else, and that it could therefore never form part of any person. But if we take such an indeterminate entity as a presupposition, we need to know why some people can think they have any kind of relation to it, and why they should think it is in some sense 'in' themselves at all. And, once again, who or what makes all the mistakes concerning identity which result in the world-illusion?

There is also the question as to what religious experience can mean to those who believe Divinity to be without qualities. In non-dualism private mystical experiences are of central importance, because neither reason nor Revelation can provide what they really need. These mystical experiences are not believed to be given by God, but rather to be obtained through the efforts of the one who experiences, like those of a mountaineer getting to the top of a mountain. (The assistance of a Master makes as much and as little difference to this as the assistance of a mountain guide makes to the achievement of the mountaineer.) But these experiences can only have the ultimate status that followers of *Advaita* ascribe to them on condition that God either does not exist, or is transcended as being merely one part of a relative duality with the created world. Conversely, if we are created by God, these non-dualistic experiences could not coincide with ultimate reality, even though, with the right intentions, they could be a realization of the spiritual potential of the human state. At worst, however, they would only be the psychic equivalent of feats of physical strength.

Identity and Illusion

Of course, nobody with any belief in God would deny that God might allow someone to experience some very high reality, like St.Paul being taken up to the Third Heaven, but even where this is the case, mystical experiences still could not have the same meaning for non-dualists as for theists. For the latter, the self or soul is not on the same level as its contents and experiences, since the former is always the container while the latter are always contents. In this case, the soul-container cannot be sublated by anything among its contents, or subsumed into its own ideas. No matter how powerful the experience, even if it is enough to smother self-awareness for a time, the relation between soul and contents cannot be reversed by any possible experience.

This does not mean that one cannot be lastingly changed by experiences, because they can always reorientate the will, but such effects are necessarily made possible by the free will of the person. This centrality of the choices of free will lies at the foundation of personhood, just as much as does the soul's status as container of its world. In relation to the will, mystical experiences occupy a certain portion of time in the interior biography of the person, like any other experiences. They are events in the development of a particular representation of the world, formed in and by the soul. This means that no kind of experience can prevent the resumption of the same identity and biography into which it entered. Even if it caused death, the same resumption could just as well take place in the soul in its *post-mortem* state.

This also explains why, for Christians and all other theists, no kind of mystical experience can be taken to be an automatic passport to salvation. The element of absolute finality necessary for that could not be possible in this world for the reason given, that the inner life must continue after them, and so it is not surprising that Catholics have always been dubious about the value of mysticism. For the followers of Shankara, however, appearance and reality are profoundly different, and from that point of view, the need for illuminating mystical experiences is paramount. In this case, the most positive things we perceive could just as well be the most negative, and vice-versa. This is involved in the idea that the world as such is an illusion, and that when true enlightenment comes, it is supposed to disappear altogether.

This would be all very well if there was never any point at which the Advaitists themselves needed to be able to take appearances as being equivalent to reality, but of course there is. For example, it would appear where a non-dualist mystic was recognized by his followers as being a source of wisdom and virtue. They could not be free to regard his perceived qualities as mere masks for ignorance and folly, or their system would not survive. Similarly, they also have to accept the coincidence of appearance and reality where opposing doctrines were encountered, such as dualism. But if *all* were illusion, the apparent falsity of dualism could just as well be masking the truth, while the (to them) apparent truth of their own could be a mask for falsehood.

This shows that the Advaitists' position cannot be argued for unless they were to accept, as common sense would suggest, that the world is a mixture of reality and illusion, rather than purely the one or the other. But this acceptance would still only mean that they were logically in a position to argue for a particular doctrine; at the same time, the monistic doctrine itself would be overturned by this realistic view of the world, as this would exclude the idea of universal illusion. Conversely, if illusion were upheld as a basic premise, neither monism nor non-dualism need be the only conclusion, because no part of an illusory world can have a stable identity. This shows non-dualism to be self-contradictory. Unequivocal distinctions are necessary for any doctrinal position, and they are only possible for those who accept that the world contains reality along with illusion.

To this it is sometimes objected that to find reality in the world is to treat it as though it were God, in the belief that absolute reality and absolute unreality were the only alternatives that God could devise. This also reveals an ignorance of the difference between created and uncreated reality. Things which exist by an act of the Divine Will are necessarily real as being manifestations of that Will. Given that there are such qualitatively different orders of reality, the crudely-understood idea that there is only one reality is either a truism, where 'reality' is a collective name for all the different levels of being, or it is an assertion that there is but one mode of reality, which is obviously untrue. For those who think in terms of a simple dichotomy between the All-real and the all-illusory, there could not be the kind of ordered distribution of being and reality 'downwards' from God, which is one of the central postulates of Neoplatonism. The general monistic dogma that the reality of the Absolute is exclusive must rule that out, whence this doctrine must in reality exclude the idea of the Great Chain of Being, despite its being the most universal belief among the traditional religions.

So fundamental is the Chain of Being, with its many levels of reality, to traditional metaphysics that even belief in God is no more universal. For this reason, non-dualists who deny its implication of countless degrees of reality cannot have a right to speak as though they were the most authentic representatives of traditional religion, such as they often believe themselves to be. By the standards of a universal orthodoxy, if there is such a thing, non-dualism, with its essentially monistic idea of reality, could not be sufficiently comprehensive, no matter how carefully one distinguishes one's position from that of pure monism.

Spiritual Self-Knowledge

If the body, and the psycho-corporeal aspect of personality, is set aside, it might appear that the deepest self-knowledge should be made much easier. Why should not a purely spiritual part of the self know itself in the fullest possible way? The pursuit of this could possibly be taken for a justification for the rejection of the body which was considered above. There is certainly an awareness of the fact that if the mind could know itself as such, it would have a claim on divinity, as instanced in the following:

Disciple: Who is God? Master: He who knows the mind. Disciple: My mind is known by me, the spirit. Master: Since the Shrutis declare, 'God is only one,' you (as the knower of the mind) are really God. (Ibid., p77)

Everything depends on what one means by 'knowing the mind'. What has already been said in Chapter 3 shows how little scope there is for any meaning in this which would go beyond the common sense ideas of knowing one's mind. For practical purposes the mind can be known in tangential ways which fall far short of knowing what it actually is as such. 'Knowing the mind' typically means a knowledge of its existence, the thoughts in it, and the things it can do. If anything more than this was involved in the above quotation, we are not told, and if this were the case, the essential issue is ignored. If the mind possessed an absolute self-knowledge, it could well be identifiable with God, but that has already been excluded for the reasons given in the same chapter.

Nevertheless, non-dualism is tied to an implicit claim that there is no reality beyond human consciousness, and this has an impact on the role of experience in religions of this kind. *Advaita* and Buddhism depend almost wholly on private mystical experience, but experience depends in turn on a relation between a subject and an object, that is to say, on a duality, which is the last thing one wants in a context of monistic thought. This duality itself depends on the existence of an individual, regardless of the fact that individuality is not admissible in these religions. The ideal of non-dual experience would have to be a self-revelation in and by consciousness or awareness, but one in which there would be no difference between the subject and the object. This would be like thinking about something without thinking about it, as F. Copleston puts it.

In connection with getting rid of the distinction between subject and object, Copleston points out that there is a wholly unmysterious and natural way in which that could be understood:

> The emergence of the distinction between subject and object is contingent upon the existence of beings who are capable of exercising the function of subjects, distantiating themselves, from the epistemological point of view, from the object of awareness. Is it not natural to claim that the underlying unity is simply the common world, within which and out of which the distinction emerges?' (*Religion and the One*, chap. 8, p187)

Despite the fact that a state in which there is neither subject nor object could thus be even more easily inferior to them rather than superior, further affirmations of a similar kind are made, like the following:

> Great texts such as 'Thou art that' which proclaim the identity between the individual self and Brahman completely root out from the body and the senses 'I' and 'mine'.... (Ibid., p150)

The elimination of the 'I' and 'mine' referred to above is not the same as the elimination of the individual self, because 'I' and 'mine' are only terms which express the relations of the self to itself and to other persons and things. If these relations were in abeyance, the possibilities underlying them would still exist as long as the self does. The reality of the 'I' and 'mine' is besides presupposed by morality and moral responsibility, which are as necessary for monistic religions as for theistic ones.

In the text just quoted, the subject-object relation must have been overcome, and not necessarily in the reductive sense indicated by Copleston. This can be understood in different ways: from a creationist point of view, the higher unity of subject and object would be in the God who created them, and a mystical vision of God would, among other things, be a vision of this higher unity by which subject and object were created. But this could only be thought of as a sublation of the individual person if the difference between Creator and creation is a relativity. For those who believe in God, this communion with God is a sufficient answer to the problems raised by the subject-object relation, but for those who do not, or who believe in a non-personal divinity, the resolution of subject and object can only take the form of a mergence of the same kind as that between two quantities of liquid.

This is because the pantheistic or non-personal ideas of divinity are not ultimately different from the world, or the non-dualistic idea of 'realization' would not be workable. On this basis, the individual self can be seen as a superfluous entity which can only disturb or confuse the order of real being, like a wave on the surface of water. When it is finally disowned, there will be peace. However, from a theistic perspective, this precarious state of individual being, which makes it vulnerable and always liable to suffer, is something which we were put into this world to learn to cope with and live out to the full, and convert its troublesome accidentality to something of real substance, through the grace which is offered to all who believe. That is a very different kind of 'realization', and one which is profoundly creative by nature, and therefore a worthy response to the creative act which brought the world into being. God's creative act is then vindicated, which it could not be if we refused the Cross and just slipped back into the state which preceded our creation.

The Function of the Ego

In the same text, it is said that 'In whatever way it may be examined, the ego with all its faculties turns out to be unreal, a momentary limitation, inert, insentient, and incapable of realizing the One.' (Ibid., p151) If we leave aside the question of finding an agreed meaning for 'realizing the One', or of saying what should be meant by the 'One', there remains the implicit idea that the ego and its faculties are conceived as being like a collection of natural phenomena, and not as different functions of the soul. The soul is ignored, and the attack is focused on the softer target of the ego. To make sure the ego is reducible, it has to be conceived as something too limited to constitute a person.

If in fact we may believe that the ego and its faculties express certain powers of the soul, their diversity would be no argument against them, only in this case the soul would allow a conception of the individual person which transcended the multiple contents of the phenomenal realm, one which could not be dismissed as 'ego'. Besides traducing personality by ignoring such facts, the Advaitists reduce the ego to something even less than itself by equating it with the function of carnal desire. This point is explained by Joseph Campbell as follows:

> [In] the Indian myth the principle of ego, 'I' (*aham*), is identified completely with the pleasure principle, whereas in the psychologies of both Freud and Jung its proper function is *to know and relate to external reality* [my italics] (Freud's 'reality principle'): not the reality of the metaphysical but that of the physical, empirical sphere of time and space. In other words, spiritual maturity, as understood in the modern Occident, requires a differentiation of ego from id, whereas in the Orient, throughout the history at least of every teaching that has stemmed from India, ego (*aham-kara*: 'the making of the sound I') is impugned as the principle of libidinous delusion, to be dissolved. (*Oriental Mythology*, chap. 1, iii, p15, Penguin Books, London, 1976)

Subject to the psychologists' conception, the ego is the soul's instrument for the purpose of interaction with the outside world, and that interaction can vary from that of sensual pleasure to the exploration of external realities in the manner of science. If, however, the ego is understood only as the agent of carnal desire, the non-dual conception itself will be dependent on a mutilated conception of the ego. In this way it creates a simplistic dichotomy between divinity and unalloyed mortality, between which the idea of personality is lost, leaving no place for the Christian idea of a self defined on the basis of the soul.

Denial of the Physical Self

Since the *Advaita* doctrine asserts this extreme and irresolvable duality between the true self and the sense-perceptible self of common sense, the result is an inability to explain how the two ever came into any kind of association in the first place, or how this relation is preserved. This problem is much the same as that of explaining how the body and the Cartesian soul are related. Given the Cartesian idea of the soul, which does not have any attribute in common with the body, it is but a small step to the Advaitist conception of the Self. The fact that Descartes was not trying to formulate a spiritual doctrine makes no difference to this point, because in either case, the true self is conceived as detached and essentially disincarnate.

Accordingly, non-dualists can, consistently with this conception, teach their followers to:

> Give up this false physical self, just as an actor gives up his role and remains himself. By knowledge acquired through Self-enquiry discard both the microcosm and the macro-cosm as unreal and, abiding in the unbroken stillness, remain ever at rest in the perfect bliss as Unqualified Brah-man. (Ibid., p151)

If we should experience a state of lasting or unbroken still-ness, we obviously have a right to see it as a grace, but to actually identify it with Brahman is a different question, apart from the uncertainty as to its immediate cause. In any case, the identifica-tion of the state of peace with Brahman must involve an attempt to equate the real self with one of its states or part of its con-tents. But the self is a being in a different category from that of any of its states, however spiritual, because it is their container or theatre. In opposition to this, Ramana Maharshi follows Shan-kara in equating the self with its own contents, the conception of the self which was taken up in later centuries by Descartes and Hume.

There appears to be no effective proof for the idea that the self is nothing but its contents, although there is instead a more or less question-begging analysis of the self which reaches the conclusion that there is no real self because it cannot be found among the mind's conscious contents. This kind of thinking is a slightly more sophisticated version of the contention that there is no God because He has not been seen above the earth by an astronaut.

Given this reductionist idea of the self, the Advaitist position requires us to believe that the individual self can be sublated or subsumed into one or other of its conscious states. We are told in the above to 'discard both the microcosm and the macro-cosm,' but who is it that discards them? Is it the Self? In that case, the Self would be a conscious individual agent, and therefore part of the world which is declared to be illusory. If it were the individual self, this self would be denying its own reality by its own lights, which is clearly self-contradictory; if it is unreal, its mentation must be unreal likewise, and if its mentation is valid, it must be real. In the former case, the non-dual Self has by defi-nition no need or reason to discard anything in the natural world, since it is in no way involved with it. Either way, then, the above statement is quite outside logic.

Elsewhere, the relation of the body to the Self is treated in a way which would be better suited to that between the body and the soul, since soul and body at least have enough in common for there to be meaningful relations between them:

> While in fact the body is in the Self, he who thinks that the Self is within the sentient body is like one who considers the cloth of the screen which supports a cinema picture to be contained within the picture. (Ibid., p97)

I too have used this comparison between a projected picture and the screen, as a means of clarifying the distinction between the soul and the representation of the world it contains. The soul is in a sense both screen and cinema in this context. But this is a strange comparison to use for the purposes of a philosophy for which the mind is its contents, for in that case it would mean that the screen really was part of the picture. The Self is not indi-vidual in any way, however, so unlike the soul, it has no intrinsic relation to the individual person, even though it may in some sense contain the latter.

The idea that the body is in the Self is taken to exclude the possibility that the Self could be in the body, but this is to think of the relation in physical terms, e.g., if the wine is in the bottle, the bottle cannot be in the wine. This does not apply in the same way to non-material things, because while the body and the world to which it belongs are comprehended in the soul, the reverse is also true within certain limits. The soul is also in the body, not in the sense of being comprehended or enclosed in it, but as being active in it and pervading it. Otherwise there would be no union between them, and the soul's comprehension of the body would be on just the same level as its comprehension of everything else in the outside world. If the soul were symbolized by the space occupied by a city, then the body of anyone who lived there would obviously be 'in' that city-space, but this implies that some small part of that space would at the same time have to be in the body of that person as well.

To that extent, then, body and soul are 'in' one another reciprocally, and if this kind of relation should apply to the Self and the body, it would conflict with the absolute transcendence attributed to the Self. To return to the relation of soul and body, the idea that the soul was wholly contained by the body would make the soul to be part of the body and therefore part of the world, as though the cinema screen was indeed part of the picture. If that were the case, there could be no transcendent property in the individual person, and so there would be no basis on which his faculties could represent the world and his relation to the Self. He would be wholly a phenomenon. Since the distinction illustrated by the image-and-screen comparison is even more valid for the soul-and-body relation than for the Self-and-body relation, it undermines the non-dualist position more than it supports it.

If one takes no account of the soul as the container and substantial ground of our perceptions and mental life, everything has to rest on some impersonal substitute, like the universal 'Self' of the non-dualists. This idea of our mental life is in accordance with the monistic position that only one substance is ultimately real. However, there are no factual grounds for believing in a universal substance which somehow thinks it is you, me, or anybody else, and the logical grounds are no better. On the other hand, the soul as an individual substance does at least correspond to experience, and can only be denied on a basis of pure dogmatism. Monistic dogma is necessarily unverifiable, because verification always requires at least two terms for comparison. Logically speaking, on the other hand, the One cannot be the negation of the Many if it is their source.

With the soul, the 'screen' on which the images are projected is a property or function of the individual self, and the objective or veridical nature of its perceptions is owing to the *synteresis*, with which the soul interacts with Intellect. This property is individual, and is compatible with each soul having a place in the hierarchy of being, whereas there could be no hierarchy or Chain of Being if the only ground of objectivity was a non-dualist Self, identical in all. This anarchical property of non-dualism has been observed in non-Advaitist Hindu tradition, and its political consequences have been drawn before now by the 'Levellers' of the Seventeenth Century, who also denied the difference between God and man.

Identity and Self-Differentiation.

The denial of meaning to the body as such, if believed, means that we could be free to think of our identity as having no concrete basis, and endlessly modifiable. Once man's identity is no longer the Formal cause of a specific physical nature which manifests it, new identities can easily be assumed:

> Giving up the separate identity of yourself as distinct from Siva, meditate constantly on the non-dual unity: 'I am He who is known as Siva. (*Ramana Maharshi*, ibid., p107)

A soul or self which was so impersonal as not to be manifested by its body could just as well be reincarnated as the soul of any number of other individuals, and equally easily become the soul of divine beings. This is to assume that we do not know our own identity as any kind of determined, created entity, but that we do know the identity of the divinity, in this case Siva. But this is the opposite of what is nearly always experienced. We do not know what God is, but we do know what we are to some extent. Can anyone even try to give up a 'separate identity' unless they know enough about some other identity to make them want to change places with it? A change of this kind could not meaningfully be made unless it were possible to know what it was like to be both oneself and to be some other being at the same time.

If the change were extra-personal, like that of buying a new house, something like equal knowledge of both terms of the change could be possible, since one could know what it was like to be in both of the houses. But this kind of change applies only to things in the outside world, far short of personal identities. If, on the other hand, the change were like that of a soldier becoming an officer, or a priest becoming a bishop, an external knowledge of the new identity could suffice, but for non-dual identification we do not have even that much knowledge of what is aimed at.

For Advaitists, the existence of individual identity is an evil or an illusion, as though it were an artificial imposition subject to which we had no means of reaching the truth, and which we were free to get rid of. Superficially, this could be taken as a prospect of realizing larger possibilities, but in reality it means something appalling, namely, that man as such has no real identity at all, only a void into which identities can be inserted. To think that he could be ennobled by the insertion of a divine reality into this void is just a confusion; if his identity were a nullity, it would remain the same, no matter what it happens to be accommodating. To think that such an empty kind of being could be made otherwise by some other nature, even a divine one, is like thinking that a rusty tin can could be made into a golden bowl by having a precious jewel placed in it.

This implication is ignored by non-dualistic thinking, so much is it wedded to the belief that individual identity and its self-differentiation must be nothing more than a limitation and an affliction, as though no one had ever discovered that the self was capable of indefinite enlargement:

> It says in the Yajur-Veda: 'He who has even the slightest sense of differentiation is always afraid!' He who sees any attributes of differentiation, however small, in the Absolute Brahman will for that reason remain in a state of terror. He who locates the 'I' sense in the insentient body and its objects ... will experience sorrow after sorrow.... (*Ramana, Shankara, and the Forty Verses,* p48, Watkins Publishing, London, 2002)

This contains another implicit affirmation of belief in a divinity without attributes, as though this must be separate from and superior to any divinity with attributes, such as creating and loving anyone or anything. Two quite different ideas are joined here. The first of them is a truism to the effect that we should have no need for courage if we saw ourselves as no different from anything else, which could just as well be produced by states of reduced consciousness. This is to ignore the fact that fear is an essential part of consciousness which serves the soul in the same way as the sense of pain serves the body by enabling it to withdraw itself from injury. Even where fear is irrational and goes beyond its necessary function, it is the means whereby one can build a character able to dominate it. That is what distinguishes fear in man from fear in the animals, because it is necessary for the development of free will. Nevertheless, free will is excluded by non-dualism, because free will implies a real causality in persons, and that can only be possible for beings with some independent reality. At the same time, the above text ignores the possibility of rising above irrational fear by spiritual maturation, rather than by a surrender of the personality, as though truth required us to abandon the moral struggle before it even began.

The other idea joined to the above is that we can only identify either with our bodies or with God, as though souls had never been created and had no identities of their own. Accordingly, the teaching is apparently that to cease to identify with the body is *ipso facto* to identify with God, as though there were no other possibility. Such an outcome owes nothing to logic, whatever else it may hold, besides which, some degree of identification with one's body is both necessary and valid, since the body is the material instantiation of the soul. The only cases of real false-hood occasioned by the body are exclusive identifications with it, but the distinction between these two kinds of identification is ignored, along with all the modes of being between God and mere matter.

Further on in the same text as the above, the soul is referred to in relation to the body, but only in a way which deprives it of spiritual significance:

> It [the body] is the projecting power of maya together with its veiling power which unites the soul with the ego, the cause of delusion, and, through its qualities, keeps a man vainly dangling like a ghost. (Ibid. p49)

Here again, there is no admission that the individual self is capable of endless development and spiritualization, and instead there is only a fatalistic assumption that the self is solely a quan-tity of limitation, fixed at its own level for ever and irredeem-able. If that were believed, it would certainly be able to arouse a strong commitment to non-dualistic religion. But the question remains as to why such an idea should be believed. It is anything but self-evident, and Plotinus' thought consistently teaches the exact opposite. The idea that the body and ego as conceived in the above need some outside agency to join them to the soul (or the soul to them), appears to be equally dubious. If, in fact, the body and its ego are the manifestation of a spiritual soul, there would be no need for anything else to unite them, any more than white objects need a third part to unite them to the White Itself, or beautiful things to the Beautiful Itself.

If soul and ego are presented as disparate realities contin-gently related, we would have an idea of the soul which could easily be thought capable of reincarnation. On this basis, the individual self is in effect deconstructed, leaving no obstacle in the way of attributing all personhood to the universal Self. Only if the body is contingently related to the soul, and does not express an identity intrinsic to it, can the soul have the indeterminate nature necessary for it to be able to identify itself with higher forms of being. Here, then, we have two conceptions of the self which reinforce one another: the idea of a soul which can be the soul of pretty well any kind of living being, and the idea of a soul which is no more than the sum of its contents. Together, these two conceptions serve to exclude from the person everything which could bar the way to what this doctrine calls 'realization'. It is doubtful if anyone would be willing to believe either if it were not for the way in which they support the non-dualist agenda, as it is expounded in the texts quoted here.

These texts include clear examples of the way in which Non-dualism employs the related ideas that the self is nothing but the mind, and that the mind in turn is a more or less artificial combination of contents, such as passions and habits, which would be open to literally any kind of reconstruction:

> Because the individual self, which is nothing but the mind, has lost the knowledge of its identity with the real Self.... The mind is a unique power (shakti) in the Atman, whereby thoughts occur to one. On scrutiny as to what remains after eliminating all thoughts, it will be found that *there is no such thing as mind apart from thought* [my italics]. So, then, thoughts themselves constitute the mind. (Ibid., p40)

This is exactly the doctrine of both Shankara and Descartes, as discussed in Chapter Four, and Hume could not have put it better, albeit in a philosophy which has no pretense to spirituality. The individual self would have no identity or created nature, but only an endless fluidity or capacity for change, of much the same kind as Platonism attributes to its conception of matter. What is most strange about this is that consciousness is of ultimate importance for this kind of wisdom, while the individual self it tries to eliminate is the only known source and vehicle of consciousness. There is something clearly self-destructive about this, and in a way, naive. It may be argued that the supposed lack of identity in the self will be made good when it identifies with the Self, which must have a real identity which will be shared by the non-dualists who assimilate to it. But in reality, the Self or Absolute of non-dualism is a divinity without attributes, so no identifiable identity can be communicated to those who can claim some deep relation to it.

Since one cannot explain what one means by experiential content in monistic mysticism, it is a spirituality which could not be expected to modify any human attributes. Not only is it apparently impossible to say what consciousness is, but for the followers of Shankara there is nothing definable for it to be conscious of, at least not in the state which their doctrine aspires to. Nevertheless, some minds are able to see salvation in the discarding of an identity which is known, however imperfectly, in favour of one which is beyond human conception.

Self-Creation not Sublatable

If there should be something in the identity of God which cannot be subject to sublation, the same would have to apply to human identity, given that man is made in the divine image. This divine attribute, once it is identified, will confirm what has already been argued against monism.

From the foregoing it can be seen that the operative factor in monistic thought is an idea of personal identity which is conceived as though it were a material substance like metal or plastic which can be made into different objects equally easily. Only if the self is this kind of object can monism be sustainable. The idea that the identity of the self is like that of a material object which can be melted down and made into other shapes is one which appeals to common sense. For unthinking common sense, one's own self appears as a physical object in a world of other physical objects; it is taken to be what the senses make of it. Monistic esotericism merely transfers this deceptive half-truth from the sense-world to a world of abstractions, where the same falsehood makes the self an abstract object among other abstract objects. In the light of this parallel, monistic or non-dualistic systems of spirituality are collections of abstract objects arranged in various sequences, and presented so that unwary minds will see themselves as enclosed in them, and not vice-versa, just as the physical ego is seen to be enclosed in the physical world. This abstract self-identity is then felt to be under the power of the other abstractions, with the result that it completely belies the creative dynamism which is the essence of every soul and person, and treats it as an illusion.

To clarify the issue involved here, we need to relate it to what God's identity consists in. On p142, I referred to the idea that a denial of identity with one's body and everything to do with it can lead to a sense of identification with God or the Absolute. If the intellectual faculty in man was wholly unrelated to the body and the individuality, then, its sublation to the Absolute would be possible. What could prevent it? A fundamental objection to this idea of Divinity has been given in a classic work on Jacob Boehme by H.L. Martensen, and it is one which further develops the idea that the inmost nature of the individual person is a self-reflective act. This has already been discussed in Chapter 4, where it appeared as the basis of Madhva's refutation of Shankara. Self-reflection is as it were 'an inside without an outside,' and constitutes the individual as a monad. It expresses itself verbally in first-person statements like 'I know that the earth goes round the sun,' compared with which, third-person statements like 'The earth goes round the sun' are impersonal and lacking in the dimension which would link them to the mind; they are common property and appear to be independent of individual consciousness.

If we want to understand what differentiates us as individuals, we will have to relate the question to what differentiates God, and forms His identity. The idea of identity based on self-reflective consciousness can be taken a stage further. The self-reflective center of the soul can be seen to be the cognitive aspect of an act which is self-creative. I have argued elsewhere (*Person, Soul and Identity*, chap. 4, vi, pp141–142, and chap. 1, v–vi) that the

essence of every soul is a continual flow of volition, whence follows the idea of 'self-creation' as its effect. In man, the self-creative act is relative, since it must always have something upon
which to work, but it is perfectly real within its limits. All our
choices and decisions take our personality from potentiality to
actuality, and thus create it out of the God-given raw material
with which we begin. This attribute follows from man's being
made in the image of God, since the essence of Divinity is an
absolute self-creative act. It was Martensen's great insight that
this divine attribute is a fundamental objection to Pantheism
and other monistic forms of thought which deny the Divine
transcendence. He begins by making explicit the Christian idea
of God:

> We have to emphasize the fact that God, as the absolute
> Spirit, must be self-powerful, self-conscious and self-defin-
> ing prior to the nature which He posits outside of Himself;
> and that there can be no single aspect or element of His
> being which is not irradiated and encircled in perfect clear-
> ness by this self-consciousness. We must insist that God be
> conceived as the *Causa* of Himself, or, as it may also be
> expressed, that He be conceived under the title of *Aseity*
> (Self-caused, independent being); . . .

One could add that Christ as Divine Logos is both God's own
self-knowledge and the primary agent of God's creative power.
(Col. 1:15–6). Martensen goes on to show how this excludes pantheistic sublation:

> Pantheism is unable to apprehend God as the Cause of
> Himself, or as the eternally Self-positing and Self-produc-
> ing. It is only the ethical conception of God, the conception
> which views God as the eternally self-realizing, and in Him-
> self eternally realized Goodness and Love, that can hold
> God to be His own cause (both "efficient" and "final")."
> (*Jacob Boehme*, chap. 3, (ii), pp 73–74)

Such is the attribute which makes God absolutely individual,
unlike the attributes more commonly thought of, such as infin-

ity, perfect goodness, eternity, or omniscience. Therefore monists have to ignore it because it cannot be reduced to a mere "determination" of something else.

In case this is not sufficiently clear, this conception of God's essential nature, (and of man, by reflection), as *an internal activity from and to itself,* excludes monism along with Pantheism because they both require a one-dimensional conception of God and man, one which is confined simply to cognition in a purely third-person sense, like the picture formed by a camera. As opposed to first-person consciousness, third-person cognition, as expressed in reported speech, ignores its origin. This is why those who follow pantheistic or monistic religions are taught not to use the word 'I'. Every statement in the first-person involves something these doctrines cannot acknowledge, namely, *self-reflection,* and therefore our natural transcendence. If, then, a self-reflective act cannot be converted to any other being, how much less could a self-creative act be so? This is what lies in the essence of the Divine identity, and it is consequently in the essential nature of beings created in the Divine image, and which is manifest in the soul's self-motive power.

7

Dream and Reality

Oriental Ideas of Personality

The counter-arguments of Theistic religion were articulated and established by teachers of Vedanta who came after Shankara, but their teachings do not appear among the versions of Hinduism which dominate modern neo-traditionalist thought in the West. The question of whether the self contains spiritual and unspiritual parts which are physically separable was answered by Ramanuja, with the idea that in God, 'Sat' (irreducible stuff), or substance 'is inseparably related to its innumerable attributes of infinite perfection.' This is an outline of his answer to Shankara's reduction of the divine attributes to the most purely undetermined among them. That doctrine, we are told, 'was anathema to Ramanuja' (see Eric Lott, *Vedantic Approaches to God*, p130), where Lott also says that 'For him (Ramanuja) the reality of Sat is not pure and infinite Being, but infinite being *in inseparable relation* to finite beings [my italics].' This would obviously exclude the presuppositions that the personal and impersonal aspects of God are objectively separate realities, and obviate the parallel belief that man's intellect and ego are similarly separable.

Furthermore, according to the same author, this implies that 'It is precisely his related-attributes of compassion, lordship, and so on, that distinguish the Supreme Being most clearly from other beings, and thereby establish his supremacy (ibid., chap. 8, p134). In Jewish tradition, it is similarly understood that the nature of God requires creation rather as the nature of a king requires a kingdom, such that God has some kind of dependence on created being. (see Angelo Rappoport, *Ancient Israel*, chap. 1) This strongly suggests that Ramanuja would have endorsed the argument that the absolute Principle of consciousness is only conceptually separable from its contents, but not in objective reality. This inseparability does not mean any confusion between the abstract and the concrete, or between the conceptual and the phenomenal, but only that their several natures logically imply one another. The doctrine of their physical separability may well have originated in an attempt to express rhetorically the deep qualitative difference between the intellectual and the sensory faculties; their supposed physical separability could thus have been a metaphor to convey their deep difference.

As a way of symbolizing the difference between orders of being, the above expression would be harmless enough, but it is a metaphor which non-dualists take literally, making the ego separable from the intellect, and so inadvertently sharing with materialists the single-subject idea of the person which was discussed above, because this is all it can amount to if it has no intrinsic union with the intellectual function. In this respect they share with modern philosophy the reductionist idea of the person, which indicates that neo-traditionalist rejections of modernity are less deep than they profess to be.

Conversely, once the spiritual soul is taken into account, it is far less easy to treat individual persons as mere relativities, and that would explain why Guénon and Schuon have little or nothing to say about it, and prefer to speak only of the 'ego' instead, when reference to the individual person is unavoidable. This use of the 'ego' idea clearly corresponds to an idea of the Absolute which would be the sole possessor of real being and immortality, with a 'creation' alongside it which had no spiritual principle of its own or any substantive being.

For those who can believe the world to consist only of egos and animate bodies and their subjective phenomena, this conception may sound reasonable as long as one does not enquire as to how it is known. The ego is not the kind of entity to be capable of reflecting universal reality, since the only kind of self capable of this belongs to the realm of spirit. But in this case, the created world must include beings which transcend it while also being individual persons, and as such they could not be equated with the non-dualists' idea of 'ego'.

There is a very great difference between relegating an external and material creation to near-unreality, and including in this conception the intellectual powers which conceive it. To include intelligent spiritual beings with creatures which have no such property is to confuse categories. Consequently, a disproof of the belief that the self is solely its ego, such as I have given elsewhere (see *Self and Spirit*, chap. 2), must also therefore be to the same extent a refutation of non-dualism at the same time. This has consequences in two opposite directions, so to speak: on the one hand it establishes the spiritual dimension of individuality, as opposed to non-dualism, and on the other it excludes a materialist and reductionist idea of the self and its activities.

Dream and Reality

The monistic alternative to the naturalistic conception of the person lies in the assumption that uncomfortable realities can be tamed by bracketing them as 'illusion,' or at least excluding them from the eternal verities, as for example, where Schuon says that *Maya* means 'illusion' in *Gnosis: Divine Wisdom*. There he also quotes the Hindu formula that 'All is Atma' (ibid., p68), which is an explicit affirmation of the monism which is never far beneath the surface in non-dualist thought. Clearly, if this were true, everything apart from 'Atma' could hardly be anything but illusory. Accordingly, Schuon defends the idea of world-illusion by means of the hypothesis of a 'collective subject' which experiences 'solidarity within a cosmic dream.'

This conception appears to be an inversion of some of the basic facts about dream and waking: it is when we are *awake* that we are able to enter a world of shared experience, whereas it is when we go to sleep and dream that we each go away into a separate world as Heraclitus observed. Consequently, this idea of Schuon's stretches the idea of 'dream' so far as to make it useless.

It is, besides, based on the premise that a common or collective object of experience, even of a whole world, must correspond to a common or collective subject. But the subject-object polarity means no such thing. This basic polarity only requires that a common object (common to a number of minds), be known to a certain number of subjects, from one upwards, but with no commitment as to any number exceeding one; one subject could suffice. Naturally, one subject can relate to many objects, but if many subjects relate to one object, the oneness of this object can create no unity among the subjects apart from that of the contents it gives them.

Taken literally, the idea of a 'collective subject' is self-contradictory, because a collectivity has no mind or soul of its own; it is only a single thing by convention. Understood more freely, it could be a metaphor for many people having closely-related experiences at the same time, as with the word 'unanimous,' but the impossibility of a literally real or substantive 'collective subject' makes the idea of it ineffectual as an argument for illusion.

Moreover, in a real state of dream, we cannot conceive of any other state, or, if we do, we start to wake up. Conversely, when we know we can think of different modes of reality, i.e., awakened, dreaming, and dreamless sleep, we know thereby that we are awake. Thus what Schuon says about the 'collective dream' can only mean that his use of this expression is metaphorical. He allows that 'the word "dream" is only another term for "illusion" or Maya.' (Ibid., p69) Note how this statement equates Maya with 'illusion'; this is not consistent with more fluid meanings, like 'unfolding' or 'magic', and from what Schuon says here (ibid., p69, footnote) he assumes that world-illusion is the only alternative to 'the absolute reality of the ego.' This is a case of argument by attributing untenable beliefs to those who think otherwise. This conclusion could only be valid if there were no alternative to a crude dichotomy between the Absolute and the ego, as though there was no such thing as a scale of being, with different degrees of reality.

Schuon says that it is 'universal Man' who 'dreams', and that we dream 'in him' and 'with him'. If that was what our Archetype did all the time, we would have to dream with him, of course, but what does universal Man do apart from dreaming? If he never did anything else, by reference to what other known possibilities could we say that he was dreaming, or draw any conclusions from the fact? If, on the other hand, he does other things, we are never told what are these other activities are represented by in human life, or how are they could be distinguished from the 'dreaming' kind.

If we knew that universal Man was dreaming all the time, we would know more than he did, since dreaming is not knowing. But in this case we would not be dreaming, and we would thus not be instances of him. Conversely, if we were only dreaming that he was dreaming, there would be no reason to believe it to be true, although our being in a dream state would follow from the premise that our Archetype and Formal Cause dreamt all the time. Without labouring the point any further, this should suffice to make clear the incoherence of the dream metaphor where one attempts to account for personal identity.

The use of the idea of 'dream' in metaphysical thought is based only on the popular misconception that nobody can ever be really sure whether they are dreaming or not. This is untrue for the reason given above, and because in the dream state we never have the use of all five senses. Having the use of five senses defines us as awake; in our experience in the dream state we have only sight, hearing, and a much reduced sense of touch, while the senses of taste or smell are absent. In effect, we have only two-and-a-half senses instead of five, which is enough to prove the objectivity of the distinction of dream and waking.

Mystical Consciousness

Because it assumes a naturalistic single-subject idea of the individual person, non-dualism appeals to the common sense idea of a self which must make it look like an insignificant part of the world as a whole. On this premise, that man is solely a phenomenon, the non-dualist idea of self-transcendence can easily appear to be both necessary and well-founded. The materialist ethos of today creates a great deal of tension between what people are misled into believing about themselves and what they know at the deepest level. In those whose intellect is not wholly stifled, this tension can be unbearable, and its resolution, when found, can easily go to extremes which cannot be corrected by the knowledge that is popularly available today.

Where there is only a materialistic idea of the self or person, therefore, the discovery of transcendence can come as a complete negation of the self thus misunderstood. When one tries to understand mystical union in terms of this mindset, there is no awareness of the way in which this union must form part of the development of an indivisible spiritual substance, along with all its other experience. If there were such an awareness, it would be seen that there was now a second reality besides that of the union between man and God, namely, consciousness of this union in a rational soul, as well as in the mind of God.

It is therefore not hard to understand why monistic mysticism should appeal to those with a scientific background in today's world: both scientism and theological monism make the same assumption about reality as a whole, that it is a system in which the Whole is everything and the parts are next to nothing. For scientists, the Whole is an object without a subject, while for Advaitists it is a subject without an object, because for them the world disappears at the highest level of reality. (This is the point behind my remark to Charles Upton at the start of our correspondence, that 'you are thinking it, and that is something else again.' If he were right, there could be no room for this consciousness). In either case, therefore, there would be only one reality, with one specific nature to the exclusion of any others. Although the idea of object-without-subject and vice-versa is a contradiction in terms, since 'object' and 'subject' are each definable only in terms of the other, this misconception has a psychological appeal because it conceives a world of pure order with no observers to dilute the picture of absolute rigor.

For the sake of this vision of unity, many minds are willing to forget that this requires them to base their understanding on something which can be neither object nor subject. The highest reality, being one and one alone, must therefore be either the Creator of subject and object, or be the cosmic condition from whence subject and object arise in this world. Neither of these two alternatives is open to any kind of literal identification that human beings could be capable of, since all such identification depends on something common to both sides of the issue.

In the world as we know it, the conception of real things as unions of subject and object reveals something about the structure of the universe which J.W. Dunne has called 'The Serial Universe'. Pictures typically attempt to convey in their own way an object without a subject, rather like the scientist's phenomenon and the monist's One. But every attempt to approach full objectivity by including the observer creates a new and deeper level of duality, according to the sequence: scene; scene-being-painted-by-artist; scene-being-painted-by-artist-being-painted-by-artist; and so on. In the real world, the criterion of the real phenomenon is a bipolar compound of object and subject, and the structure of such a world consists in just such infinite regresses of representation.

If one is aware of X, one can be aware that one is aware of X, and so on, and this is a condition inseparable from consciousness of the world as we know it, but the objective world itself is not separable from the consciousness which comprehends it. This is about as far as possible from the idea of an 'elegant solution', but it follows from the inclusion of the subject along with the object as an equal part of reality.

In *Self and Spirit* (p130, footnote) the case is considered where some mystics are enabled to separate pure consciousness from all its objects, even though the mystic's consciousness is able to resume its normal course afterwards, and he is able to communicate his experience afterwards. This indicates that the separation achieved by the mystic was a transitory state within the life-story of the self and not something other than it, but what would be the point of such an experience? It might make someone nearer to God in some bare, ontological sense, but hardly in any personal or moral sense. It is, of course, a proof of spirituality, but spirituality alone can equally well be demonic.

More generally, such things could be demonstrations of special powers, like those of certain yogis intending to show that they could survive being buried alive. But however humanly interesting such things may be, they have little or nothing to do with what God requires of us, and are of no more spiritual help to others than feats of strength of any other kind. One thing certain about a supposedly ultimate experience of a subject without an object, or of an object without a subject, is that it is not an experience.

The common assumption that unity is more real than duality is based on the fact that one can have unity without duality, while one cannot have duality without unity, since every duality is a binary system which must in some sense form a unity as well. Therefore, non-dualists think that if they reject duality they will be able to identify with a unity which is exempt from all the determinations that could give rise to dualities. This is mistaken, however, because the independence of unity means only that it does not depend on duality in the same way as duality depends on it; unity determines the existence of duality, and if it could not do so, it could not be itself. In this way, therefore, unity does depend on duality.

A Two-Way Dependence.

The above idea that the One could be in any way dependent on the Many is contrary to some of the usual habits of thought which can make monistic religion feel natural and congenial. The normal conception of the relation of the One to the Many is asymmetrical, in much the same way as the relation of a Form to its instances is asymmetrical; the Many depend on the One in a way which cannot be mutual. This truth is enshrined in the first proposition of Proclus' *Elements of Theology*, according to which we are only able to speak of 'a multitude' if we can think of it and its members under an imposed and overriding unity, because pure multitude seems not to be conceivable:

Neither this manifold as a whole, nor any of its several parts will be one; each part will be a manifold of parts, and so on

to infinity; . . . For each part of the manifold — take which
you will — must be either one or not-one; and if not-one,
either many or nothing.' (Proclus, E.T., prop. 1)

Each member of the multitude must be one thing through
participation of the Form of the One, that is by being an instantiation of it, so that as a whole and in its parts it depends on the
unity delegated by the One, if it is to have any reality at all. In
this case, it appears that there are no grounds for conceiving the
One as dependent on the Many, so that if in fact there were, it
would have to be a dependence of a different kind. While the
Many depend for their existence on the One, the existence of
the One would seem to be unconditional, because if the Many
were annihilated permanently, the One would still exist, would
it not? But here is the counter-force: though the One would still
exist, it could not exist in the same way as before, because its
nature would be altered in a radical manner, there being no
longer any multitude, or even the possibility of one, to which it
could impart some degree of unity. It would thus be deprived of
all power of causality, and therewith its substantive being.

In this case, the One would be little more than an abstraction,
a shadow of itself. Consequently, there is a sense in which the
One must depend on the Many if it is to remain what it truly is. If
the dependence of the Many on the One is *a priori*, the dependence of the One on the Many is *a posteriori*, but just as really so in
its own way. This may be illustrated by a concrete comparison, if
it is not too misleading: all the points on the surface of a globe
are fixed by and dependent on the North (or South) Pole, and
the circles of meridian and latitude which radiate from it. At the
same time, the position of the Pole is independent in relation to
all the other points. But, if it could be separated from all those
other points, the pole would still be a point, but for all other purposes, nothing.

This conception of the relations between the One and the
Many is the basis of my discussions of the non-dualistic treatment
of the individual self hitherto, as well as in the next section.

I would leave this aspect of the One and the Many at this

point, but for the fact that there will still be some minds who will regard this reasoning as an attempt to prove the impossible. The One must be absolute by definition, it will be said, and any deviation from this must mean polytheism. This difficulty can be answered from the way in which the One is defined. The One which has a dependence on the Many, as shown above, is defined as the negation of the Many, or as the exact opposite of it, and for this reason it ought to be called 'The Relative One', or 'The Pure One'. If this definition is borne in mind, we can proceed to a conception of the true or Absolute One as a union of the Relative One with the Many. This resultant entity would truly have no dependence on anything external to it, and in this way the absoluteness of the One can be maintained without conceding anything to monism or non-dualism. Theologically, this does not mean attributing pluralism as such to God, because God is both One and Three, and therefore transcends the phenomenal distinctions of unity and plurality.

Non-Dualism and the Self

From a personal point of view, the most essential presupposition for the Shankaran doctrine is that the individual self or person as such has no metaphysical basis for identity, and that only the common intellectual faculty can have such identity. The person as such must therefore be purely and simply a natural phenomenon, and the fact that this entity is mysteriously tied to a transcendental 'Self' or *Atman* adds nothing to it, because the true reality cannot qualify it, let alone unite with it. (This is the same in principle as the total disjunction between the Cartesian soul and body, and is open to the same objections.) In this respect, the *Atman* differs radically from the orthodox idea of the immortal soul, because it can only mean that the individual is faced with the stark choice of identifying either with his mortal rind or with a non-personal transcendental principle. In either case, individual identity on a spiritual level has no meaning; there could only be one Identity, which is why I apply the term 'monistic' to this kind of doctrine.

It is for this reason that the conception of the soul as a monad or indivisible substance, containing its own equivalent of all realities, is a fundamental alternative. In the light of this conception, each person would not be just an individual, but a world, in which case the non-dualist dichotomy of matter and universal spirit would be excluded. Thus Non-Dualism has no adequate answer to the traditional conception that the individual self has an immortal soul which is also its Form, a soul which both relates to the universe and reflects it, and on this basis the self-aware individual person as such is a spiritual reality.

Although it is known under the heading of 'Dualism', this conception does not mean that the person consists of two separate substances, but that there are dualities, firstly between the psychic and the corporeal levels of being in one and the same person, and between his soul and God. In the light of this conception, the Shankaran doctrine can only be persuasive for those whose understanding of the individual self does not go beyond common sense. Consequently, for all its identification with the esoteric, monistic religion is still closer by nature to the exoteric than to the esoteric. This is also shown by its identification of man with his temporal condition, since it treats the person only as a subject of limitation, corruption and transience. This perspective results from the absence of a metaphysic which would include the immortal soul and the hierarchy of spirits.

The most essential non-dualist presupposition referred to so far is the idea that 'all determination is negation.' That, if true, would make personality a negation, and would take away any reason for trying to find any ultimate meaning for personality. Because they think of the self in this way, advocates of non-dualist spirituality speak of a literal 'annihilation' as necessary for 'salvation', as if that were not a flat contradiction: Christ, it is said, was annihilated on the Cross, and He was in some way recommending a comparable self-annihilation, at least for Christians who are willing to mentally bracket the Resurrection. No deductions are drawn from the fact that this annihilation is also believed to be the fate of everybody by materialistic people who have no religious beliefs. Equally, no notice is taken of the manifest fact that this flower of pure spiritual religion and devotion should thus blend seamlessly with the outlook of simple pagans, although it must surprise anyone in whom the sense of wonder is not quite dead.

Consequently, it is assumed that our individual identity must be given up, on the grounds that it is only a natural phenomenon to which we are irrationally attached. But far from being highly spiritual, this thinking reveals nothing more than an absolute disbelief in the possibility of redemption, strangely adorned with the garments of religion, because the subjective connection between religiosity and its doctrinal content is weak or non-existent in many persons. The very fact that this school of thought can use the word 'annihilation' in a natural and apparently literal sense is enough to prove that their real doctrine is indeed Monism, without even the refinements of non-dualism. Only if there was in fact ultimately only one reality and one substance alone could annihilation be a legitimate or necessary requirement for created beings. This is why the exclusion of personal immortality follows as rigorously from a spiritual Monism as from materialism.

The non-dualist conception of annihilation is never taken so literally as to imply any termination or curtailment of anyone's existence in this world, however, whether consistently or not. This raises the question as to how an annihilation of the inward and essential part of our identity can happen without any corresponding disappearance of the outward person; if the soul were the Form of the body, it would have to do so. It may be said that the *Nous* or *Atman* will remain in the same relation to the body, and that that alone can sustain the physical life. But this brings us back to the unprovable presupposition that the soul and its intellectual faculty are two separable things which are not subject to any unifying principle of their own.

This kind of thinking, with its despair over the possibility of redemption or spiritualization of the individual person as such, is consistent with the Manichaean doctrine that there are two Gods, an evil one who creates the natural world, and a good one who neither creates anything nor has anything to do with the world created by the other one. In this case, salvation could only consist in a radical rejection of the created world and a self-identification with the 'good' God who does not create. This was an essential feature of the Manichaean religion in Roman antiquity, as it also was of the Albigensian religion.

The Manichaean form of dualism has been said to be the most convincing of all theological systems, in view of its repeated reappearances in different forms over the centuries. This is because it offers a very drastic simplification of the real world and a spiritual commitment which does away with all compromises, and in a way which does not depend on any kinds of social or institutional involvements. It appeals to a taste for the heroic and the authentic, as well as to an impatient desire for perfection. This calls for an act of faith in return for which one becomes at once a member of an elect, in which one is free to practice individualism in the concrete while condemning it in theory.

A Spiritual Evolutionism

Those who interpret all religions in terms of non-dualism believe that they can justify the making of assimilations between deeply different doctrines such as those of creation and emanation. This raises the question as to whether language can transcend the conventions of usage and connect with essential and universal realities. If non-dualists were right, it would appear that language must in fact be a matter of convention. Nevertheless, there is one difference between the above two doctrines which cannot be talked away, namely the idea that a created world results from a conscious will and purpose, whereas the emanation or cosmic illusion idea involves no conscious or voluntary act at all. Therefore to assimilate these two doctrines would be to say that intention was the same as no intention, or in other words, that something was the same as nothing. This conclusion would not be altered by the fact that one's denial of the Divine purpose results from a belief that the highest reality transcends all purpose along with all other determinations.

Those who originally taught the doctrines of creation and emanation believed, on the one hand, that they were affirming the world to be an intentional act of God, and on the other, that the world just happened for no particular reason, very much as pagans and evolutionists do. This is why it is strange that the modern followers of Shankara are mostly anti-evolutionists, but this may have more to do with a hostility to science as such, rather than to what it says in this instance; an illusory world such as they believe in cannot yield real knowledge, whence science would have to be an imposture. Ramanuja, who rejected Shankara, was consequently able to affirm that the natural world was a source of knowledge, as indeed it must also be if we are to have any right to make deductions from scriptural texts, whether for the purposes of Monism or of Dualism. Darwinian evolution and the Shankaran non-dual doctrine are clearly compatible, since they both deny creation and Divine purpose in the world, besides which they both self-destructively subvert the capacity for the knowledge on which they depend.

Their compatibility could go as far as identity, because non-dualism is by its very nature a kind of transformism by default, even though its world-process is said to come from mind rather than organic matter. If human beings can spiritually evolve across the species barrier between man and God, why should anyone want to deny that apes should be able to evolve across the species barrier between them and human beings? The same lesson follows from the ideas that reptiles can evolve into mammals, and fish into amphibians. If, on the other hand, we believe in a rigorous doctrine of creation, for which the species are unalterable, as most neo-traditionalists do, the idea that man can mystically evolve into God can only be an anomaly.

It is not enough to object that nothing of a biological nature is involved in the goal of non-dualism, on the grounds that the goal of this change is not a physical one; that would require a hard and dualistic distinction between mind and matter. It must be understood that this is a distinction that neither monists nor non-dualists have a right to draw, since their ideas of spiritual evolution cannot logically be separated from evolution of the biological kind. By its very nature, there is nothing to prevent evolution from being relevant to all levels of being, whether subtle or gross; logically, it should embrace all modes of being or none.

The belief that a world of rigorously separate species could come into being without any creative design, whether because all is matter, as Darwinists think, or because all is spirit as non-dualists think, is the absurdity of demanding a universal miracle while denying the existence of a Creator who could perform it. Some traditionalists try to solve this problem by restoring the Creator in a role like that of Plato's Demiurge, but this kind of being is clearly not equal to God. In this case, the Creator would really be a creature, and therefore still a sublatable being on non-dualist premises, along with the rest of creation, and therefore he would remain as unreal as anything else.

The basic tendency of evolutionism or transformism is unmistakably monistic, as it conceives all things emerging as temporary modifications of a single material substance which is as indifferent to them as the monistic Absolute is to the world. Creation and emanation are mutually exclusive, since one side affirms that the world results from God's design, while the other believes itself to be affirming that the world results from something fortuitous and unintended, like the casting of a shadow, or a reflection on water. To say that two such opposed conceptions can mean the same thing is really a disguised form of scepticism, because one can only assimilate such ideas on the basis that neither side knows the truth, but that both have merely projected their own subjectivities onto the real world, rather as one culture has called a group of stars the 'Great Bear' and another one called it the 'Big Dipper'.

This would rule out the possibility of metaphysical knowledge, which must be the most paradoxical result possible for the *Advaita* Vedanta school. Needless to say, non-dualists do not abide by the logical result just outlined, because they demand that their side of the issue be literally true, and that only the others' must be figures of speech.

The Meaning of Survival

Personal immortality is not only not believed in by modern people, but is very often not even felt to be desirable, which is an incredible reversal of the historical norm. In this respect, pillars of neo-traditionalism like Guénon and Schuon and their disciples are typical modern men, which raises a question as to how real their traditionalism was. What is a traditionalism which rejects the historical norm just as much as does materialistic modernism? They profess not to wish for any personal life or survival in the next world, just like pagans, but unlike worldly pagans, they cling to a strong religiosity, and adopt a doctrinal position where some kind of spiritual sacrifice is equal to truth, and on this basis take their denial of a personal hereafter to mean that their belief must be more true than that of those who believe in personal immortality. Non-dualists draw no conclusions from the obvious fact that there are literally billions of other human beings who have little or no belief in the immortal soul either. If they did, they would see that this state of mind reveals only a lack of grace and not a higher wisdom, and they would see that they were uncomfortably similar to this unspiritual majority. They cannot know that their particular lack of belief in the immortal soul is really any more spiritual than that of the majority, since no faith is required in either case.

A further similarity between the materialistic majority and the non-dualists appears in the fact that neither can count as authentic persons in this realm because authentic persons are not interested in compromises like quasi-survival; they will either believe in personal immortality or they will believe that death is final extinction. Similarly, there is nothing authentic in rejecting the individual self because it is flawed and relatively unreal. On the contrary, the authentic choice is to stand by it and accept the suffering that that will lead to, until in God's good time it finally is fully real, whether in this life or in the next.

The potentiality for developing into a true individual is one of the chief marks of man's spirituality, and that is why it is so sadly ironic that the disciples of Shankara can only denigrate it. They may promise some greater spiritual good instead, but without individuality, human beings could hardly differ from animals, regardless of what they are supposed to believe.

If they wanted to convince anyone that they could be truly spiritual while wanting to go on living here, they could be in some difficulty if this appeared to be short of sacrifice. What *moral* difference is there between a Shankaran non-dualists's claim that he has a right to go on living in this world and a Christian Platonist's claim that he had a right to believe in personal immortality in the next world?

Morally and psychologically, natural life and eternal life would appear to be inseparable, because the desire to live at all is by nature open-ended, not bound by any given period. It may be objected that the life which one wants to continue here is something well known, whereas life in the next world is not known, and so cannot be desired in the same way. Nevertheless, however little known the next life may be, it must include continuity of consciousness, and therefore of personality. To believe in it does require faith, however, over and above the proofs that can be provided for it, whereas it takes no faith to believe in a non-dualist 'salvation', apart from a will to show oneself unchallenged by orthodox religious belief.

Without personal immortality as part of its structure, religion loses its substance, since there would be no basis for any ultimate experiential knowledge of God or Heaven, nor any individual substance in which the religious life could realize its transforming action. Instead, it would be reduced to a cult of rhetoric and poetry aimed at fostering a feeling of the spiritual, and possibly inducing some obedience and self-denial. Apart from that, it could easily descend to the level of the worst kind of philosophy, that is to say, a cult of verbal forms without substance.

Nevertheless, religion emptied of substance can be of interest to some kinds of partial believers who have a fascination with religion. For many of them, a religion can fill a need where the difference between God and soul is not clearly perceived. Instead of speaking of 'salvation', therefore, neo-traditionalists prefer to say 'realization,' which, when thus used out of relation to anything else, is so little definable that one cannot deduce a meaning for it, even from the writings of those who most profess belief in it. (It is not necessarily meaningless, since some idea of a meaning for it can be found in the writings of Maurice Nicoll, who never uses the word 'realization' or preaches non-dualism.) In general, it can only be taken to mean 'private mystical experience', and therefore an assertion of individualism, despite the declared intentions of non-dualists.

The urge to deny individualism is typically an individualistic trait, and its imprint on non-dualists is unmistakable. Their beliefs are focused on the achievement of a metaphysical goal which is not performatively verifiable in the way that moral attainments are. Since it involves some kind of identification with a divine principle which is without attributes, all attempts to find definitions or even objective criteria must be a waste of time. This is what creates significant parallels with the rise of the Protestant doctrine of salvation by faith alone. The claim to have a 'realization' in this mysterious sense of the word is just as indefeasible as an Evangelical Protestant's claim that he is saved, or a theosophist's claim that he or she is some famous historical personage reincarnated. In particular, those who believe themselves to be reincarnations of great or glamorous persons can have a subjective security similar to that of non-dualists, because of its degree of untestability; reasoned argument is of no use against them, since that does not apply to what never pretended to be reasonable in the first place, and that can appear as unassailable truth to those who maintain such positions.

To return to the question of survival, the modern mentality has another kind of problem in relation to survival in the next world, one which must be relevant in this context, if I am right in thinking that this same mentality now affects everyone, whether they are practising members of religious traditions or not. This problem is identified in one of the truest observations made by Gurdjieff, namely that modern man's spiritual inertia comes from the fact that he is unable to imagine the process of his own death. This is no doubt a result of an intense repression of awareness of this reality, which has arisen in the last hundred years *pari passu* with the collective waning of belief in the next life. Without that belief, the truth about any human life as a natural thing is unbearably tragic, if it is faced at all, whence the only non-spiritual defense against it is all-out repression. The result of this is the absurdity of the 'pseudo-aseity' of the profane ego, according to the expression frequently used by Alphonse Levée.

In addition to this, the young have always tended to feel as though they were immortal in any case, and this can only be reinforced by the near-universal repression just referred to. For this reason, it is highly unlikely that terrorists, for example, really believe that they are going to die, no matter what they may believe in the top of their heads. The same applies to other kinds of person, such as non-dualists, who are not consciously suicidal but regard the extinction of the individual as an ideal. In short, they are able to think in this way because they are insulated against any effective apprehension of non-existence by the ruling modern repression.

Under these conditions, one can think of self-extinction with a certain sense of satisfaction and justification, because of a belief at gut level that one will somehow always be there both to supervise one's 'annihilation' and to enjoy its good effects afterwards. Although that is complete nonsense for reason, it is not too foolish for the subconscious, nor for minds which are more than usually distorted by the emotive repression of awareness of the fragility of our mortal being.

Free Will and Personal Reality

Denials of free will involve much more than the will alone, because they also have a negative impact on the reality of individual persons. Free will and personal reality are in fact inseparable, even though that may be ignored by Calvinists, who think they can deny free will and still believe in real personality. Conversely, when one starts with a denial of personality, as with monists and non-dualists, they usually do not consider that their denial of the reality of personality means a denial of free will, as much for themselves as for anyone else.

The connecting principle involved is that of causality, because whatever actually exists has *ipso facto* some power of causality, and the causal power in man is exercised and manifested in his free will, free because it is self-originating in the person. If one can originate an action in oneself, one must therefore be able to make different responses to any given stimulus, without that implying that all such responses could be made equally easily. Thus no free will means no agency, and no agency means no causality, and that in turn means no being. The nondualists' denial of the reality of individual selves is therefore a denial of free will at the same time.

It has often been believed that man cannot have free will if he is the creature of an all-powerful and omniscient Creator, inasmuch as man is conceived to be purely finite and God purely infinite. But this comes from a very crude idea as to what God can create. The answer to the confusions that surround free will and Providence has been presented in a convincing manner by Stephen Clark, where he says that God can just as well create beings who share in God's uncaused causality as create beings who are without causality and who are therefore solely altermotive by nature. In this case, the supposed conflict between grace and free will is an irrelevance, caused by a materialistic idea of creation which equates it with the creation of passive objects.

The relevance of this argument used by Clark appears in connection with an argument used by Professor Jean Borella to justify non-dualism in the context of Catholic doctrine, and to distinguish it from monism. He says that non-dualism is nothing more than what theology affirms of the relation between God and the created world. The two are separate from the point of view of the created beings, but the world has no being apart from God, and so is not really a separate reality. This cannot be true, however, because the separate natures of God and creation must exist for God also, on pain of the absurdity that God would be unable to distinguish Himself from His own creatures. God and the world cannot be the same thing for God for the further reason that God is transcendent in relation to the world, just as a Form transcends each one of its instantiations.

There is a certain question-begging in this argument, which is much the same as the one indicated above in relation to free will, i.e., the notion that because we are created beings, we must be purely and simply objects with no causality of their own. But it is pointed out that, besides creating mere objects, God can also create beings who share in His self-caused causality, and in the same way there is equally no problem with the idea that God can include a degree of self-existence in the existence given to created spiritual beings. There is no more reason why created existence should always mean the bare existence of purely contingent things than that it should mean the passivity of things with no causal power. These two cases are clearly very closely related.

Consequently, the fact that the created world cannot exist without God will not mean that its relation to God must be non-dual, because the relationship must be more dualistic than that, as a consequence of the fact that God has created beings which are given a share in His own necessity-of-being. This is no more than what is implicit in the concept of immortal souls, which are such that they could not cease to exist, except by a special miracle of destruction. This property resolves the apparent contradiction in the idea of 'conditional self-existence'; self-existence, like infinity and self-caused causality, can be relativized to various degrees, being perfectly real in more restricted realms.

On this basis, there are adequate grounds for saying that the relation between God and created beings is a relation between different substances, even with full allowance for the fact that the latter owe their existence to their Creator. What this relation is not like is the relation between soul and body, which indeed is non-dual in the manner in which Borella understands non-duality. Body and soul are not different identities and even less are they different subjects, because their relation is that of Form to instantiation, the soul being 'the Form of the body', and this is precisely the kind of relationship to which the non-dualist analysis applies. The body is essentially a prolongation of the soul in matter and is instrumental for it. The soul's use or direction of the body does not therefore mean action upon anything alien to it, but only a combined mode of activity between them.

The fact that the non-dualistic conception is wholly appropriate for the soul-body relation, then, is precisely the reason why it cannot be used to account for the relation between God and creation, at least if we are trying to speak for religious orthodoxy, and do not believe the world to be God's body. Attempts by neo-traditionalists to equate the orthodox doctrine of creation with non-dualism are therefore implicitly heretical, not least because at bottom, they mean that God no more creates anything than the soul creates its own body. Non-dualism could only be right, therefore, where we were free to believe that the universe was God's body. No matter what arguments may be offered for that, it is a conclusion which could not be either Christian or Islamic, being all too clearly pantheistic.

8

A Debate
Concerning Non-Dualism

Introductory Note

What follows is the text of a debate between myself and Charles
Upton, as it appeared in *Sacred Web 17*, where it was headed 'On
Vedantic Non-Dualism and Christianity'. This was started by a
message of mine about *Advaita* to James Wetmore, and it was
subsequently answered by Charles Upton, another author with
whom James Wetmore was in correspondence. Most readers
will take it for a debate between Theistic and Pantheistic ideas
of religion and no more, and to them it may appear evenly bal-
anced, even to the point of being indecisive. However, the more
philosophically alert will see that at a deeper level it turned into
a debate about personal identity, and what constitutes it.

While I defended an idea of the self which gives full scope to
the idea of the soul as a microcosm, along with the permanence
of all temporal states of being outside the range of sense perception, Upton's replies were based on an idea of personal identity
which does not go beyond what it appears to be for common
sense, a collection of ego experiences, the very existence of
which is disputed by some modern philosophers.

That is why I believe his replies failed to make their point. It
can only be a waste of time to teach the idea of some ultimate
transformation of the self when one does not have a true idea as
to what this self, this 'I', this 'me', is. On the common sense level,
very little is known about the self, and next to nothing about

God, and that is no basis for the divinization of human selves, if it is supposed to be objective and not subjective. We must know what is related to what if any light is to be shed on such things.

The Debate as Published

Bolton to Wetmore
February 18, 2005

I used to be a keen believer in the Non-Dualist esoteric, and this book (*Christianity and the Doctrine of Non-Dualism*)[1] is giving me a lot more ideas about why I broke with it. The first principle, that the highest impersonal reality must be more real than the highest personal one, is strange because we never know the impersonal except as a part of the inner life of persons. For all I can see, the impersonal out of relation to the personal is simply a self-contradiction, since it is an object without a subject. (And by the way, if the Non-Dualists have an effective answer to this, that will be the behavior of persons as well.)

A significant peculiarity of the Guénonian Vedantic esotericism is the way the Vedantic dichotomy of everything between the Godhead and illusion matches the dichotomy in exoteric religion, of a purely infinite God and a purely finite creation. The resolution of dichotomies like these are precisely what we have the esoteric for! Facts like this tend to justify Borella's idea of the esoteric as an exoteric with an extra big ego. At any rate, there is definitely something sub-esoteric in Guénon's thinking.

Another point, according to this system, the universal mystery of creation is to be explained by an analogy with the way light is reflected on water, in which case a child could understand it. So

---

1. *Christianity and the Doctrine of Non-Dualism*, by 'A Monk of the West', translated by Alvin Moore, Jr. and Marie M. Hansen, Sophia Perennis, 2004, was reviewed by Harry Oldmeadow in *Sacred Web 15*, June 2005.

what would we want the esoteric for? In fact, this conception of creation absolutely excludes creativity on all levels, since it would require neither intelligence, nor power, nor will, nor purpose. That would be a religion without mystery, and a God capable of much less than we know humans can do.

Upton to Bolton
February 19, 2005

I was moved to reply to your e-mail to James Wetmore, which he forwarded to me. As I see it, your idea of the Vedanta — though one might make the point that this is actually the way Guénon presents it — contains certain misconceptions which seem to be very common among Christians. They are: (1) that the Vedantic Absolute is strictly 'impersonal'; (2) that the Vedanta divides everything between an infinite God and an illusory cosmos; and (3) that the Impersonal Divinity must be an 'object', since the Personal Divinity can be nothing other than a 'subject'.

(1) The first misconception, on the sentimental extreme of the spectrum, becomes the Chestertonian image of the Mysterious East as an abyss of numb impassivity and terrible, impersonal heartlessness. This simply indicates that a personalistic sentimentalism must see all that transcends its own level as a demonic emptiness, void of all life, love and relatedness—and this may indeed be the realm encountered by some westerners who have been attracted to the eastern religions because they are basically in flight from God. To them, an impersonal Absolute seems less threatening than a personal God who is *watching* us, and Who may even require something of us. An impersonal Absolute seems much less inconvenient; as C.S. Lewis said about the God of pantheism, 'He is simply there if you need him, like a book on a shelf, there is no danger that heaven and earth will flee away at his touch.' I would hazard a generality that Christians, or those with a Christian cultural background, will tend— consciously or not—to view the Vedanta as if it as were a kind of Greco-Roman pantheism, which is certainly not the case. And

this misconception will present itself equally to those attracted by the Vedanta and to those repelled by it. I'll deal with this misconception in greater depth under item (3); here I only want to say that to us westerners the word 'impersonal' denotes something on a lower level of being than personhood, like 'the Force' in the Star Wars mythology, something on the order of electricity or magnetism or nuclear energy. But the 'impersonal' Absolute is actually *transpersonal*, otherwise the Personal God could not be its first and highest intelligible manifestation. The Absolute transcends what we know as personhood in the same sense—though to an infinitely greater degree—that you or I, as persons, transcend a stone. To say that God is only or essentially personal *may* be to imply that He is no more than we conceive Him to be; it may be to imprison Him on our human level of understanding, to deny that He opens out 'beyond' into the Infinite. But of course we habitually do the same thing in our conceptions of other people and ourselves; we treat others as if they were no more than our ideas of them, and ourselves as if we were limited to our self-images; we forget that *all* persons are, precisely, personal faces of the same Transpersonal Mystery, because they are made in the image and likeness of God. As an icon of Christ is not Christ Himself but a window opening onto His Reality—which is ultimately the reality of the Father Whom 'none has seen at any time,' given that 'I and the Father are one'—so you and I are 'icons' of the Universal Humanity, as Paul indicated when he said, 'It is not I who live, but Christ [Who is One with the Father] lives in me.'

(2) The Vedanta does *not* strictly divide reality between an Infinite God and an illusory cosmos. To begin with, *Maya* does not mean 'illusion'; it means 'manifestation' or 'magical apparition,' deriving from the root 'to measure'; *Maya*, then, is the Infinite when seen according to any finite conceptual or perceptual set. God creates the universe by His *Maya*-power, projecting it as something which exists in one sense, and in another sense does not. The classical metaphor for the action of *Maya* in the Vedanta is 'to mistake a rope for a snake.' The 'snake' is clearly an illusion; the 'rope' is not. Maya is a manifestation of the God

Who is unknowable in His Essence. If we take the universe as something existing in its own right, as something which would continue to exist even if God were to withdraw His attention from it, then we are deluded by *Maya*. The universe does not exist in its own right — it is a creation of God, Who has not simply created it in the past, but holds it in existence in this moment. It is created *ex nihilo* in the sense that God creates the universe from nothing *other* than Himself, since only He possesses Being intrinsically; the universe does not. In one sense it is a manifestation of Him: 'the heavens show forth the glory of God, and the earth declares His handiwork. In its own right, it is nothing. And if we believe that it exists in its own right, then *Maya* has deluded us; in this sense alone can *Maya* be translated as 'illusion'.

Furthermore, the Vedanta does not make a strict separation between God and cosmos. If no separation at all were made — if the level where such a separation applies were not recognized — then the Vedanta would indeed be pantheism. And, as you say, if the Vedanta were to absolutize this separation in a simple way, then it could in no way be called an esoterism. In reality, the Vedanta recognizes four levels of consciousness, which are equally four ontological (or trans-ontological) levels: (a) 'Brahman is real, the universe is unreal'; (b) 'There is only Brahman'; (c) 'I am Brahman'; (d) 'All this, too, is Brahman'. And the earlier levels are not negated by the latter, but rather contained within them. Thus level (d) is not pantheism, because it embraces level (a) which negates pantheism, nor is level (c) megalomania, because it embraces level (b), where the individual self does not appear, as well as level (a) where, though it appears, it is recognized as illusory.

To say 'the reality of the universe is like the image of the Sun reflected on the water' is not, in my opinion, simplistic; rather, it is *simple* in the sense of immediately efficacious and accessible. Any child could understand it — in a childish way — but how many of us can really see the world around us, and our own phenomenal selves, as direct reflections of the Absolute? We can only pray that a lifetime of spiritual purification will enable us to

catch a glimpse of this level of Reality. Here we come to one of
the great apparent divides between the Vedanta and what some
would call 'exoteric' Christianity—or that between, say, Plotinus
and Semitic monotheism: the seeming conflict between 'emanationism' and 'creationism'. For God to 'emanate' the universe
rather than creating it, as in the case of the appearance of the
image of the Sun in a motionless body of water, seems to make
creation an 'automatic' reflex of the Divine Reality, and thus to
constrain God by something less than He is, something that is
merely on the order of natural law—as if God were helpless *not*
to create the universe, and thus, in effect, helpless also to deliberately create it. On one level, we can say that whereas Beyond
Being emanates the universe—if we can actually place Beyond
Being in relation to its own emanation as 'other', which strictly
speaking we cannot—the Personal God, or Pure Being, creates
it. In other words, the Absolute (as it were) brings the universe
into being by first 'emanating' Pure Being, the Creator. In
Vedantic terms, the first 'reflex' of Brahman is Ishvara, who does
indeed plan, create, govern and maintain the visible universe;
even Ramana Maharshi asserts this—though he adds that, from
the standpoint of *jnanic* realization, Ishvara is simply the 'last
thought'. While we experience ourselves as actors, God is the
Supreme Actor whose actions supersede ours; by our own
actions we can create only certain modifications in the conditions of our lives, while God the Creator has established both
the entire range of those conditions, and ourselves as acting subjects with free will. But as soon as we transcend the experience
of ourselves as authors of our own actions—by means of the
realization that, in reality, God is the only Actor—then (paradoxically) we have also transcended God as Actor and Creator,
at which point all things are viewed not as objects created by
Him, but rather as direct emanations or reflections of His essen
tial nature.

(3) To say that the Impersonal Absolute (presumably Nirguna
Brahman or God-without-attributes) is Object, while the Personal God (Saguna Brahman) is Subject, is not what the Vedanta
teaches. It teaches precisely the reverse: that Nirguna Brahman,

as the Absolute Witness or Atman is, in Frithjof Schuon's phrase, 'the Absolute Subject of [or behind] our contingent subjectivities,' whereas the world of conditions, taken (on one level of consciousness) as Saguna Brahman, is *objective* to this Witness; Beyond Being is the Absolute Witness of Being and all It creates—with the understanding that it does not witness Being as *other* than Itself, but rather *as* Itself.

At this point we can come to a deeper understanding of the Vedantic Absolute, in the mode of Atman, not as impersonal, but as transpersonal. That in me which witnesses things is my very power of consciousness, my very Self, the furthest thing from anything impersonal. And yet that Self nowhere appears in the total field of the possible objects of consciousness, since anything I witness out there as 'myself' is not my true Self, but merely a self-image, or a sense-image of my body; (remembering Blake's doctrine, from *The Marriage of Heaven and Hell*, that 'the Body is the portion of the Soul perceived by the five senses'.) Who I Really am never appears, *cannot ever* appear, as an object of consciousness; in Vedantic terms, 'the eye cannot see itself.' The very essence of my personhood is thus not *impersonal*, but rather *transpersonal*.

What could be more obvious than our Self? And what is more hidden, to our passion-darkened habitual consciousness, than the obvious? It is not I who see the world, and the self I think I am, but Christ who sees it through my eyes. If I seek to retain my soul, the self I think I am, I will lose it. But if I lose it for His sake, I will find it (as the Self). Three (or four) levels of consciousness are described here. The first is the level of 'seeking to keep our souls,' the level of our habitual egotism where we, in effect, believe that we have created ourselves, or at least that it is up to us to define ourselves, and to maintain our identities as so defined. (If we cannot transcend this level we will lose ourselves anyway, not by self-transcendence but by eternal self-destruction; we will fall into the world where everything is defined by the ego in its failed and despairing attempt to create and maintain itself—this being the state of hell, the 'darkness outside'). The second level of consciousness is where we lose our souls for

His sake; this corresponds to the second level of consciousness posited by the Vedanta, the level of 'there is only Brahman,' as well as to *fana* (or 'annihilation') in Sufism. And the third level, the one where, because we have lost our souls for His sake, we now 'find' them, corresponds to 'I am Brahman,' and to the Sufi *baqa* or 'subsistence-in God'. (The fourth Vedantic level, the level of 'All this, too, is Brahman,' corresponds to everything Christians mean by Apocatastasis.) The same passage from self-defined subject through annihilation in the transcendent Divine Object to the unveiling of the Absolute Subject is also encapsulated in the hadith of the Prophet Muhammad, may peace and blessings be upon him: 'Pray to God as if you saw Him, because even if you don't see Him, He sees you.'

And it is certainly true that an 'esoteric' ego is a much bigger and more savage beast than an exoteric one. 'To whom much has been given, much will be required.' All that is required of the exoteric believer—and it in itself is no simple task—is sincerity and humility; the esoteric *jnanin* must submit to total annihilation and 'objectification'; if he fails in this he will rebel like Lucifer, and fall as just deep.

Bolton to Upton
February 21, 2005

I was surprised that you should have replied to my comments to James Wetmore at such length. I have just read your letter, and am not sure if I can provide a detailed response at the moment.

I am sure there must be many theoretical arguments against what you have said, but more important than any of them is what G. K. Chesterton called 'the little dumb certainties of experience.' These are things which you appear to have exterminated so that you could contrive to put a world of phantoms between yourself and reality, which to me is merely to abuse one's sanity.

You speak so confidently about 'the Vedanta', although when we speak of it in relation to what I was addressing, this really only means the Vedanta as interpreted by Shankara. What we are talking about would not be possible, subject to the interpretations of

Ramanuja or Madhva, I believe. Both Guénon and Schuon ignore that as well.

With what you say about all the levels to pass through, and the mysterious processes through which something or other (the ego?) must pass, it looks as though you have summed up the system of the truly real, but for one thing, namely, that *you are thinking it*, and that is something else again.

Upton to Bolton
February 21, 2005

To disagree with you is obviously to invite you to disagree with me, hopefully in the spirit of exposing error and serving truth.

So: What 'little dumb certainties of experience' are we dealing with here? Could you be more specific?

Your point is well taken that I have unthinkingly identified 'the Vedanta' with the non-dualistic, Shankaran Vedanta alone. I will be more careful in the future.

You ask if it is the *ego* that goes through all those levels of consciousness. Good point! Language undoubtedly constrains us to speak as if the 'little me' were realizing God, as if it were capable of encompassing Him. But as is made clear in the First Chapter of John, the little me cannot realize God, and insofar as that little me remains—which it always seems to, for almost all of us, at least while we are still in this life—then it is a servant of God, in need of His grace and helpless without it.

So the question is, are my ideas 'phantoms'? And if they are, are *all* ideas then phantoms?

Or all metaphysical ideas? I suppose you mean to challenge me to ask myself whether all this metaphysical mumbo jumbo is simply a kind of information acquired by mental effort which lives nowhere but in my temporal memory which will perish with my mortal flesh. Undoubtedly some of it is. It is certainly possible to 'learn metaphysics' by rote—but it is also possible to speak out of realization, to express a metaphysical truth that is 'before one's eyes' in as concrete a way—in even more concrete a way—as the coffee cup on the desk.

Bolton to Upton
February 23, 2005

Thank you for your reply. I will try be more specific.

You challenge my use of the word 'impersonal' rather than 'transpersonal' in regard to the Absolute, but I can easily concede that, because it too is something known on the basis of the personal and not ontologically separable from it. That is important for what we believe about God: whether God's unity embraces the personal, the transpersonal and the impersonal, or whether God-as-personal and God-as-transpersonal are ontologically different realities.

This is probably the essence of our disagreement. To begin with, you seem to come out against the latter alternative, referring to C.S. Lewis' remark about the pantheists who treat God as though He were just a book on a shelf But are you not actually committed to a position for which the personal God who can require something of us is nevertheless the lesser of the two realities?

You say that all persons are 'personal faces of the same Transpersonal Mystery', when we should really say that they are all images of the archetypal humanity of Christ—and that humanity cannot be regarded as a mere mask, as the Monophysites believe.

You say that Vedanta (according to Shankara?) does not divide reality between and Infinite God and an illusory cosmos, and that *Maya* does not mean 'illusion'; that is the opposite of everything I have been able glean on this subject, so the interpreters must be deeply divided. Do any creatures exist in their own right? That is very much an issue in modern Catholic theology, which may be influenced by the Vedanta in dividing everything between an absolutely self-existent God and an absolutely contingent creation. Being a Platonist, that means for me that in this case there could not possibly be any relation between them. All things are joined by means. Thus the highest members of creation share to a large extent in (created) self-existence, and only the lowest members are completely contingent. Hence the

Great Chain of Being. Just to say that the soul is immortal is to say that it has a degree of self-existence. (Actually Aquinas affirms this.)

You say very emphatically that 'Who I Really am can *never* appear as an object of consciousness,' although by holding this position, you undermine some other things you say: you mention the four levels of consciousness through which Vedantists progress, but we cannot know what levels we are on if the 'I' cannot be an object of consciousness to itself Similarly, where you say that we can only save our souls by losing them (into God's hands, presumably), we cannot know whether we are doing that or not, if the self is not an object of consciousness to itself. Perhaps you mean we just have to hope that we are doing so in the conduct of our lives. Losing one's soul in order to find it raises a logical problem, by the way: if we mean it literally, we are not really doing so, if we are hoping for anything—losing one's soul (literally speaking) must mean losing it in order to lose it. But in reality, the meaning of this expression is strictly of the moral order, not the ontological order.

The word Apocatastasis is used in a good many ways, but no Christians, apart from, possibly, Origen, have used it to mean that there will ultimately be nothing but God. That is Monism precisely.

Back to the 'two Gods' issue: the Transpersonal God who 'creates' a world by something as casual and contingent as causing a reflection, and the Personal God who creates the world on purpose and sees that it is good—these are either two antagonistic Gods, or this is all just a way of saying that, while God really is the Creator, He has other activities which have nothing to do with creating. If man can have a private life, why not God as well?

I am a Christian Platonist, and that allows a certain kind of esotericism, which has very sound credentials. But the esotericism of Guénon and Schuon seems to me to owe too much to the 'tradition' founded by H.P. Blavatsky. We are clearly a long way apart, but I hope that this will help you to see what the issues between us are.

Upton to Bolton
February 28, 2005

I will respond shortly in greater detail to your latest (more challenging) letter. For the present, I want to share this with you: last night, my wife and I attended a theatrical version of C.S. Lewis's *The Great Divorce*, and I was conscience-struck by one of the characters: the painter for whom the love of light had been replaced by the love of paint. As Rumi says, 'When I came to Love, I became ashamed of all I ever said about Love.' And yet (like Rumi, who in his *Mathnavi* keeps saying 'Enough! Now all is silence . . .' and then goes on to compose another thousand lines) we continue to write. I think it was Li Po who made the same comment about Lao Tzu: If he believed that 'those who know don't speak and those who speak don't know,' how came he to compose a book of 5,000 characters?

Bolton to Upton
February 28, 2005

Thanks for your latest, but for this time will just clarify my original reply. I had no intention of disparaging metaphysics as such—ideas are not just thoughts, but realities reflected in thought. My reference to the 'world of phantoms' was projecting something of my own experience. In my younger days there was something which inclined me to Solipsism without my realizing it, and the Guénonian Vedanta blended with that trait, so I was a keen consumer of this Oriental mysticism. Solipsism gives one a world full of emptied beings, devoid of inner reality, inner worlds, or mystery. Those are the phantoms which one would be putting between oneself and reality. If you have no such problem with this doctrine, I would not know whether that was to the credit of your doctrine or of your psychic self-defences.

This is all of a piece with the 'little dumb certainties of experience.' Monism/Non-Dualism, if taken seriously, has an effect of devaluing the reality of things we naturally take to be real, as though we could only make God look more real by making creation look less than real. That may be helpful for people who are inclined to make a God of the world, but I do not include myself there. On the other hand, if the 'illusion' doctrine is really just another way of underlining the difference between creation and the uncreated God (as you seem to suggest), do we really need it?

Now the ego or the 'little me', as you call it: this perception of the self is wholly owing to sense-perception, which is deceptive in many ways, and most of all when it pretends to show us our own selves. We cannot base deep metaphysics, let alone initiatic knowledge, on sense perception—and untrained common-sense perception at that. And yet, it seems to me that most of the impact of Vedantist mysticism depends on our taking this average man's sense perception of finite beings, passing into and out of existence like shadows, as though it were a revelation from God. But metaphysical knowledge must get behind these appearances, and the esotericism I have in mind does that. Conversely, if sense perception rules, it must define knowledge as such, and our metaphysical knowledge may well be phantasmal.

Here we get to the main focus of our differences: there are deeply different ways of defining the esoteric, and they depend in turn on how we define man himself There are two diametrically-opposed ways of doing that, one of them of Indian origin, as adopted by Guénon and Schuon, and one of Egyptian origin. For the Indian doctrine, man is in essence the same as God, but cosmically polluted in the course of arriving in this world. So, then, we just have to scrape off the pollution, and there will then be nothing but God, just as it ought to be. This is practically the same as saying that man as such is not real at all.

The opposite of this is a conception for which this multi-leveled, microcosmic nature we have is not accretion, but is our very essence, created by God. Consequently, it would be self-contradictory to try to fully realize that essence by trying to be a pure spirit, like God. I could say more about the real or esoteric nature of the individual self, if need be.

Upton to Bolton
March 7, 2005

You ask me whether God's unity embraces the personal, the transpersonal and the impersonal, or whether God-as-personal and God-as-transpersonal are ontologically different realities. That is an extremely good question. I would say that It/He does embrace all these levels of reality. Yet (paradoxically) we can still discern these ontological levels within that Unity (though to strictly identify them with the Persons of the Trinity is not warranted.) I share what is perhaps your concern about some of Guénon's and Schuon's formulations of the ontological distinction between Saguna Brahman and Nirguna Brahman, or the Personal God as Pure Being and the Godhead as Beyond Being, which sometimes seems in danger of degrading the Personal God to some kind of independent, created demiurge. That is sometimes a problem with their language, though not (I trust) with their substance.

I certainly agree that we are not mere masks of the Transpersonal (despite the etymology of 'person' from the Latin for 'mask'; literally, something that is 'sounded through'); rather, we are individual instances of It: unique instances of the Human Archetype, which in itself 'opens up behind' into the Infinite. God Himself is not merely universal; He is also unique, is Uniqueness itself.

Do creatures exist in their own right? I would say that nothing created by God exists in its own right—at least in the same sense that God does—but for the fact that God confers that right upon it. In my own religion (Islam), the absolute sovereignty of God over creation—a sovereignty that is both willful and ontological—is emphasized to such a degree that some schools of thought seem to deny secondary causation. This, however, is not literally the case, no tradition that doesn't allow for secondary causation could have so advanced the human understanding of natural law. It's just that the First Cause is seen as absolutely superseding and dominating all secondary causes, though He chooses to allow them to operate, or actually wills them to operate. To say that God 'turns existence over' to secondary causes, however—which also implies that He turns it over to beings who (now) exist in their own right, and can thus create in their own right—opens the door to Deism. Sentient beings choose and create, natural laws operate, but always as created, witnessed, allowed, and ultimately willed by God. (When we will something, it is really God Who is willing it—*not* because we have no free will, but because, as we draw upon God's gift of His Own Being for our very existence, so we draw upon God's own power of willing for our actions and choices: if 'it is not I who live but Christ lives in me,' it is also not I who act, but God acts in me—action being an essential aspect of life. Yet God does not impose His Will upon us; this is the principle expressed by Ibn al-Arabi as 'the determined determines the Determiner.') So everything, on all levels of the Great Chain of Being, is absolutely contingent upon God; on pain of Deism we must assert this. God's free gift of His own autonomy is the source of whatever autonomy we have, and such autonomy varies vastly in degree, from that of the Seraph to that of the falling rock. Both are equally contingent upon God in this present creative moment. He wills both to be, and could at any moment will them not to be. And both are totally free to be what they are as he has made them. Yet the freedom and autonomy of the Seraph immensely surpasses that of the rock.

You are right in saying that if we try to lose our life in order to find it, then we have defeated our own purpose—but then why did Jesus say 'he who loses his life for My sake shall find it', if he was not somehow recommending a kind of self-annihilation, of which His crucifixion was the clearest and most complete example? Jesus obviously knew that He would rise again, that He possessed eternal life, but that didn't prevent Him from going straight through the experience of 'My God, my God, why hast Thou forsaken me?' Yes, we must lose ourselves completely in God, as if we never knew that we were immortal, because we cannot at the same time hold on to our desire for the continued existence of our individual identity, and really let go of that identity. We may plan to do this kind of letting go in the future, in hopes of obtaining something infinitely better; the spiritual life would be impossible without the theological virtue of Hope. But when the moment of truth arrives, we have to (in Rama Coomaraswamy's colloquialism) 'fish or cut bait.' In that moment, the one we imagined 'obtaining' something is no longer the old 'me', but rather One for whom nothing need be obtained because, to Him, all eternally is. The life we regain is His life, not ours (and, in truth, it was always His). But since there is no continuity between my individuality and the Absolute, I really do have to die 'without hope,' as hope is defined by my mortal thoughts and desires. Conversely, because there is nothing real that does not partake of the Absolute and is not supported by It, my human individual personhood is itself eternal—eternal as long as I have really died to it, died to its concupiscence, its pride, its temporality and its mortality.

Here you bring up one of the real paradoxes of mystical experience, or at least of the kind of mystical theology which says things like: 'I cannot know God, but God knows Himself in me.' You are absolutely right that, if the individual self cannot be an object of consciousness to itself, then there is no way we can experience its loss to, or in, God. So the only way our life can be lost and regained in God, in full consciousness, is if the experience is ultimately God's own consciousness—not that of a strictly transcendent God, but of a God who is immanent, at this moment, in me. This immanent God is the Absolute Witness, the Atman: 'It is not I who live, but Christ lives in me.'

You say that in reality, the meaning of this expression is strictly of the moral order, not the ontological order. But can there be anything moral that is not, on another level, also ontological? If so, it wouldn't be real. (So much for the false voluntaristic exoterists who deny the Hierarchy of Being.) And can there be anything ontological that is not, on another level, also moral? If so, it wouldn't be good. (So much for the antinomian pseudo-esoterists.) I say that the exoteric meaning of 'to lose one's life for Christ's sake' is moral, while its esoteric meaning is ontological. And the two are not ultimately separate (which, incidentally, is why both Elijah—symbol of the esoteric, ontological dimension—and Moses, symbol of the moral, the exoteric—appeared next to Christ in His Transfiguration). But who else says this? Probably not even Dionysius the Areopagite. Perhaps only Eckhart is explicit about it, when he says 'My truest "I" is God.' In my view, this is precisely the esoteric exegesis of 'he who loses his life for My sake shall find it.' I define Atman as the 'I' Who knows Itself essentially—by being itself, not by becoming an object of consciousness to itself—which is not to say that It does not also (partially and imperfectly) become an object of consciousness to Itself, thereby manifesting the universe. In other words, we cannot say that before creation God was ignorant of His true nature, that he manifested the world as a kind of creative Self-exploration. We may learn more about ourselves in the act of creating something (though I believe that we often forget nearly as much at the same time, if not more), but God does not need to practice art therapy in order to better understand Himself, His Being is His Knowing.

You say: 'The word Apocatastasis is used in a good many ways, but no Christians, except, possibly Origen, have used it to mean that there will ultimately be nothing but God. That is Monism precisely.' If by Apocatastasis we mean that all things will be restored to their original form and stature as God created them, then this implies that human consciousness will also be so restored. I maintain that such restored consciousness sees all things in God. 'All this is Brahman' is not strictly Monism, since there is still an 'all this', a 'ten-thousand things', and since, as I said in my earlier letter, this fourth level does not negate the earlier three levels, but embraces them. This is what Schuon means by 'maya-in-divinis', and it is maya-in-divinis which negates strict 'literal' Monism. In the (Shankarian?) level two, 'there is only Brahman,' all individual distinctions disappear; but here they are restored, as manifestations of God, not as veils hiding Him—as is the case with level one, 'Brahman is real, the universe is unreal.' Only a universe of veils need be negated in favor of God; a universe of theophanies need not be. It seems to me that the experiential 'realization' of Monism is represented by those enraptured saints, much in evidence in India, to whom the particulars of the world, other people and themselves, have disappeared, the ones immersed in *nirvikalpa samadhi* and therefore totally unable to deal with practical affairs. Traditions which recognize the existence and validity of such ecstatics usually speak of them as inferior to those sages who, while they may have passed through an ecstatic stage, have now 'returned' to the conditional, manifest world, seeing it all as a theophany but not for all that ignorant or unable to deal with the particulars of other people and of changing situations—even more able than most to deal with such things, some would argue, since they no longer view them through the obscuring veils of subjectivity. So Monism, though false as a description of the essential nature of things, does represent what the Sufis would call a *maqam*, a 'station', a proximate stage-of-realization, whereas the sage who sees all things as participating in the divine theophany, in their total depth of particularity, but without this veiling to the slightest degree the Presence of the Absolute, sees things as they really are, and so is beyond all stations. This is what I believe is indicated by 'And all this is Brahman.'

With regard to Guénon, Schuon, and Blavatsky, exactly how do you see Guénon and Schuon as part of an esoteric tradition 'created' by Blavatsky? Doctrinally, which is what we are talking about here, they are poles apart. Of course Guénon investigated many occult organizations in his earlier life, and may have retained certain accidental habits of mind from those years, but that doesn't mean he shared any doctrinal common ground with the Theosophical Society, except by virtue of what the Society stole from the Vedanta (by 'stole' I mean 'appropriated for their own purposes, and in so doing took totally out of context). Guénon wrote an entire book exposing the Theosophical Society as a pseudo-religion; are we to believe that he had no doctrinal reasons for doing so, that their disagreement was a mere turf-war among rival gurus? It is true that Blavatsky on the one hand, and Guénon and Schuon on the other, spoke of a Primordial Tradition (in Hindu terms the *sanatana dharma*), but this, in Blavatsky's rendition, is something that is destined to replace the revealed religions in the near future, while Guénon and Schuon maintained that it was manifest in the revealed religions, and was only spiritually effective within the bounds of one of them. This is the great divide between Blavatsky and Guénon. Guénon's teaching reached back to the days 'when God walked with man in the cool of the evening'; Blavatsky's went back only as far as the Tower of Babel. Guénon speaks (at his best) out of the Primal Word, Blavatsky only from the Confusion of Tongues. You can legitimately disagree with Guénon's position, but no well-informed person can confuse his teaching with Blavatsky's, except in accidentals.

When you refer to 'the Transpersonal God who 'creates' the world by something as casual and contingent as causing a reflection,' and the Personal God who creates the world on purpose and 'sees that it is good', where you see 'casual and contingent,' I see 'inevitable, effortless, and perfect.' Do you think God has to struggle to create the universe? Wrestle painfully with His materials like some tormented artistic genius? Raise a sweat like a carpenter or bricklayer? As the Qur'an says, 'He needs only to say to a thing "Be!", and it is.' Once all is already created, in a moment of eternal time, then God's creative power extends further, toward bringing 'out' into existence what has been created, and finally toward working on, and with, what already exists. (Here we can see the operation, on three distinct levels, of three of God's Ninety-Nine Beautiful Names: the Creator, the Producer, and the Fashioner.) Perhaps on certain levels God is a Workman, but if we take the level where He (apparently) must struggle against the chaotic inertia of matter to build the cosmic harmony, then we deny His Omnipotence (besides starting to sound an awful lot like Freemasons), which is instantaneous and ontologically absolute.

Man truly would have a private life—if it were not for God. God is the only One whose private life is absolutely private. (I love your metaphor, by the way; it is worthy of C.S. Lewis.) Certainly, He has many other 'activities', or modes of Being, than those defined by His role as Creator; and yet all His activities are subsumed under the definition of God as 'pure Act'. In God, all possibilities are actualized—by His nature, not by what we would think of as discrete, particular actions, in which what is first a mere potency is later made actual. The motion from potency to act happens in the already-projected reflection of God in the sea of cosmic *prima materia*, where the creative aspect of Him 'stands out' as Creator.

Only when a Creator is confronted with a mass of possibility which has yet to be actualized can we speak of such a motion. But in the depths of the Godhead, all is actualized already.

The Creator, in essence, is the Godhead itself—yet, as you say, that Godhead also has a 'private life' beyond His creativity. To speak of this 'private life' is to speak of the Divine Essence *per se*— but truly there is no separation between this Essence and the Creator Who is Its manifestation—Its manifestation to us as creatures. The Creator is fully Godhead, and yet Godhead is not limited to Its creative function. God Is, Perfectly, in His Own nature—and since He Is (nothing else than) *that* He Is (to quote His Self-description at the Burning Bush), He is also Beyond Being. He is Beyond Being by the fact that He is neither this nor that; by the fact that, since He Is by His Own Essence alone, He is not one among the various things that possess Being; and by the fact that He is neither contingent upon some other Being, nor is He 'contingent upon Himself'. He has not created Himself and so need not maintain Himself He need not Be. He is Beyond Being.

Again, those writers I follow—the Traditionalists, Ramana Maharshi, and others—do not define *maya* as 'illusion', but as the 'magical' self-manifestation of God. If we think that the universe is literally God, we are deluded by *maya* (*aviaya-maya*), whereas if we see the forms of the universe as nothing other than manifestations of the very Godhead, Who can never be defined in terms of that which manifests Him, then we are witnessing *vidya-maya*. And this is the furthest thing from stumbling around in a world of contingent, illusory, dying phantoms: rather, it is a witnessing of the Real, as if face-to-Face, and of all forms as living, breathing instances of Life Itself It is poles apart from an alienated vision of things; it is a vision of all things restored. In Blake's words, 'If the Doors of Perception were cleansed, all would appear to Man as it is, Infinite.' In the same vein, Olivier Clement, in *The Roots of Christian Mysticism*, quotes from Vladimir Maximov: 'it is as if I were seeing the forest for the first time. A fir tree was not only a fir tree, but also something else much greater. The dew on the grass was not just dew in general. Each drop existed on its own. I could have given a name to every puddle on the road.' In Buddhist terms, this is a vision of the union of 'suchness', *tathata*, and 'voidness', *shunyata*. This shunyata is not some horrible, dead emptiness—only thought thinks that. It is rather an 'emptiness of self-nature' in things, which means that things are not hidden from us, and from themselves, by some obscure sort of self-involvement, but rather are exactly as they appear, as they appear to the eyes of Truth Itself They are not *mere* appearances; in all their uniqueness, they are the very appearance of the Real. This is their suchness, their *tathata*.

I'm sorry, but I just can't see how the Advaita Vedanta could be based on naive realism taken to its metaphysical extreme, as you have suggested; that would be materialism. It is true that Hinduism and Buddhism—Buddhism in particular—tend to emphasize the passing impermanence of things, but they do so as a spiritual method: If we witness our phenomenal selves as impermanent, for that precise reason we will not identify with sense experience or seek to hold on to old self-concepts, which are the chief among those lifeless phantoms you mention. When the phenomenal self is allowed to pass, when it is clearly witnessed as passing, then the noumenon shines clear.

With regard to your reference to cosmically polluted man scraping off his pollution, here is where we run into the whole idea of reincarnation—which Guénon, rightly or wrongly, denied was ever taught by the legitimate Vedanta—which may seem to deny the eternal immortality (rather than the indefinite temporal extension) of the individual soul. Here is where we must ask the question: what incarnates?, which is another way of asking: 'who am I?' Guénon emphasizes the doctrine of the Advaita Vedanta that 'the Self (or Brahman) is the one and only Transmigrant.' Only He passes (or appears to) from form to form. On a less absolute level, however, we could say that what 'reincarnates' is my physical and psychic *materia*, which, like my clothes and books, may pass on to new owners after my death. My form, however, is never repeated. And what is never repeated is, thereby, immortal form the standpoint of God's consciousness in the eternal present. Exactly how Hinduism expresses this kind of immortality on a doctrinal level I am not entirely clear on—like most Westerners I jumped directly to the Vedanta; fool that I was, I didn't want to busy myself with with concepts that seemed no better than Christian—but it is clear that the sages of the past, who can intercede for the living, are conceived of as immortal on some level; Ramakrishna himself has visions of those immortal exalted sages who are higher even than the gods. Likewise the dying Ramana Maharshi, when asked by his disciples where he would 'go' after death, replied: 'Go? Where could I possibly go? I will be "here", even where I am now.'

The individual, form-bound self can never become pure Spirit (it is Luciferian to believe it can)—except as witnessed by pure Spirit, Who, while remaining totally aware of all form-and time-bound particulars, in essence (and paradoxically) sees nothing but Itself. The created, form-bound self remains a servant of its Creator. What happens, however—if it happens—is that the Absolute Witness is unveiled, after which point it is not I who witness myself, but He who witnesses me. I am objectified before the face of God, Who Alone knows me perfectly, precisely as I am. Before this metanoia, my contingent self is 'me' and God is 'He'. After it, my contingent self is 'he', while God is 'I'—again, in Eckhart's words: 'My truest "I" is God.' In this state our individuality remains; it is not merged or blotted out in the Formless. Rather, it is witnessed by the Formless, which (paradoxical as it may seem) by Its witnessing both reveals my form-bound, witnessed self to be totally contingent upon the Formless, and at the same time sees it as being, in all its synthetic complexity, transparent to It. By becoming fully objective to the Absolute Witness, that self becomes most fully itself, and at the same time is revealed as fully 'void of (contingent) self-nature'. Its uniqueness is known as a unique instance of the Absolute Uniqueness of God. Thus what once appeared as various layers of cosmic accretion and pollution, obscuring the face of Truth—which is exactly what we seem to be (and, effectively though not essentially, what we are) when perceptually limited by our passions and egotism—is now revealed as a manifestation of all it once seemed to hide—a manifestation in which nothing is hidden. When veiled we are veils—when unveiled, unveilings— of the Truth.

What you have to say is profoundly true to the dark, alienated ways in which abstract thought can construe spiritual truth, and to what so many westerners have actually found who have turned to Buddhism and the Advaita Vedanta in flight from Christ (in the case of Christians) or Yahweh (in the case of Jews). But Christ, Yah-weh are there too, if they only knew. And undoubtedly many Hindus have the same alienated relationship to their own tradition, as do many westerners to Christianity and Judaism, and many Muslims to Islam. The Advaita Vedanta is old, in cultural terms. But the Truth Itself, though old, never becomes old. The Ancient of Days is also archaic and, simulta- neously, Ever-Young. Ibn al-'Arabi met him at the Kaaba.

Bolton to Upton
March 16, 2005

In arguing for the Guénonian idea of the Vedanta, you are argu- ing for a form of mysticism which requires that the world should result exclusively from emanation and not creation, and so this discussion will have to be mainly concerned with the question as to whether there is a real creation or not. Your latest reply begins by agreeing that God is really one, and so comprises everything personal and transpersonal, so here is at least one orthodox belief about God on which we are agreed.

However, the 'two Gods' idea, and the Non-Dualist doctrine of 'identification' appear to stand or fall together. If God cannot be divided into one half which is above Maya and one which comes under it, because the determinate and the indeterminate aspects of God are equally real, God must be outside this con- ceptual framework. Why then may not everything else be?

You have said before that 'Maya' does not really mean 'illusion,' but in that case, you are parting ways with Schuon. He affirms that it does in Chapter 5 of his book, *Gnosis: Divine Wisdom*, and he says that God as Creator is 'determined by Maya' in his book, *Survey of Metaphysics and Esoterism*, at page 55. For Schuon, 'Maya', 'illusion', and 'collective dream' all mean the same thing. He relates this to 'All is Atma,' which implies that everything but the Absolute must be illusion.

In any case, you would be right to discard the doctrine of Illusion, because it is really just a monument to bad logic. Its premise is that the world cannot be as real as God is, but illusion does not follow from that. There are so many relevant examples: for example, as homes go, mine is not much compared with Buckingham Palace, but that does not mean it is not a home, or that it is anything less than a home; practical arithmetic is not as advanced a subject as algebra, but it is in no way less mathematical. In fact, God gives everything the exact amount of being and reality which is appropriate for it.

Where you say that 'we are individual instances of It,' you appear to be excluding the idea that we are individually created, and this is a case where an implicit emanationism is evident. You state that 'nothing created by God exists in its own right.' Not in the sense of self-created, of course, and most modern people are completely blind to this. But you add that if God 'turns existence over' to secondary causes, that 'opens the door to Deism.' But it is a principle in Scholastic tradition that God never acts directly in the world when He can act through some subordinate agent. Since you reject the idea of God creating the world laboriously, you should accept this idea of causal delegation.

When St. Paul said 'it is not I who live, but Christ lives in me,' he was not saying that he was Christ, or that he was incapable of sin or error, but the use you make of this text does imply both that and that we could say the same of ourselves. But if we deny our independent being or substances, we may well have to so speak of ourselves. Nevertheless, the idea of created beings with some degree of absoluteness is to be found in Aquinas:

> But to be simply necessary is not incompatible with the notion of created being.... Again. The more distant a thing

is from that which is a being by virtue of itself, namely, God, the nearer it is to non-being; so that the closer a a thing is to God, the further it is from non-being.... Thus some created beings have being necessarily. (*Summa Contra Gentiles*, vol. 11, chap. 30, [5] & [6])

This text excludes the idea that while God has absolute self-existence, everything else has only absolute contingency (if that could be more than nothing). There are many degrees of real and necessary being in creation, and that is why it manifests its Creator. God does not make rubbish, and Moslems and Christians should be able to agree about that.

Later on, you speak of 'a kind of self-annihilation, of which His Crucifixion was the clearest and most complete example,' but He only submitted to that and did not do it to Himself. When He rose again He was still Himself, with the same recognizable human personality, the Wounds, and the same relationship to the disciples. If that was annihilation, we all get annihilated every time we go to sleep at night. The idea that 'we must lose ourselves completely in God,' can be understood in a moral sense without an ontological one as well. One can be 'selfless' in a moral sense, and still have a real self physically, and one can be 'of one mind' with one's associates when all have real minds of their own. If you insist on the idea of 'losing oneself in the ontological sense, you are ignoring the distinction between the corrupt and selfish self, and the virtuous self, and treating them both as the same kind of evil to be eradicated equally, as though God made a mistake in creating, and as though nature was evil in itself. This results from following a doctrine which does not distinguish between the Creation and the Fall, and which therefore has something unmistakably Manichaean about it. In any case, what you are affirming here could only mean physical death.

This does not mean that I am unaware of the need for theoretical truth to be 'realized', but I have a different idea as to what that means, but one which is still traditional. It is more like a slow 'assimilative conversion' which calls for more patience than modern people can find. This belongs naturally with a Platonic intellectual basis, and the point of departure for that is the immortal soul, and to pretend that that did not exist would be as pointless as pretending that God did not exist. On this basis, 'losing oneself' cannot have the same meaning, because the 'losing' would have to be something going on in the self or soul that is supposed to be getting lost. Your doctrine applies to the self's ego, not to the self or soul. I have worked out some consequences of this in 'Dualism and the Philosophy of the Soul,' which appeared in *Sacred Web 4*. These were opposed to the Guénonian Vedantist idea of the individual self, because the latter is tied to the common sense idea of self-as-ego, and that the world containing the ego is made up of things just as one perceives them. These perceptions are assumed to be shared by everyone else, and to be the causes of their experiences, just as much as of one's own, when they are in any case only the final effects of the objective world, and not causes at all. Each person is thus conceived solely as an object contained in a common world which is really only one's own. If each soul in reality contains its own representation of the world which contains its ego, the self-annihilation idea must mean something quite different. It need not be crudely untrue, of course, but just more limited and more psychological.

But if our psycho-corporeal being is thus, must it not still be mortal and perishable, even if the soul itself is immortal? Possibly even that is only an appearance which deceives the senses. Esoterically, the person who appears to perish is really only a minute part of the real person which extends as a continuum through countless states over different times. That would not be literally open to annihilation on any natural level. I gave some explanation of that in 'Life, Death and Resurrection,' in *Sacred Web 7*. This is the reason why I said that the Non-Dualist doctrine depends on an idea of reality based only on sense-perception. Besides, it is so largely expressed in terms of temporal processes that we should be warned not to take it too literally for that reason alone.

The position you are defending would be sound enough if Eckhart's saying 'My truest "I" is God,' were literally true just as you quote it, but in reality the literal sense could only amount to one of two absurd alternatives, either: (1) (assuming that we are real beings) that God was divided up into little bits (by whom, or by what?) for the private use of creatures, in which case God could not be separate from creation; or: (2) that God is not really divided, and the world and ourselves are just illusions, and there is no creation. Phantoms only. But what Eckhart was really referring to here was not precisely God, even though it is in many ways Divine, but what is known as the 'eye of the soul', or the 'Divine spark', or the 'synteresis', of the soul. This is necessary to complete the human microcosm, and its nature is the next reality to God, that of the Uncreated Heaven. I give an explanation of this in Chapter 8 of my next book which is in preparation at the moment, but if that had to be adapted for popular consumption, one would end up saying that the highest part of the soul was 'God', just as Eckhart did. When we judge statements, we must also consider those to whom they were addressed before we take them literally.

Then there was my remark about H.P. Blavatsky and the Traditionalists. I do not see why the idea that Guénon's break with the Theosophists as 'a turf war among rival gurus' should be so obviously wrong. *L'Erreur spirite* is mostly an attack on the shortcomings of other Theosophists and not an attack on Theosophism itself, if I can read French. That is why it is so tedious—four hundred pages of hacking away at other people's inadequacies, and no attempt to engage with the fundamental issues of Theosophism. It all amounts to proof of a lot of very soured personal relationships and disillusionments, I would say.

It is very likely that, when Guénon ceased to practice his Catholicism, he compensated by intensifying the inner mindset behind it, the passionate interest in orthodoxy and fear of losing it. He may thus have seen heretics everywhere and ignored the possibility that he was one himself. Similarly, many Protestants who lost their faith used to compensate by working harder at Christian morality. This is a well-known religious phenomenon. At any rate, Guénon ended up claiming to speak for orthodoxy from a position above orthodoxy, rather as the Theosophists were doing in their own way. We have no way of knowing that this was not just the latest version of the Serpent's 'Ye shall be as gods,' so I do not see how you can feel so certain that he was right.

Guénon was in some respects a typical intellectual of his time, influenced by the way in which metaphysical thought in Europe had already moved in the direction of monistic Pantheism under the influence of nineteenth-century German idealism. Blavatsky just had to connect that with the Shankaran Vedantic tradition. That meant that European intellectuals would assume from then on that the most monistic interpretations of Indian thought must be the most authoritative.

Where creation is concerned, and you ask 'Do you think that God has to struggle to create the universe?' That would be clearly anthropomorphic, but something of that problem remains even when we say the He creates it with the greatest of ease, because that is human as well. Some degree of anthropomorphism is in fact necessary in view of man's 'Theomorphism', as Schuon would call it. As for effort, I suppose Omnipotence must be able to create challenges for itself, as the state of the modern world seems to confirm.

One objectionable aspect of the 'reflection' analogy of creation is that it excludes the idea of there being any intention to create any specific beings. The personal relation between God and man would therefore have no basis, and the saving of the soul would be purely and simply a matter of human activities, as Guénon evidently thought it was. Another objection to it is that it explicitly confuses the creation of the world with the procession of Christ from God the Father: 'He *reflects* the glory of God and bears the very stamp of his nature, upholding the universe by the word of his power.' (Heb. 1:3, Catholic R.S.V.) If this can be said of the processions of the Trinity, it can *not* be said of the natural world—except on the emanationist assumption that there is no essential difference between God and creation.

The same view of God and creation appears where you say 'Here we must ask the question: what incarnates?' The one coherent consequence of the reincarnation idea is that there are no personal identities, because all apparent identities are just so many ephemeral disguises for God. So to affirm reincarnation is to affirm the doctrine of Illusion and deny the reality of creation, although both our faiths affirm the reality of creation.

Similarly, where you say that 'The individual form-bound self can never become pure Spirit,' you are denying theoretically something which Non-Dualism affirms in the concrete with its belief in an 'identification' of the self with God, who is necessarily a pure spirit. But regardless of any supposed reincarnation, man's not being a pure spirit is not an accident, since he is specially created as an epitome of all levels of being. Each person is therefore a world, so that the real objective world consists of the sum total of all these worlds, and of which one's own world is just a tiny part. Such is the true Macrocosm, known only to God. (The smallness of the ego in relation to its world reflects this on the empirical level.)

If you can say that you are aiming for a state where 'my contingent self is "he", while God is "I",' this would mean that God is either unwilling or unable to confer real being on anything. We may, of course, say that God wants to confer on us something much more important, namely, Himself, but even Omnipotence cannot confer itself on nothing. There must be a common measure between the recipient and the Received, and that is why created personal identities must be real, and why they must have appropriate degrees of infinity in them, as instanced in their comprehension of worlds. The Vedantist (and Moslem?) perspective is so much centered on man-becoming-God that there is no room for the complementary Christian doctrine of God-becoming-man. This issue must make a very serious difference to what it is that one is supposed to 'become!'

Bolton to Upton
March 18, 2005

This is to complete what I was saying in the previous letter. Just to add something to the idea of 'illusion:' Schuon, in *Gnosis: Divine Wisdom*, admits that the usual arguments for it are not very good, and then goes on to offer one of his own for it, which is one of the worst he ever used. This is the idea that we are all in a collective dream because our archetypal Universal Man, is 'dreaming', and thus making us all dream with him. Considering that we are speaking of an eternal Form, this is like saying that the Square on the Hypotenuse is feeling sick. He must have known that archetypal and physical realities could not be conflated like that.

This idea involves a denial of our own faculties which may as well be a denial of our sanity. It is utterly irrational to think that we shall wake up and get real when some big mystical revelation comes. Why should that not be a dream as well? Besides, if we can only dream that we have a desire for reality, we probably do not have one. As Schuon himself says somewhere, a being who is inherently absurd cannot have the possibility of ceasing to be so.

Although we may try the alternative of avoiding the word 'illusion' by speaking of 'the magical self-manifestation of God,' and being able to 'see the forms of the universe as nothing other than manifestations of God,' we are not much further on. At best, this is a way of speaking about heightened forms of experience, such as poets have, but even so we do not have a right to take such things as encounters with God, because God has no sensory or sensuous attributes. In such experiences, what is really happening is that the mind is struck, not by God as such, but by the eternal Forms of the things observed. They are experienced so intensely that the individual properties of their instantiations are forgotten. But God is not the world of Forms, even though He is ultimately the cause of the relationship of our faculties to the formal causes of the world. In any case, the difference between 'illusory' and 'magical' is mainly semantics, and there is no great mileage in it.

My attitude, you suggest, is owing to 'the dark, alienated ways in which abstract thought can construe spiritual truth.' Nevertheless, I construe a lot of other kinds of spiritual truth with the same mind, but with very different results. If conceptual thought indicates something dark and alienated in connection with Non-Dualism, it would be more natural to assume that that is the fault of Non-Dualism; but if we must allow at least the possibility that it is owing to this kind of thought, one still cannot assert that it is so without proof. If one does, it could only mean that Non-Dualism is being put beyond the range of discussion—that is, set up as a dogma.

Another reason as to why logical analysis might find something negative about Non-Dualism, from a Christian point of view, is that it requires one to discard a doctrinal truth, i.e. that the world is a real thing, created by a personal God Who transcends it. Having done that, it would not be surprising if the new outlook appeared dismal. It is far easier to be an ex-Christian than to acquire another and commensurate truth. 'The way down is easy,' but the way back up may not be recognizable.

There is a problem with Indian thought here, which is not just mine. Europeans are spiritually Egyptians—the Judaeo-Christian tradition, Platonism, Pythagoreanism, and Hermeticism are all of Egyptian origin. The fact that God acted in history through Moses and in Christ clearly did not alter its essential nature. Therefore, trying to graft Indian spirituality onto people with that heritage is really just a way of increasing the amount of confusion in the world.

Upton to Bolton
April 4, 2005

Responding to your criticism of Schuon's arguments regarding 'illusion', Schuon here is using the word 'dream' metaphorically. He doesn't mean that God dozed off after dinner and helplessly dreamed the universe. By the word 'dream' he means 'a world created out of one's own substance with no immediate perceptual relation to any outside reality.' When we, as limited and imperfect beings, have dreams, these dreams are highly subjective (though as I pointed out earlier, they can also contain certain objective elements) and are thus less real than the waking world around us. But when God dreams, His dreams are as real as can be; not as real as Himself, of course, but in no way less real than some other more objective world, because—given that God creates *ex nihilo*—there is no such *other* world.

Your comment that 'it is utterly irrational to think that we shall wake up and get real when some big mystical revelation comes' seems to deny the universal testimony of the mystics. When St. Paul was hit by God's light on the road to Damascus, though his fleshly eyes were blinded by it, the eye of his Heart was opened. Given that he passed from being a persecutor of Christians to the premier Christian missionary and proto-theologian, I don't know how you can call that anything other than a great awakening. And as for dreams, I can only quote the words of William Butler Yeats to the effect that 'In dreams begin responsibilities.'

And where does Schuon say that human beings are 'inherently absurd'?

Certainly we do not see God directly; in God's light, we see the Forms or *logoi* of things as symbols of Divine realities. In St. Paul's words (Rom. 1:20): 'For the invisible things of Him from the creation of the world are clearly seen, being understood by the things that are made, even His eternal power and Godhead.' And yet, does not the Christian assert that, since the Incarnation, it is actually possible to see God in Christ ('Who has seen Me has seen the Father')? That Christ is the *ikon* of the Father? And that the cosmos, in Christ, is transfigured, until it is all theophany? Maximos the Confessor says: 'He, the undifferentiated, is seen in differentiated things, the simple in the compound. He who has no beginning is seen in the things that must have a beginning; the invisible in the visible; the intangible in the tangible. Thus he gathers us together in himself, through every object . . . enabling us to rise into union with him, as he was dispersed in coming down to us.'

With regard to your comments regarding abstract thought and spiritual truth, abstract thought does not only construe Truth darkly; it can also, within its limitations, open to spiritual Truth; when logically sound it is an inescapable sign of that Truth, as C. S. Lewis brilliantly demonstrated in his book *Miracles*. Nonetheless, clear, valid logical thought is only a tiny part of our (potential) spiritual experience; most of what we experience on all levels, not just the spiritual—cannot be expressed in any human language.

One cannot, by definition, logically prove the doctrine of Non-Dualism, since arguing from premise to conclusion is dualistic in essence. Non-Dualism is, and must be, the First Premise as well as the Ultimate Conclusion, and premises, in the sense of axioms, are never arrived at logically; they are understood through direct Intellection. If it were not for axioms witnessed via Intellection, there would be no axioms at all, and therefore no logic. In the case of axiomatic knowledge, proof proceeds from certainty, which is prior to it. It manifests certainty; it does not establish it.

With regard to the comment about 'the way back up' being unrecognizable, I concur that, once having gone down, the way up is totally unrecognizable—without spiritual Guidance and the virtue of Faith: the evidence of things not seen. And once again, I do not see Non-Dualism as asserting the literally illusory nature of the world in every sense. The introductory essay 'Shankara's Doctrine of Non-Dualism' to *The Crest-Jewel of Discrimination*, translated by Swami Prabhavananda and Christopher Isherwood, explains it like this:

> When Shankara says that the world of thought and matter is not real, he does not mean that it is non-existent. The world-appearance is and is not. In the state of ignorance (our everyday consciousness) it is experienced, and it exists as it appears. In the state of illumination it is not experienced, and ceases to exist. Shankara does not regard any experience as non-existent as long as it is experienced, but he very naturally draws a distinction between the private illusions of the individual and the world-illusion. The former he calls *pratibhasika* (illusory) and the latter *vyavaharika* (phenomenal). For example, a man's dreams are his private illusions; when he wakes, they cease. But the universal illusion—the illusion of world-phenomena—continues throughout a man's whole waking life; unless he becomes aware of the Truth through knowledge of Brahman. Shankara makes, also, a further distinction between these two kinds of illusion and those ideas which are altogether

unreal and imaginary, which represent a total impossibility or a flat contradiction in terms—such as the son of a barren woman.

Here, then, we are confronted by a paradox—the world is and it is not. It is neither real nor non-existent. Any yet this apparent paradox is simply a statement of fact—a fact which Shankara calls Maya. This Maya, this world-appearance, has its basis in Brahman, the eternal. The concept of Maya applies only to the phenomenal world, which, according to Shankara, consists of names and forms. It is not non-existent, yet it differs from the Reality, the Brahman, upon which it depends for its existence. It is not real, since it disappears in the light of knowledge of its eternal basis. World-appearance is Maya; the self, the Atman, alone is real.

I would add one further dialectical step to Shankara's (or the translators') argument: that the world-appearance both disappears and does not disappear in the light of the knowledge of Brahman. In the *nirvikalpa-samadhi* it disappears; in the state of waking consciousness of a sage like Ramana Maharshi it obviously reappears, but is directly recognized as illusory in itself and not other than Brahman in its essence. Ramana Maharshi could recognize individuals, respond to specific questions, walk deliberately from point A to point B; his perception was not absorbed in an undifferentiated field of Divine Light. Yet the disappearance of the world-illusion that he had already experienced, and undoubtedly often returned to, was always there in the background of his day-to-day experience of the world-appearance; it was this very realization which revealed that appearance to be illusory.

With regard to your comment that Europeans are spiritually Egyptians, there was an age, before the tower fell (or before the vision fell that tempted man to try to 'put Humpty-Dumpty together again' by building such a tower), when 'India' and 'Egypt' were one. In the spiritual Heart of man, that age is with us still.

Bolton to Upton
April 21, 2005

In reply to your question about Schuon, I do not remember where that passage was, but only that Schuon was speaking conditionally, as in fact I was: given a certain idea of the human condition, then must follow absurdity, etc.

Granted that Schuon was using the word 'dream' metaphorically in this context, the implication of this metaphor, 'a world created out of one's own substance,' is that the world is not a result of creation but of emanation. What happens in dreams has no more relation to our conscious intentionality than the shadows cast by our bodies. Such a conception clears the way for a mysticism of identification, but the word 'creation' in this context could only be rhetorical.

You say further on that my arguments about the collective dream 'deny the universal testimony of the mystics,' rather as though there were only one such testimony, and that perfectly clear. What happened to St. Paul does not amount to a universal testimony. The great majority of mystics, in Catholic tradition at least, did not take their experiences as a basis for changing their ideas of reality, but were rather reluctant even to speak of them. This was because their experiences gave them a new dimension to what was contained in their faith in any case. St. Benedict and St. Teresa of Avila were typical in this respect. One could only say I was denying their testimony by drawing conclusions from their visions which they did not draw.

On the question of seeing God in nature, it is true that we do not perceive the Forms exclusively, because God relates to all the Forms as each one of them does to all its instantiations, so God is seen in an implicit way in every Form. A Unity which contains too much for human minds can be known in a divided and serial manner. However, I do not follow the transition from the Incarnation's manifestation of God the Father to His being manifested by all nature as well. If God were manifest to that extent, would the Incarnation have been necessary?

Concerning proof of Non-Dualism, you say that it must be

'the First Premise as well as the Ultimate Conclusion,' and that it is an axiom 'witnessed via Intellection.' However, if you wish to claim that, you must show what your axiom actually states. From what you say, you believe its truth to be self-evident, which looks highly unlikely, because there is no agreement as to whether even so basic a statement about God as 'God is' is self-evident. In fact, it can only be so if one accepts Anselm's Proof, and that in turn requires Platonic premises.

On the other hand, it is easy enough to see one basic proposition for Non-Dualism, namely, 'God is, therefore nothing else is,' but there is no self-evidence there. If true, it would mean that 'God is the Creator' was self-contradictory, which logicians have never suspected it of being. It is also hardly self-evident that the self and God each consist of two separate things: the one, a metaphysical part and a collection of psycho-biological junk, and the other an undetermined Absolute and a personal Creator; and that the two metaphysical parts fuse while Maya disposes of the biological junk and its Creator.

This is not to deny a strong form of psychological self-evidence in this connection, which is true in general, even if not of you in particular. If one takes the position that there is no creation; no one to pray to; no redemption; no immortal soul; and no eternal life for human beings as such, one has given up a lot (and even more if one had some belief in them in the first place). That kind of asceticism creates an unshakable sense of moral superiority over those who do not follow this path, and this combines powerfully with the mind of the unconverted and despairing pagan who remains somewhere inside even the devoutest of us. He always thought that life came from nothing and returned to nothing, and now he can come back home to stay, with a spiritual role to play. No one can deny the strength of this combination.

This underlines the fact that Non-Dualism does not require any faith, such as one must have to believe in personal salvation. It also begs the question that we might, after all, be created, and created specifically for the purpose of finding individual salvation and immortality in Heaven. (I know Non-Dualists believe that Heaven is only for stupid people, but if they are so intelligent, one would expect them to be able to see that this opinion of theirs results only from an idea of Heaven they acquired in childhood and never developed further.)

I remember once explaining Guénon's Non-Dualist gospel to someone who knew nothing about it, at a time when I still believed in it. To my amazement, he said it was hardly any different from Communism! But later on, I was not so amazed, when I saw how both systems attack people through their moral sense with a cult of self-elimination, where they find the idea of personal redemption completely incredible. In either case, this despair gives rise to a rejection of individuality as such, and with it any spirituality of creativity.

Concerning what you say about reality and illusion, and the text you quoted about it, it is not yet clear to me how far that coincides with what Plato and Aristotle have said about the way in which nature falls short of the reality of the Forms instantiated in it. To try and see how near or far apart we may be on that subject had best wait till another time.

A general point about Non-Dualism is that, if it were true, one would expect that finding God and finding one's own real self would be one and the same thing, whereas real life shows again and again that they are not. It is possible to find God in a sad and frustrated kind of way without finding one's real self, and those who go too far down that path end up as the 'holy idiot' types found in religious cultures. Conversely, those who find their real self often fall into the trap of thinking that they must have found God as well. Possibly Gurdjieff did that. At any rate, his usefulness is mainly for those whose need is to find their real self.

Upton to Bolton
April 21, 2005

Your experience confirms so much of my own when it comes to certain 'Traditionalists.' The egotism based on a tendency to despise all that is created and all that is personal—and which is in fact scandalized by the least mention of love, whether human or divine—is certainly the worst form of egotism I can conceive of. 'Blessed is he who is not scandalized in Me.'

I assume the 'self' you are speaking of here is the psychic self, the soul. The Self the Advaita Vedantins speak of is the spiritual Self, the Atman, which is closer to what Christians mean by 'synteresis' or 'Nous', though the two may or may not be strictly identifiable. (Most Christians, I'm sure, would not strictly identify them.) You touch here on the all-too common tendency of those attempting to follow a spiritual Path to use that Path as an excuse not to understand themselves in human, creaturely terms, and then to justify this flight from self-understanding by pontificating as to how the Atman or Nous so vastly transcends the 'mere' soul or psyche. But it is this 'mere' soul which is saved or damned, which means that we had better understand ourselves on this 'all-too-human' level as well as we possibly can. The fact that the Atman is undamnable and eternally one with God, and that we are host to it intrinsically, is a 'mere' truism which has nothing to do with the salvation or damnation of our immortal soul. If we are so involved in the passions—chief of which is the passion of pride, whose metaphysical expression is the error of solipsism—that we are set to inherit Hell, then there is no way we can realize the *moksha* of the Advaitins. And to use the mere mental knowledge, the mere belief, that 'my truest "I" is God' as an excuse to not even begin the path of self-purification, the 'unseen warfare' against the passions for the purpose of realizing the virtues—which absolutely *requires* human self-understanding, as well as all conceivable humility and gratitude to God for His grace and help, without which we would be irretrievably lost—is nothing short of sacrilegious. It is also inconceivably foolish. To think that you can read some books on the Vedanta, understand them well enough mentally so that you can expound them, do maybe a few meditation exercises, and thereby become a realized Non-Dualist Sage—without ever having confronted the spiritual darkness in your own soul, not to mention having gone through the metanoia that such a confrontation calls for but cannot by itself accomplish—is just plain dumb. 'Paper cakes do not satisfy hunger.' This is the ingrained foolishness of so many of these 'Traditionalist' wise men. Thank God I have been privileged to meet certain other Traditionalists who have not been deluded by ideas. I am thinking of one person in particular, a saint in the making, the most canny and inglorious of men, whose presence nonetheless radiates, in spite of himself, the Uncreated Light.

As a member of an email group dedicated to the teachings of René Guénon, I just answered an email from a Rumanian Guénoniste who is preparing a bibliography of texts from all the world's religious on the theme of 'the Truth is beyond words.' So this would probably be a good time to bring our dialogue to a close, since I haven't said much in this exchange that I haven't said in earlier ones. Feel free to reply, of course! I'm not trying to put you off, just sensing that we are starting to get a little repetitive. It's clear that we agree on some things and disagree on others, and that this will probably not change all that much. In the words of the Holy Qur'an, in the next world 'God will enlighten us as to wherein we differ.'

Logic and Transcendence

There are many points left over from this discussion, some of which will be looked at in Chapter 9, but for the moment I would only draw attention to the apparent contrast between a very inclusive mode of thought, which asserts a unity regardless of questions of logical possibility, and one which asserts the need to accept one alternative or another. These contrasting points of view have determined a good deal of what has been said. In Chapter 1, it was acknowledged that there is a supra-logical unity in which many conflicting realities are reconciled, even though in some cases the unifying factor consists only of the fact that both sides of the issue were created by the same God.

The principles of logical inclusion and exclusion must form part of the higher unity, which is the cause of both sameness and difference. Consequently, many of the things which appear to us to be incompatible will be present in a higher synthesis, even though it be known only to God. But this fact is of no profit to monism or non-dualism, because man has to make his choices among things which are radically different for the human mind. In the realm of the spirit, he is not free not to make such choices, because it is not possible to evade them on the basis that one believes in a transcendental unity which makes them all the same. Since we do not share the mind of God, we must judge and choose with our own minds, even if the consequences are constricting.

9

Some Final Reflections

The Non-Dualist Strategy

Charles Upton's replies reveal a significant feature of non-dualist thinking in the places where it could be necessary for him to concede a point: in all such cases, the concession is taken back at once on the grounds that the point made against non-dualism is doubtless true of many morally corrupt, ignorant, or confused non-dualists, but not at all true of those who really understand the doctrine. For this reason, it appears to be a doctrine which can only be professed by intellectuals or qualified experts.

If so, it forms a complete contrast with Christianity or Islam. A profession of Christian or Muslim faith by a simple but sincere believer is nearly always as valid as any that might be made by a theologian. The question, then, is why is this not true of non-dualism as well. Why should its lofty spiritual wisdom and all-embracing idealism so easily descend into something too amoral, incoherent, or blasphemous for its fastidious exponents whenever there is no trained advocate on hand to mould it into morally edifying shapes? Real doctrines always have a coherence of their own, which they can impart to human minds; it is not human minds which have to put coherence into them.

At this point, it may be objected that I am merely arguing for a religious formalism and rejecting the esoteric. After all, why may not the esoteric aspect of non-dualism account for its problems of expression? It would accordingly be said that non-dualism is concerned with the wholly supra-formal reality which transcends everything that can be named, and that without this, religion must be without depth. Nevertheless, the truth is quite different: the forms of any revealed religion are by definition manifestations of supra-formal realities which join them to God, or else they would have no salvific power at all.

Thus they are a class of forms which contain their own guarantee of the supra-formal. In this case, the addition of a purely and designedly supra-formal doctrine, such as non-dualism, must be a redundancy which must change the nature of religion by substituting itself for the metaphysical content implicit in its revealed forms. For those who nevertheless believe this substitution to be valid, religion becomes equated with the collection of phenomena it appears to be for casual observation. One could say that its transcendental dimension is in a sense ingested by the non-dualist, while the religion itself is relativized. This is what lies behind the objections to formalism by which a non-dualist idea of the autonomy of the individual is conceived.

Absolute Dependence

A significant coincidence between non-dualist doctrine and the fashionable modern theology can be seen in the emphasis on the way in which the world depends on God. This dependence is so complete that the dependent reality could hardly be said to exist at all, which I have already questioned on the basis that God is able to create relative self-caused causes and relative degrees of self-existence, or otherwise there would be no immortal souls or spiritual beings. There is also the principle that every degree of assimilation to the Divine nature is necessarily an assimilation to the absolute independence of God. Everything depends on God as its ultimate source, but both modern theology and Advaitists understand this dependence in a very crude manner, possibly in the hope of correcting the imaginary self-sufficiency of modern man, which is really based only on the physical security brought about by applied science.

There is also a moral dimension to this question, because the more we emphasize the direct, immediate, and instrumental dependence of the world on God, the more we involve God in all the things that are being done in the world. If the total-dependency thinkers were right, then, God would be directly involved in the crimes, injustices, and disasters of the modern world. He would, of course, be equally involved in all the good things that were going on as well, but that would mean a God who was not necessarily good as such, but one which was good, bad, and indifferent equally. For the ancient Greeks, that kind of God was recognizable as Pan, who was really a personification of nature. One does not hear anyone declare that the total-dependentists are substituting Pan for God, but this conclusion is hardly avoidable. Worse still, this doctrine would mean that God was directly active in the sufferings of the souls in hell and purgatory. God would have to be the author of their sufferings in a very real sense.

There remains the well-established argument that a perfect and all-powerful God must be able to create a world which can function without continual manipulation to keep it going. To do this would require more power and wisdom than it would to create one which was never really separate from its creator. God's power, wisdom, and perfect goodness do all thus depend on a creation which is relatively independent and therefore real.

Moral and Ontological

These two criteria are by no means bound to one another, so it is not true to say that if something is true in a moral sense, it must be true in an ontological sense, and vice-versa. For example, one can be morally 'selfless' while having a very real self in physical fact. Conversely, someone may be literally selfless owing to some mental disorder, but that does not by itself bring any moral virtue with it. Likewise, a devout person who always tries to do what he believes to be God's will is at one with God in a moral sense, but obviously not in an ontological one, for the reason just given. Where religion is concerned, the state of moral union is the one which really matters; for example, one may be ontologically or existentially a member of the Catholic Church, but if one is a member of it only in that way, and not in a moral sense as well, it could well be worse than nothing. For this reason, Upton's objection that the moral and the ontological are inseparable is mistaken.

No Role for Creativity

The problem Upton referred to in his creative work (Feb. 21, 2005) results directly from the fact that creativity can have no meaning in the context of a Non-Dualist metaphysic. If the world itself is not created, but only emanated, like a collection of reflections in distorting mirrors, there can be no point in expecting to find anything qualitatively superior to that kind of origin in any particular part of the non-dual world. Consequently, there would be no point in expecting there to be any merit or spirituality in what one would like to call one's 'creative' activities. For this reason, the non-dualist metaphysic is a prescription for inertia, and so it is liable to cause or worsen cultural and political decadence. This doctrine does not mean simply a harmless absence of the creative principle, because no exclusion of this principle can ever be harmless; the reality involved is too fundamental for that. In practice, this deficiency will unleash the opposite of creativity, destructiveness, as can be seen in countries where a religious rigidity has been turned into a practical Monism.

The Evil 'Ego'

Both Guénon and Schuon frequently use the word 'ego' in ways which appear to denote the individual self or personality, but without ever offering any definition of it. Whatever it may be exactly, it is unquestionably held to be evil as such, and so not capable of being saved, but only of being eliminated. A representative view of it by Schuon is given as follows:

> The second—the great—humility is spiritual death, the 'losing of life' for God, the extinction of the *ego*; this is what saints have had in view in describing themselves as 'the

greatest of sinners'; if this expression has a meaning, it applies to the *ego* as such, and not to such and such an *ego*. Since all sin comes from the *ego* and since without it there would be no sin, it is indeed the *ego* which is the 'most vile' or the 'lowest of sinners'; when the contemplative has identified his 'I' with the principle of individuation, he perceives it as it were in himself the root of all sin and the very principle of evil. (*Gnosis: Divine Wisdom*, p133)

Considering the intensity with which this ego is denounced, it would be desirable for us to know more about what it is. Rather than speak of the individual self, Schuon uses the word *ego*, as though there were some unspoken understanding about it which excused him from being any more explicit. In view of what was said in Chapter 4, there need be no doubt that this demonization of the individual self is not on account of its sins and crimes, but because it is the possessor of the self-reflective, world-representing faculty, which is not subject to the monistic sublation or transcendence on which the non-dualist position depends. Not surprisingly, it is detested, therefore.

Even if it were true that without the individual self 'there would be no evil,' one would not need to be a great metaphysician to see that there could be no virtue without it, either. In reality, both evil and goodness exist in the fabric of the world independently of the persons in whom they may be manifest. To take the individual self as such to be 'the very principle of evil' can only be done by those who believe in a God who creates evil, that is, by Manichaeans. However, even classic Manichaeism did not go so far as to make individual persons the source of evil, no matter how evil they were supposed to be in themselves.

As for the claim to be 'the lowest of sinners,' this is not verifiable if taken literally, but it can easily be meaningful on an emotional level, especially in those who experience a strong fear or horror of sin in themselves. But for the same reason, it is of no use for constructing metaphysical conceptions as to the source of evil. On the contrary, every admission of one's personal badness presupposes a relatively incorrupt part of the self which can understand what is bad about it and react feelingly against it. No such mixed self as this could ever be 'the root of all sin' that Schuon takes it to be.

Freedom from Ego

It is easy to deduce from Upton's insistence on the 'annihilation' of the self necessary for his kind of salvation that non-dualism finds its way into many people's minds by working on their moral sense, rather than by anything directly rational. It starts from the well-known truth that an excessive reality attributed to one's own ego must mean moral badness, and suffering besides, while an equality of status for one's ego and those of others will mean justice, and that consequently an even lesser status for one's ego than for those of others will result in something higher than justice, namely, charitable behavior. This progression tempts some minds to think that if one were therefore to elimi-nate the ego altogether, the result would surely be perfection.

If 'ego' is taken in the usual pejorative sense, this would be almost a statement of the obvious, but if ego is confused with the individual self as a whole (of which the ego is the part mani-fest to sense-perception), one would eliminate the very condi-tion by which anything could be either good or bad. A certain 'salvation' would thus be guaranteed on the grounds that there was no longer anything to be saved, and there is clearly no rea-son why Divine or even angelic help should be needed to help bring about something like that. This kind of mysticism is pre-cisely an example of 'entropic collapse' between religious belief and paganism: the religious dedication to salvation is somehow mated with the pagan's belief that everything comes from noth-ing and goes back to nothing. This kind of religiosity cannot be called Faith, and therefore grace is not necessary for it, which is why unbelievers can become converted to it without any sense of crisis, as I indicated to Upton in my reply of April 21, 2005.

Illusion and Instantiation

In the place where we discussed the Forms and their relation to the natural world, it can appear that what Shankara means by his Advaita doctrine is possibly the same as what Plato means about the imperfection of the physical world in relation to the Forms. For Plato, the visible world and everything in it always fell short of the reality of the Forms which were instantiated in it, and this is why he put phenomenal beings in a mid-way position between Being and not-Being, as in the *Republic* (477a). For both Plato and Aristotle particular things are not knowable as such, but only by means of the Forms or objective universals instantiated in them. For Aristotle, everything in the physical world was subject to 'privation', which meant that none of them ever contained as much of the Forms as they could have done. The natural world was thus permeated with voids, owing to which it was never fully coherent with itself, and so was always liable to corruption and dissolution. In Plato's terms, this meant that matter was never completely mastered by the Forms, and that this deficiency meant that they must eventually be dislodged from the things in which they were present. The mere fact that the world is in constant change thus means that it has no stable hold on Being, but must constantly lose it and regain it at the same time.

Whether this is the same as saying that the world is an illusion, however, depends on whether the changing image is mistaken for the unchanging object which causes it; it cannot be called an illusion as such, simply because it happens not to be the realm of Forms or God. An illusion is something which exists solely in the mental activities of those who wrongly believe they are perceiving something real. As such, it is something which can only happen in the experience of isolated individuals. However, the Shankaran idea of illusion requires that it be extended from the individual case to the entire collective state, which would negate all normal definitions of the illusory, which always depend on the existence of the realities corresponding to them, whether they are correctly perceived or not.

Shankara's doctrine requires that there be a deeper sense in which common shared experience can also be an illusion, and that in turn requires that the natural functions of perception and cognition should be flawed, even when they do what they were made for. That, however, raises a theological issue, namely, whether a good God could create a world which by its very nature served to deceive the rational creatures for whom it was created. The Shankarans can avoid this issue, because they do not believe in creation, but think the world results only from something like a reflection of light on water. Christians, on the other hand, have the belief that the world is designed and fully intended by God for His own purposes, and that means that, however restricted the truth it may manifest to most persons, it cannot be a collective illusion, except in regard to what it may conceal.

Illusion, if that were in fact the nature of things, would include all religion, tradition and culture, not least those which taught the idea of illusion. The most essential point about illusion (where it is not deliberately created), is that it is the fault of those subject to it, whether as isolated individuals or as a collectivity, and not of reality itself. From a Christian point of view, then, world-illusion is an attempt to project a subjective deficiency onto the outside world, and, in a certain sense, on God as well, ignoring the distinction of objective and subjective. This is not the same as the deficiency in the world according to Plato, for whom it never ceases to be joined to the reality it partly hides.

Non-Dualism and Evolution.

The same monistic tendency can be seen in both non-dualism and Darwinian theories of evolution. The fact that the former envisages the monistic sublation in terms of a spiritual reality, while the latter does so in terms of a material one, makes no difference in this respect. In either case, the knower of the doctrine becomes absorbed without remainder into the conception of a world which he has chosen to rule his mind. The hostility shown by non-dualists towards Darwinism is much more a hostility towards a heretical form of one's own beliefs than towards something truly alien. No doubt Darwinists would express the same attitude to non-dualism if they were sufficiently interested in metaphysics, or had any belief in the importance of non-material reality, and for similar reasons.

Monism and Non-Dualism were first popularized in the West in the context of Theosophism, when the difference between them did not seem important. They were made known in H.P. Blavatsky's *Secret Doctrine* and *The Veil of Isis*. In Theosophism, monism was combined with both reincarnation and evolution, and it made a coherent combination with them. The Darwinian belief that all living things are caused by mindless and purpose-less material forces, is particularly well-adapted to reincarnation, with its belief in endless successions of spent and discarded lives which have no ultimate purpose of their own. This combination of beliefs obviously supports a monistic idea of reality, with its belief that only the *Nous* or *Atman* can be 'saved' or be worthy of salvation, and that all persons are mere masks, hiding one and the same reality. Likewise, if we believe that persons result only from a mindless process of natural selection, we need have no qualms about believing that these biological 'masks' are expend-able, as non-dualism also requires from its own point of view.

These facts make it appear extraordinary that Guénon should have eliminated all positive reference to both reincarnation and evolution from his own expositions of Advaitist doctrine. By so doing, he reduced the doctrine almost to incoherence, since it is now applied to lives which are conceivably specially created, and which are not mere extensions of previous lives, inasmuch as evolution is denied. This can only turn the doctrine into a purely dogmatic denial of the reality of personality, since the natural reasons for this denial are ignored. It is hard to think of any theoretical reasons for this different approach, but on a practical level, it would make sound enough sense if the aim was to convey Non-Dualism to people who were inclined to reli-gious orthodoxy. The absence of any direct denials of creation and of personality would remove two of the main sources of resistance to the monistic ideas of self and salvation that would be felt by such persons.

At the same time, the inerrancy of orthodox religious tradition is asserted at every opportunity, so consistently that it becomes hard to think that Guénon's writings could be heretical. Besides, the issue is clouded by the fact that there are numerous things in most traditions of which the verbal forms can be taken to be monistic, even though there be no such intention in them. (Hinduism is unique among the religious traditions in having its *Advaita* school of doctrine which identifies man and God.) Nevertheless, the inmost content of these apparently orthodox ideas implies a denial of any hope of redemption for the believer himself, and a conviction that any kind of 'good news' for mankind as such must be inconceivable. Devotion would have to be inspired by a belief in being nothing, despite the fact that one must be something in order to feel that kind of attraction to nothing. The kind of wisdom which these ideas enshrine is one which has no role or meaning for charity, and that is anything but harmless, since that must ultimately develop into hate, at least in the outer layers of its sphere of influence.

This teaching is well-suited to the modern mentality, despite all the anti-modern commitments that usually go with it, because modern man differs from his ancestors in no longer seeing life as a gift, but only as a problem. For the less thoughtful majority, the life-problem is seen rather as a danger, for which constant precautions and protective measures are necessary. When things are seen in as negative a manner as this, it is easy to present the ideal solution to the problem of existence as that of non-existence. 'Nothing,' as a kind of ideal, has a strong magnetism for those who cannot see meaning or value in life, and this condition is very much part of the liberal tendency to invert values, e.g. to represent defeat as victory, loss as gain, control as liberation. But this reveals only world-weariness.

The Bugbear of Morality

For modern man, the Good News of salvation is no longer thought of as good news, firstly because salvation has become conflated with physical security in the popular mind, which is of

222   The One and the Many

course much more widely available than in earlier times. Secondly, it is not good news today, because the promise of salvation has to bring to mind the deficiencies for which salvation is necessary, and thence the dangers of disregarding it. But physical security allows us to ignore our limitations, whereas an orthodox religious message would not allow one to do that. Besides, with the idea that one's moral limitations are caused by a supposed Darwinian origin, there would be no reason for taking moral responsibility for our own condition. Conversely, a belief in creation implies that we must have a moral duty to obey the laws revealed by the Creator.

The moral issues referred to in general terms so far are not exhaustive, however. The issue of sexual morality as a factor in religious belief as a condition of salvation is not acceptable to most modern people, for whom sexuality is identified with its unrestricted physical expression. That is a result of self-ignorance, which is not compatible with the deeper kinds of spiritual life, although people today are determined to ignore that, and they seek doctrines which allow them to do so. As if in answer to such needs, sexual morality does not raise problems for non-dualistic religion, any more than the moral issues mentioned already, because from a non-dual position, both chastity and the denial of it merely belong among the contingencies affecting an individual ego, which has no destination as such in any case.

The modern naturalistic attitude to sexuality reveals a state of mind which is neither willing nor able to rise above the level of the ego, which looks very strange alongside the prevalent passion for self-transcending forms of religion. Nevertheless, to see hypocrisy in this would be superficial, because real hypocrisy demands a coherent self-awareness; it must be whole on a natural level, however little it may be on the moral level. This contrasts with the much more usual case today of an ego which really consists of a cluster of more or less unrelated secondary egos, which are activated in turn by the changing contents of their surroundings, more than by the will of their nominal owner. (Gurdjieff illustrated this insight with the case of someone who has one ego for making resolutions, and another one for carrying them out, with the result that the resolutions are never carried out.)

This condition rules out any central over-view by which one's attitude to any one kind of thing could be affected by one's attitude to anything else. The result is an attitude of apparently complete sincerity towards each positive option one encounters, no matter how much it may conflict with other options which are not being thought of at the time. In this way, one can behave in ways which are materially hypocritical while having no need for any intentional hypocrisy. At the same time, this can blend with a passion for self-transcendence, which in many persons feeds on an actual lack of self. Consequently, the question of internal coherence among one's values is ignored without any sense of discomfort.

The idea that the moral codes of religious orthodoxy are the key to developing a real self is found unbelievable today, partly because of the negative image of orthodoxy, and partly because modern religion chooses to ignore the connection between itself and 'self-help' and self-realization, owing to the social morality of those who control it. Consequently, all kinds of heterodoxy are eagerly believed in instead as a diluted orthodoxy creates openings for them.

A Non-Dualistic Reply

It is possible for non-dualists to adopt the position, implicitly taken by Charles Upton, that most of the criticisms made by those who disagree with them are really beside the point, because, even where valid, they apply only to those who adopt non-dualism in ignorance or from unworthy motives. Such dubious exponents of the doctrine could not therefore amount to an argument against the doctrine itself. Are bad Christians an argument against Christianity? However this counter-argument depends on an analogy with established and institutional forms of religion, which breaks down because bad Christians can be so-called by reference to a well-defined body of Christian doctrine, whereas there is no such means of judging supposedly bad non-dualists, because there is no agreed body of doctrine there, no agreed religious or sacramental practice, and no central teaching authority.

Consequently, the possibilities of being 'good' or 'bad' in this field depend solely on the opinions of one's fellow practitioners, and in this case it is almost inevitable that the more doctrinaire adherents will disown those who do not share all the complexities and commitments to which they attach importance. The latter are those who feel most able to rebut criticisms of their beliefs, and they will profess that true non-dualists must be sincere practising members of traditional religions. Their Non-Dualism must be professed in addition to this, and under the supervision of a Master or Guide. Thus an assurance of truth is created by a process of increasing the demands and the complexities of their faith, which is in reality no guarantee of truth, and could be Pharisaic. In the final extreme, however, the defense of this position would have to equate it with sainthood, i.e. the only category of person who could not be excluded on account of some moral or spiritual flaw or other.

The security against criticism obtained in this way results from little more than making the target so rare and elusive that it is impossible to hit. Tightening the definition of 'true' non-dualism ends by making rational discussion impossible. Following this tendency, Frithjof Schuon was among the first to reject categorizations such as pantheism, on the grounds that such categories were too simplistic, while the true doctrine combined properties which conventional thinking took to be incompatible.

In fact, non-dualism is distinguished from pantheism and monism inasmuch as it does not assert univocally that there is only one real being, but modifies it to the extent of allowing some kind of meaning to the created world, which is allowed to be alongside the supreme Reality, at least from our point of view. This is a formula which is less likely to prompt objections from the religiously orthodox than plain pantheism or monism, despite the fact that the concession to creation is trivial and indefinable. At the same time, if one were to be more a monistic pantheist than a non-dualist, one could still adhere to one's belief in an orthodox setting without much discomfort.

The success of non-dualism in convincing many thinking people in the West and in India is largely owing to its being a default position resulting from the absence of metaphysical ideas in modern culture. It is significant that Guénon's work began to appear in the Nineteen-Twenties, when the traditional role of philosophy in the West was coming to an end, as far as the universities and mainstream culture were concerned. In the absence of metaphysical knowledge, God tends to be conceived exclusively as an individual agent, while everyone and everything else are also conceived as individual concretes, which is deeply misleading, no matter what practical uses this idea may have. If it were true, it could only mean pluralism, that is, a thinly-disguised materialism, but the cure for this error is not the opposite extreme of Monism, but a middle way, by which the different orders of reality can be reconciled without being reduced to one another. As Berdyaev has observed, the absence of real metaphysical teachings results in a pragmatic wavering between the false extremes of monism and pluralism.

The non-dualist idea of truth is also successful because it agrees with the modern idea that truth must needs be simple, and the more simple, the more true. This is a piece of modern ideology which is not supported by either logic or experience. The belief that truth must mean simplicity would have at least two absurd consequences, namely, that no one would need any intelligence, and that everyone should know everything, or at least everything of any importance. But this shows that it is not traditional wisdom, but rather the entropic flow of culture into increasingly simplified and popularized forms, which undoubtedly create the conditions which covertly work in favor of non-dualistic ideas of religion, despite all its professions of allegiance to traditional authority and its doctrinal rejection of modernity. These professions are made according to one's own personal choice, and not in obedience to any authority which could have a right to require it. Whether it be right or wrong, therefore, it is individualistic, and so not part of the non-dualistic ethic. That can also be seen from the paucity of traditional religion which requires any assent to non-dualism itself.

The non-dualist refusal of classifications like 'pantheism' and 'monism' rests on the apparently reasonable grounds that the ideas of both theism and pantheism have limitations which prevent either of them from corresponding to the whole truth; the fullness of truth must require something of both of them and something more. I have argued for a complexity of this order in connection with personal identity, where the ego-self of common sense has to be conceived as combined with the larger self in which the ego-self and its world are contained. On this basis, the real self must be the sum total of these two levels of identity. Similarly, ought it not be arguable that a complete belief in God ought to combine theistic doctrine with pantheistic? This would be so if the element of unity between man and God as understood in theism were to require a separate theological conception, like that of pantheism.

The Independence of Dualism

In reality, dualistic doctrine is more self-sufficient than that, not least where it includes its own principle of unity which subsists between God and creation. But far from being a compromise with monism or non-dualism, this principle of unity is not a reality superior to God and creation, because there is no necessity for it to be so. For example, gold and silver are united by the concept 'metals', but 'metals' is an abstract idea which is not a superior being in relation to any actual metal. Similarly, an apple and a bar of soap have a unifying principle in the idea of 'things', without that meaning that the concept 'things' is necessarily more real than either fruit or soap.

That the unifying principle can just as well be inferior as superior to the things it unites is not usually understood by monists and non-dualists, and so they assume that the unity that subsists among all things must require some ultra-divinity above even God. As opposed to this, the ambivalence of the unifying principle just indicated above should make it clear why dualistic or theistic doctrine does not require a pantheistic conception of God to complete it. One has therefore every right to think in terms of 'God and creation' without absurdly putting God in a relative category.

The above is the last of a number of subtle questions which I hope will be given some consideration where the merits of metaphysical religion are discussed in future. No one in today's world can be reproached for being unaware of the conceptual and moral mine-fields which questions of the One and the Many involve us all in, as long as the unawareness is involuntary. Those who are attracted to non-dualism, but without being completely committed to it, would do well to think through the implications of this doctrine in the light of what has been said earlier concerning creation, and the consequences which follow from it, which I have tried to make clear. There remains one final doubt which can briefly be answered, namely, that criticisms of monistic religion could all be mistaken, because behind its verbal expressions there was an inexpressible reality which far outweighed anything that could be said against its expressible forms. But in just the same way, however, Theistic religion ought to be immune from criticism because its expressions also rest on an inexpressible reality, with the further advantage that it does not violate the sense of reality which one needs so as to be able to believe in it. This is an age where false lights shine from every quarter, so that the pursuit of truth can seem to be hopeless. Eventually, all this will have to give way to a reinstatement of the hidden truth, and what has been explained here may prepare some minds for that, and help them see how they can bring that time nearer.

Afterword

Ranters: Non-Dualism and the Law

Theological monism, or non-dualism, is the only heterodox form of religion to have been made illegal in England since the Reformation, and as this historical occurrence can shed some light on the anarchic effects it has had on those who believe in it, I will end with some relevant quotations from a history of the subject. According to Norman Cohn, (author of *The Pursuit of the Millennium*, Paladin, London 1972), ever since the non-dualist doctrine arose in Europe in the twelfth century, its devotees have been divided into two sects or schools, one of which follows the implications of self-deification ruthlessly and without regard for social consequences, while the other does all it can to disguise itself, making a zealous practice of religious orthodoxy, so as to be more orthodox than the orthodox. René Guénon and his followers clearly belong to the latter sect, and are therefore the better able to form relationships with devout people who could be converted.

If we call these two the Social and the Antisocial sects, it is not hard to perceive the attitude of each of them to the other. The Antisocial would be sure to see the Social as fainthearts and compromisers who do not dare follow the doctrine all the way, while the Social would see the Antisocial as barbarians who exploit the doctrine for their own personal gratification, even though *they* would say that it was not theirs but God's. In the mid-seventeenth century, both of these sects were rapidly gaining in strength in England towards the end of the Civil War, at which time they were known as 'Ranters'.

Norman Cohn says that,

These people (the Ranters), who were also known as 'high attainers' or 'high professors', became very numerous by about 1650. Some were to be found in the army—one hears of officers being cashiered and publicly whipped and a soldier being whipped through the City of London 'for ranting'. (Ibid., Appendix, p288)

The situation caused by this doctrine was felt to be so serious that a law was passed against it by the Rump Parliament in 1650, the second year of the Commonwealth, while Cromwell was engaged in the Irish wars. Extracts from this Act of 9 August 1650, 'for the punishment of Atheistical, Blasphemous and Execrable Opinions' are given by Cohn as follows:

The Parliament . . . Enact and Ordain. . . . That all and every person and persons (not distempered with sickness, or distracted in the brain) who shall presume avowedly in words to profess, or shall by writing proceed to affirm and maintain him or her self, or any other meer Creature, to be very God, or to be Infinite or Almighty, or in Honour, Excellency, Majesty and Power to be equal, and the same with the true God, or that the true God, or the Eternal Majesty dwells in the creature and no where else; or whosoever shall deny the Holiness and Righteousness of God, or shall presume as aforesaid to profess, That Unrighteousness in persons, or the acts of Uncleanness, Prophane Swearing, Drunkenness, and the like Filthiness and Brutishness, are not unholy and forbidden in the Word of God . . . or (those who profess) the acts of Murther, Adultery, Incest, Fornication, Uncleanness, Sodomy, Drunkenness, filthy and lascivious Speaking, are not things in themselves shameful, wicked, sinful, impious, abominable and detestable in any person or persons: Or . . . that the acts of Adultery, Drunkenness, Swearing and the like open wickedness are in their own nature as Holy and Righteous as the Duties of Prayer, Preaching, or of giving Thanks to God: . . . or that there is neither Heaven nor Hell, neither Salvation nor Damnation, or that those are one and the same thing....[1]

The penalties allotted under this law were on a 'three strikes' basis: for the first offence, it was six months 'to Prison or to the House of Correction'; for the second it was banishment; and for the third, of returning without Licence of Parliament it was death.

In the same Appendix, a work by Thomas Edwards, dated 1646, concerning heresies, is quoted for what he says of the Ranters' doctrine:

Every creature in the first estate of creation was God, and every creature is God, every creature that hath life and breath being an efflux from God, and shall return into God again, be swallowed up in him as a drop is in the ocean.... That if a man by the spirit knew himself to be in a state of grace, though he did commit murther or drunkenness, God did see no sin in him ... all the earth is the Saints, and there ought to be a community of goods, and the Saints should share in the Lands and Estates of Gentlemen, and rich men.[2]

The above text shows the connection between the non-dual Ranter doctrine and egalitarianism, a kind of proto-communism. That is perfectly logical and inevitable, because the equation of all individual persons with One Being must obviously make them all equal to one another.

According to the Puritan divine, Richard Baxter, the Ranters set up 'the Light of Nature' as their guide, and rejected the Church, the scriptures and Christian ministry, and believed that God allowed 'the most hideous words of blasphemy,' and that 'Many of them committed Whoredoms commonly, insomuch that a Matron of great Note for Godliness and Sobriety, being

1. Cohn, ibid., Appendix, 'The Free Spirit in Cromwell's England', pp 295–296.
2. Ibid., p 290.

perverted by them, turned so shameless a Whore, that she was Carted in the streets of London.'

Cohn also quotes an account of Ranter doctrine given by Edward Hyde D.D., an Episcopalian:

> We are pure, they say, and so all things are pure to us, but those that believe not their minds and consciences are defiled.... God doth all things.... If he does all things, then he doth sin, he acts sin, there is not anything that is but he doth it, wickedness is that he doth.... If God be all things, then he is sin and wickedness.... That they are very God, infinite and Almighty as the very God is; that they are in Honour, Excellency, Majesty and Power equally and the same with the true God.[1]

It was clear that there was not much the law could do about this doctrine, since it could only restrain outward behavior, but could do nothing about the interior condition which gave rise to it. For all the law could do, Ranterism was still able to spread secretly, and the 'atheistical blasphemies' were often reserved for private occasions. The resolution of this issue came from Quakerism. By one of the mysterious acts of Providence, the rise of the Quaker religion began about the same time as the monistic doctrine of the Ranters. The Quakers had one thing in common with the Ranters, namely, a religion with no hierarchical or institutional structure, and for that reason they were able to get close to the Ranters and reason with them. George Fox himself records an encounter with them, which is quoted here as follows:

> When I came into the jail, where the prisoners were, a great power of darkness struck at me, and I sat still, having my spirit gathered into the love of God. At last these prisoners began to rant, and vapour, and blaspheme, at which my soul was greatly grieved. They said they were God; but

1. Ibid., pp 291–292.

that we could not bear such things.... Then seeing they said they were God, I asked them, if they knew whether it would rain tomorrow? they said they could not tell. I told them, God could tell ... after I had reproved them for their blasphemous expressions, I went away; for I perceived they were Ranters.[1]

In the same place, it is said:

Fox saw a good deal of the Ranters in 1654–5, though by that time their influence was rapidly diminishing. At a joint meeting of Baptists, Quakers, and Ranters at Swannington in Leicestershire, he found that the Ranters 'were very rude, and stirred up the rude people against us. We sent to the Ranters to come forth, and try their God. Abundance of them came, who were very rude, and sung, and whistled, and danced; but the Lord's power so confounded them, that many of them came to be convinced.'[2]

Fox was able to confront them successfully in other places as well. Cohn says that as the Quaker movement grew, that of the Ranters shrank, until it ceased to be of any importance. From what has been quoted here, it looks as though the doctrine which the Quakers overcame was one which attracted people who in their inmost selves were not spiritual at all, but who embraced spirituality as an outward vesture to compensate for what they could feel they lacked. Only such persons as that could fail to feel the enormity of the doctrine they were professing. A consciousness of the ever-present reality of the mystical dimension of life is by no means confined to the religiously orthodox, however, in whom the discipline of religion can often stifle it, whereas it can arise with great strength in people who are almost outside religion, and usually with results which bring them into conflict with the religion whose truth they failed to recognize.

1. Ibid., p 289.
2. Ibid.

Index

www.ingramcontent.com/pod-product-compliance
Lightning Source LLC
Chambersburg PA
CBHW030715110426

42739CB00030B/436

9 781597 310819